Grant Seeking in Higher Education

Strategies and Tools

for College Faculty

Mary M. Licklider
and
The University of Missouri
Grant Writer Network
Foreword by David Attis

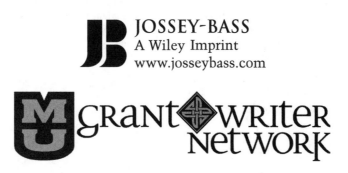

Published by Jossey-Bass
A Wiley Imprint
One Montgomery Street, Suite 1200, San Francisco, CA 94104-4594—www.josseybass.com

Jossey-Bass books and products are available through most bookstores. To contact Jossey-Bass directly call our Customer Care Department within the U.S. at 800-956-7739, outside the U.S. at 317-572-3986, or fax 317-572-4002.

Wiley also publishes its books in a variety of electronic formats and by print-on-demand. Some material included with standard print versions of this book may not be included in e-books or in print-on-demand. If the version of this book that you purchased references media such as a CD or a DVD that was not included in your purchase, you may download this material at http://booksupport.wiley.com. For more information about Wiley products, visit www.wiley.com.

Library of Congress Cataloging-in-Publication Data
Licklider, Mary M.
  Grant seeking in higher education : strategies and tools for college faculty / Mary M. Licklider and The University of Missouri Grant Writer Network ; foreword by David Attis.
      p. cm. – (The Jossey-Bass higher and adult education Series)
  Includes bibliographical references and index.
  ISBN 978-1-118-19247-4 (pbk.)
  ISBN 978-1-118-39511-0 (pdf) – ISBN 978-1-118-39512-7 (epub) – 978-1-118-47645-1 (emobi)
  1. Educational fund raising–United States.   2. Education, Higher–United States–Finance.
3. Research grants–Handbooks, manuals, etc.   4. Proposal writing for grants–Handbooks, manuals, etc.   5. Universities and colleges–Faculty.   I. Title.
  LB2336.L54   2012
  378.1'06–dc23

                                                                          2012016932

Printed in the United States of America

FIRST EDITION

PB Printing   10   9   8   7   6   5   4   3   2   1

The Jossey-Bass Higher and
Adult Education Series

Contents

List of Figures, Tables, and Boxes

Figures

Tables

Boxes

Foreword

I FIRST ENCOUNTERED Dr. Mary Licklider and her team of grant writers at the University of Missouri (MU) while researching a report on best practices in supporting large-scale multidisciplinary research. One of the challenges I heard in talking to dozens of institutions was that proposals for large collaborative grants were so labor-intensive and complicated that few faculty investigators had the time or the experience to complete them. The MU Grant Writer Network had solved this problem by distributing expert grant writers throughout the university and connecting them through the central Office of Grant Writing and Publications. The results were impressive. Prior to the launch of the network in 1998, MU had won only three large-scale multidisciplinary grants. Since then, it has won more than 25—a result of the quality of research taking place on campus and the unprecedented support provided by its network of professional grant writers. The Network has grown from one individual in 1998 to 18 individuals today. Network grant writers have been involved in over $1.8 billion in proposals and over $304 million in awards.

Not every institution or every faculty member has access to an established group of effective grant writers, and that is where this book comes in. Mary and her team have distilled the lessons learned over more than a decade of grant writing into a comprehensive handbook. Whether you are at a community college, a liberal arts college, a master's university, or a major research university, you will find helpful advice in this book. Anyone in higher education looking for funding—from foundations, state agencies, or federal agencies; in the sciences, humanities, or social sciences—will learn something valuable from this resource.

The book covers the proposal process from start to finish, with advice ranging from the strategic (how to decide if an opportunity is worth the effort it will take to apply, how to think about funding at different career stages) to the mundane (how to set up e-mail alerts with opportunities from specific agencies, how to set the line spacing in a proposal). Readers get advice on each component of the proposal—cover letters, abstracts, budgets, budget justifications—including sample text, case studies, and common mistakes. There are even sections on managing the project, including HR, finance, and data management.

A key message of the book is the importance of knowing your audience. Not only do the authors provide detailed descriptions of the grant-making process at different agencies and foundations, they also provide first-person accounts from reviewers and program directors explaining what they look for, how they read, and the fastest ways to lose their interest. The book explains the most common reasons that funders reject proposals, when to resubmit, and when not to.

Supplementing the text is an online toolkit that will save proposal writers hours of work. It includes samples of all of the components of a grant proposal—letters of support, cover letters, proposal outlines, budget spreadsheets, detailed timelines, and task lists for proposal development. The book even includes resources for building your own grant writing office like the one at MU, with grant writer position descriptions, skills inventories, and performance evaluation tools.

Competition for grants in higher education has never been tougher, and it has probably never been more critical to institutional missions and individual faculty careers. Most grant proposals (Mary estimates more than two-thirds) are turned down. Given the high stakes and the level of effort required to prepare a proposal, there is no excuse for submitting a sloppy, poorly prepared, or irrelevant application. This valuable book provides all of the information you need to make sure that you have asked all the right questions, avoided the common mistakes, and submitted a proposal that gives your idea the best possible chance of success.

David Attis, PhD
Practice Manager
Education Advisory Board

Preface

What's in a Name?

IF YOU WORK in higher education, whether a two-year, four-year, doctoral, or research institution, and your position entails generating grant proposals and running grant-funded projects, this handbook is for you. If you also have leadership responsibilities at your institution, we hope you will find the Appendix helpful and relevant to those duties. We expect that you will use this volume as a handbook, reading through the chapters, picking and choosing among the Toolkit items those that suit your needs, and perhaps going back to reread sections when circumstances or the needs of a particular project warrant it. You will encounter some repetition of concepts across the chapters. We did this deliberately so that each individual chapter can stand alone at least to some extent.

Our title tells you that this book is aimed at an academic audience. Our examples are drawn from our experience with proposals to support the research, scholarship, creative activity, instruction, and outreach of the faculty members with whom we have worked over the years. Whereas we are a network of grant writing consultants at the University of Missouri, a land-grant, Research I institution, our advice does not by any means assume that you will have access to professionals like us to help with your grant proposals. We are keenly aware that many, if not most, of our readers will be at smaller institutions without this kind of support. Indeed, survey data from the National Organization of Research Development Professionals (NORDP) suggests that the 14-year tenure of our Network is extremely unusual even among institutions that do provide grant writing support now.

A Rose by Any Other Name . . .

There is more than a little irony in the fact that, despite our success in creating what is increasingly recognized as a national model, the "grant writer" label seems to be at the bottom of the list of desirable titles for many in the emerging field of research development. The selection of titles is fraught with institutional turf wars: "Specialist" and "coordinator" may be considered lower-level positions; "officer" and "development" are reserved for those in the development division; anything with "writer" is relegated to lower salary levels. And so it goes.

In an informal survey of the members of NORDP in spring 2010, I found that, despite the use of a variety of titles, the activities which are by far the most common among the membership are proposal development, identifying and distributing funding opportunities, and pulling interdisciplinary teams together. This was reinforced when NORDP surveyed its membership in 2011: 87 percent of research development offices are editing grant proposals and helping to identify funding opportunities for their faculties.

This is not to say, however, that the grant writer title is without its issues. We settled on "grant writing consultant"—and that is the title we will use throughout this book—because we do not for the most part compose the first drafts of the proposal narratives. We are experts in process; our faculty members are the content experts. Our jobs entail helping faculty members identify funding opportunities they might otherwise miss, identifying and pulling interdisciplinary and interinstitutional teams together, organizing proposal documents, organizing the people and tasks of proposal preparation, managing the timeline for proposal preparation (read: polite, but persistent, nagging), drafting budgets and budget justifications, and conducting workshops and graduate courses in grantsmanship.

It is worth reiterating that this book will be useful to you regardless of whether you have access to grant writing professionals. This book lays out the work of proposal development and contextualizes that work in an academic environment. You may need or choose to do all of the tasks associated with preparing your grant proposals, or you may hand some of those tasks off to others. Either way, we believe the advice and tools of this book will allow you to proceed more effectively and efficiently.

Using This Book

We have organized this book into three parts: Part One provides advice on proposal development and management of the resulting grant awards. Part Two offers tools and templates to help you accomplish those tasks. The Appendix advises campus leaders who wish to benefit from our experience in building institutional grants culture.

Part One is divided into three sections: "Diving into Grants Culture" lays the groundwork for your proposal work. In this section, Chapter 1 begins with an overview, historical and current, macro and micro, that should help you contextualize your grant work. Chapter 2 walks you through the process of identifying and winnowing potential sponsors for your work. Chapter 3 asks you to look up from your desk or lab bench, look around your campus, and tap the support that is already in place for you. Following this thread, Chapter 4 examines current sponsor preferences for collaborative and interdisciplinary work. Finally, Chapter 5 moves past these more general activities to help you prepare to write a specific proposal.

The second section of Part One, "Developing Your Proposal," walks you through the key sections of a typical grant proposal. This section includes chapters on the writing itself (Chapter 6), the abstract (Chapter 7), the proposal narrative or project description (Chapter 8), the budget (Chapter 9), and the proposal package as a whole (Chapter 10).

The last section of Part One, "Next Steps," deals with postsubmission issues: what to do when your proposal is initially declined (Chapter 11) and then finally awarded (Chapter 12).

Part Two comprises a Toolkit of tested materials that we have found helpful in our own proposal work. (The Toolkit can also be accessed online; see p. iv.) This Toolkit is divided into four sections. As its title suggests, the first section, "Diving into Grants Culture," parallels the section by the same title in Part One of the book. The glossary and other materials in this section are designed to help you think about your project as an experienced grants professional would. The materials in Section Two, "Managing the Proposal Work," should help you manage the proposal process without being overwhelmed as you track all the people and proposal documents involved in the process. Section Three, "Developing Your Proposal," focuses directly on the parts of the typical proposal, offering templates, examples, and cheat sheets to help you generate a strong proposal and respond appropriately to reviewer comments.

The last section of the Toolkit, "Building Institutional Grants Culture," and the Appendix that follows Part Two are aimed at campus leaders seeking to build your institution's grants culture. We offer sample documents in the Toolkit and advice in the Appendix that are drawn from our experience in nurturing the University of Missouri's Grant Writer Network as a resource for MU's faculty.

We hope that you will find this handbook both useful and usable.

Acknowledgments

WE ARE GRATEFUL first and foremost for the creativity and dedication of the University of Missouri faculty members with whom we have worked.

We are grateful for the consistent administrative support for the Grant Writer Network from the University of Missouri's chief research officers over the years: Jack Burns, Rob Hall, Jim Coleman, and Rob Duncan.

About the Authors

THE UNIVERSITY OF Missouri (MU) **Grant Writer Network** was initiated in 1998 and has grown and thrived in the university's interdisciplinary climate. From one position in 1998, the Network has grown to 18 positions in 2012. Network members have helped with nearly 2,000 grant proposals, which have encompassed a wide range of sponsors and brought grant awards of more than $304 million to MU. This book pulls together some of the collective wisdom that has evolved through the generous collaborative relationships that characterize the Network.

Mary M. Licklider, director of the Office of Grant Writing and Publications in MU's Office of Research, provides leadership to the University of Missouri Grant Writer Network, coordinates and teaches in MU's grantsmanship courses and seminars, collaborates with faculty members on proposal preparation, and administratively oversees MU's federal priorities and limited submission processes. She has worked in education for some 30 years in roles involving teaching, writing, research, publication, and leadership at both the K–12 and postsecondary levels.

Mary holds a BA in English from Webster University, as well as an MEd in curriculum and instruction and a PhD from MU in education, focusing on organizational change. She and her husband raise alpacas in rural Boone County, Missouri, and are active in MOPACA, the Midwest's regional association for alpaca enthusiasts.

Mary Barile is the associate director of the Office of Grant Writing and Publications in the MU Office of Research. She earned her PhD in theatre history from MU, was the grant writing consultant for Family and Community Medicine, and later served as the grant writing consultant for the Center for Arts and Humanities at MU. Her interests include theatre and regional history as well as the folklore and history of the paranormal; she is the author of several books and articles about American popular culture. Mary has worked in the grants and development fields for more than 25 years and has received funding from state agencies in the areas of folklore and the arts. She teaches graduate grantsmanship courses and has been an investigator for two internal grants at MU.

Mark B. Child, grant writing consultant for the School of Health Professions, works with researchers seeking funding opportunities and assists faculty with the development, writing, and submission of internal and extramural grant proposals. Mark earned his PhD in anthropology from Yale University, where his research focused on health-related issues pertaining to the fields of ethnography, ethnohistory, and archaeology. He has written books, scientific articles in peer-reviewed journals, and edited volumes. Mark has more than 15 years of experience researching and coordinating grant-funded projects, including the acquisition of nationally competitive National Science Foundation (NSF) and Fulbright grants for his own research projects.

Bob Glidewell began his grant writing career in 1996 and has assisted various nonprofit and commercial organizations in Texas, Oklahoma, and Missouri in acquiring grant funding. Since 2007, he has worked to develop grant proposals and funding opportunities for MU's Robert J. Trulaske, Sr. College of Business. These projects include interdisciplinary partnerships with other schools, colleges, and institutes on the MU campus. He assists with the graduate grantsmanship courses and has served as a reviewer on multiple grant-review panels for the NSF.

Bob's publications include newspaper, magazine, and journal articles as well as training manuals for corporate and government clients. He is a graduate of Southwest Oklahoma State University and the University of Missouri.

Cynthia Haydon has been employed in grant writing or grants administration at MU for eight years. As the grant writing consultant for the MU School of Medicine, Cynthia currently works with the associate dean for research to prioritize projects and assist researchers in conceptualizing and completing grant proposals. She is available to investigators to help with specific questions throughout the grant process, from the funding search through the details of submission procedures. Cynthia previously worked in fundraising research at MU and at the University of Southern Indiana. She earned her BA in art history from MU and has completed course work toward a master's degree in library science.

Susan Hazelwood is now retired but was associate director of the Office of Grant Writing and Publications in the MU Office of Research for 12 years. Prior to joining the Office of Research, she was a research associate professor in MU's School of Medicine, funded on grant dollars, for 20 years. She has taught grantsmanship skills to faculty members and supported them in obtaining external funding for their scholarship and research activities. Susan has mentored and supported the newer members of the MU Grant Writer Network as they conquered the steep learning curve of grant writing positions. Susan earned her BS in life sciences at

Missouri State University and completed course work and research toward a master's degree in biological sciences from MU.

Shelley A. Hilton, grant writing consultant for the MU College of Engineering, coordinates all aspects of the preparation and submission of grant proposals, including identifying opportunities, building and managing teams, editing and writing, building budgets and budget justifications, and serving as a liaison with campus and funding agency personnel. As a member of the MU Grant Writer Network, she provides grantsmanship training to MU faculty, staff, and students.

With more than 15 years of grants experience, Shelley began her career directing grant-funded research projects in health psychology. For the past eight years, she has been a grant writing consultant at MU, starting in the Truman School of Public Affairs before transitioning to her current position with the College of Engineering. Shelley holds an MA in social psychology from MU and a BA in psychology from Creighton University.

Sheryl Koenig, grant writing consultant in the Bond Life Sciences Center, assists researchers with preparing grant proposals. With over 40 investigators from 15 departments located within the Life Sciences Center, the wide variety of disciplines brings a challenge that Sheryl finds fascinating. She holds a BS in mathematics and an MEd in educational technology and has been involved in the grants world for 14 years.

Joann Messbarger, grant writing consultant in the MU Office of Grant Writing and Publications, works closely with faculty investigators on a variety of grants campus-wide, including multidisciplinary collaborative projects. She has been a part of the Office of Research since 2005 and began working as a grant writing consultant in 2008. Joann previously worked at MU in the Department of Educational, School, and Counseling Psychology, managing the admissions process for its graduate programs. She holds a BS in early childhood education from MU and spent eight years working in the child-care industry as a teacher, mentor, and administrator.

Elizabeth D. Miller, grant writing consultant in the MU College of Human Environmental Sciences, works with faculty members to seek funding opportunities and to develop and submit grant proposals. Before joining the college, Elizabeth's grant experience included two years as a grant administrator and nearly eight years as a grant writer in public health and medicine. She holds a BA in English from MU.

Chris Montgomery, grant writing consultant in the MU Office of Grant Writing and Publications with an emphasis on the arts and humanities and MU libraries, works with faculty members to find funding sources and improve their grant proposals. She also helps with conceiving and coordinating conferences and events that highlight MU humanities programs. Before joining the Grant Writer Network, Chris served as director of a grant-supported, nonprofit art space in Chicago and as photograph specialist for the State Historical Society of Missouri. She holds a BA in fine arts.

Larry Nossaman, grant writing consultant for the MU College of Education, helps faculty and staff research funding opportunities, interpret funding guidelines, develop timelines, collaborate with other researchers, and submit internal and external funding applications. Larry holds a BA in journalism.

Diane Oerly, grant writing consultant in the Division of Information Technology, provides support for funding proposals related to information technology and resources and helps the Grant Writer Network employ technology. Diane has a BS in accounting and an MBA. She has 33 years of MU experience, including 23 years of specializing in employing information technology to fulfill the university's teaching, research, and administrative objectives. She has been a grant writing consultant since 2001.

Sherri Sachdev, grant writing consultant for the Mizzou Advantage initiative, works closely with the MU provost and collaborative, interdisciplinary networks of faculty members, centers, departments, corporate partners, and other universities to prepare major grant proposals in four areas of MU strength: food for the future; media of the future; one health, one medicine: the convergence of human and animal health; and sustainable energy. Overarching themes of the four areas include innovation and education. Sherri earned her PhD in nutritional sciences from MU and has more than 15 years of experience at the research bench conducting experiments in genetics, biochemistry, and molecular biology. She has published numerous scientific journal articles and has successfully obtained funding as principal investigator for her own research projects. Prior to joining the Mizzou Advantage initiative, Sherri served as grant writing consultant at MU for the School of Health Professions and the Thompson Center for Autism and Neurodevelopmental Disorders.

Sara Vassmer, grant writing consultant in the MU Office of Grant Writing and Publications, recently completed a PhD in health education and promotion at MU. Her background includes research in alcohol and substance use issues. In her spare time she enjoys exercising, gardening, and spending time with her family.

Bondi Wood is the grant writing consultant for MU's Thompson Center for Autism and Neurodevelopmental Disorders, a national leader in confronting the challenges of autism. Bondi helps faculty members and physicians in all phases of proposal development for collaborative research, training, services, and treatment. A freelance writer for nearly 20 years, Bondi began her grant writing career working primarily for nonprofits delivering humanitarian aid. She has written more than 200 articles for business, consumer, and women's publications. She has a bachelor's degree in English education and a master's degree in composition and rhetoric, both from MU.

Grant Seeking in Higher Education

Part One

The How-to Manual

Section One

Diving into Grants Culture

Chapter 1

Grants Culture: The Big Picture

Mary Licklider and Susan Hazelwood

AS WE APPROACHED writing this chapter, our first thoughts were that many readers would be tempted to skip it. "Cut to the chase," we could hear you thinking. "I just need to get a proposal written and submitted."

You will not be surprised to read that, as grant writing consultants, we think this focus is way too shortsighted. What you really want to do is the proposed work. So, going backward from the goal of doing the work, you need money and, before that, you need to submit a fundable proposal for the right work. Those modifiers—a *fundable* proposal for the *right* work— are where this chapter will help. To be fundable, the proposal needs an implicit but nonetheless critical awareness of its context, and that context includes the sponsor's, your institution's, and your own as an individual faculty member.

This chapter will address each of those contexts in turn. We will begin with overviews of the histories of and current trends in federal and private grant making. Then we will encourage you to look at the roles of grant-funded work at your institution and, finally, at how strategic grant seeking can advance your academic career.

Federal Grant Making through the Years

The first federal grants in the United States were land (not cash) given to reward soldiers who fought in the Revolutionary War. Land grants were later used to promote development of railroads and higher education. (A key reason for giving grants of land rather than cash was that the first effort to establish a federal income tax didn't happen until 1894. It took the passage of the 16th Amendment in 1913 to really establish a system of taxation to fund the federal government.) The point is that, even before there was a steady source of income, this country's leaders held higher education as a priority on par with recognizing the sacrifices of our veterans. Indeed, the Continental Congress spoke to the importance of education as early as 1787 in the Northwest Ordinance.

Also significant for our purposes here, some of the earliest federal cash grants had to do with the development of new knowledge through the exploration of the Western territories and the establishment of agricultural experiment stations (Morrill Act, 1862). The United States has a long tradition, then, of support for discovery. In fact, the first agricultural experiment stations were supported by state and private sources, beginning with the Connecticut station at Wesleyan University in 1875 (Government Information and Reference Services Unit, 2008). The Hatch Act of 1887 created the national network of stations and institutionalized the tie between these stations and higher education by requiring that the stations be located at land-grant universities.

These very early traditions would probably be labeled as "applied" or "translational" research aimed at "economic development" in today's jargon. The focus was on support for "agriculture and the Mechanic arts" (Morrill Act, 1862) and on exploration for the eventual development of commerce. Jefferson's instructions to Meriwether Lewis as he and William Clark set out to explore the Louisiana Territory, for example, were that "The object of your mission is to explore the Missouri river, & such principal stream of it as by it's [*sic*] course and communication with the waters of the Pacific ocean whether the Columbia, Oregon, Colorado or any other river may offer the most direct & practicable water communication across this continent *for the purposes of commerce*" (Gawalt, 1803; emphasis added).

It wasn't long, though, before the need for accountability arose. Just three years after passage of the Hatch Act, the Morrill Act of 1890 allowed the federal government to withhold funding if previous sums had been misused, and it required annual reports "regarding the condition and progress of each college" (Second Morrill Act, 1890).

In the 10 years between 1929 and 1939, federal grants rose from 3 to 39 percent of federal expenditures (Floersch, n.d.). Whereas the Depression and World War II years saw increases in federal grants for individuals and social services, the late 1950s and early 1960s shifted the focus squarely back to knowledge discovery and technology development. Sputnik, the first human-made object to orbit the Earth, was launched by the Russians in 1957 and led to a subsequent ramp-up in basic science, space exploration, and education funding in the United States.

Increasing funding in these areas and increasing awareness in the 1960s of social and racial inequities in American society proceeded in tandem with increasing concern about research ethics. This concern was initiated in large part as a response to war crimes during World War II. The Nuremberg Code of 1947 was drafted specifically as guidance for judging those who had conducted concentration camp experiments. In 1972, the US press published information about the now-infamous Tuskegee syphilis study, and in 1974, the Belmont Commission was charged with identifying basic ethical principles for biomedical and behavioral research. The Belmont Report, published in 1979, laid out the three principles of respect for persons, beneficence, and justice that continue to guide research with human subjects.

After the mid-19th century, this increasing connection between research funding and accountability seems to have been a less proactive and more reactive response to events such as the poverty of American farmers following the Civil War, the Sputnik launch, and public awareness of research abuses. This reactive stance has continued in more recent years. Protection of human subjects and financial conflicts of interest received increased scrutiny following Jesse Gelsinger's 1999 death in a gene therapy trial in which the principal investigator (PI) owned significant interest in the therapy, and the PI's university (his employer) owned stock in a company tied to the therapy (Gelsinger & Shamoo, 2008). Export control laws have received a great deal more attention (attention some would define as reinterpretation) since the 9/11 attacks. Funding for research to prevent or respond to acts of bioterrorism increased following the anthrax attacks in 2001. The wars in the Middle East highlighted again the vulnerability inherent in US dependence upon foreign oil, and funding for energy research has increased. The unresolved abortion debate ripples to make stem cell research controversial. Understanding how national events can affect the levels and targets of grant funding can help you to anticipate federal funding trends.

The United States has a long, rich history of innovation and support for innovation. US citizens want to be the shining city on the hill and see Yankee ingenuity as a vehicle for achieving that goal. At the same time, the United States is a democracy, and its citizens very much consider tax money "our money." They expect tax expenditures to reflect their values as a nation and as individuals. The US population is richly diverse, and it would be understating the obvious to say that this diversity generates controversy and sometimes-contentious debate as to the priorities for US tax dollars. Recognizing these political forces can also help you write to all of the audiences for your proposals. Proposal abstracts, for example, are often published for funded projects. When you write your abstract, you do well to consider not only the peer reviewer but also the agency staffer testifying on Capitol Hill.

It may be less obvious that these democratic traditions generate at least some of the red tape of government. To be accountable to the citizens who provide the federal grant funding, agencies solicit peer review to get professional advice as to the best value for those dollars; they require specific budget plans and regular reporting on funded activities; they require compliance with ethical standards. All this transparency and accountability does feel like red tape at times, and it helps to understand its democratic purposes and historical sources. But if you are employed at a small institution, this also serves to warn you to be careful what you ask for: if your institution is small or new, it may not have the infrastructure to provide the audits and other compliance functions entailed in managing federal awards. If not, part of your proposal development process will be to engage partners who can provide what your organization lacks.

Private Grant Making through the Years

Americans have tended to take a somewhat schizophrenic approach to giving. Calvinist traditions suggest that, through individual work in a calling, one strives to discover one's predestined state of grace (Tropman, 1995, ch. 2; Weber, 1956, p. 85). More productive and important work, higher levels of achievement, and reliable, ascetic habits characterize those in a state of grace. Poverty, dependence upon others, and the absence of rational order are indications of a lack of grace, which cannot be restored through human activity (Tropman, 1995; Weber, 1956). Why bother with charitable giving?

On the other hand, Alexis de Tocqueville (1969, p. 513) famously reported on the "voluntary associations" that Americans formed to address practical political and social problems. Today, we support private giving through more than 30 kinds of tax-exempt organizations. Over 1.5 million nonprofits were registered with the IRS as of 2008, reflecting a 10-year growth rate of 31 percent. More than 80 percent of Americans donate to charity each year. Over 25 percent volunteer an average of about 34 hours each year, and collectively, these services are valued at $3.3 billion annually. Don't underestimate the dollars you might save by using volunteers in your projects. The estimated value of volunteer work in 2010 was $21.36 an hour according to the Independent Sector (n.d.).

An annual report by Giving USA tracks the sources and recipients of private giving. According to the 2011 report, private giving comes from individuals, charitable bequests, foundations, and corporations (Giving USA Foundation, 2011). Contributions in 2010 amounted to $290.89 billion, with 73 percent coming from individuals, 14 percent from foundations, 8 percent from bequests, and 5 percent from corporations (including corporate foundations), which often provide in-kind support through donations of products or employee time rather than cash. Combined charitable giving by individuals, bequests, and family foundations amounted to an estimated $254.1 billion in 2010, or about 87 percent of the total. Family foundations provided 48 percent of all grants made by independent, community, and operating foundations in 2010.

Most individuals and family foundations do not employ staff to handle their private giving. Knowing this will help you understand why phone calls to them may not be returned and e-mails may not be answered. In these cases, you must rely on your own research to become familiar with the foundation's grant submission guidelines (if they even exist) and where the foundation has historically awarded its dollars. The IRS 990 tax returns that foundations are required to file are public information, and these can be accessed on the websites of the Foundation Center (http://foundationcenter.org/) and other organizations that provide funding information. Read the previous years' forms for foundations to which you are considering sending proposals. Look for the names of the individuals who served or are serving on the foundation's board, levels of giving in previous years, organizations and locations that received the money, and changes in the foundation's total assets from year to year.

Nationally, the table below summarizes the types of recipient organizations that received the $290.89 billion in private contributions in 2010:

TABLE 1

US Giving by Type of Recipient Organization

Percent of Total US Giving	Type of Recipient Organization
35	Religion
14	Education
11	Foundations
9	Human services
8	Health
8	Public-society benefit
5	Arts, culture, and humanities
5	International affairs
2	Environment/animals
2	Individuals
1	Unallocated

Source: Giving USA Foundation, 2011.

Total charitable giving has increased in current dollars in every year since tracking began in 1954 with the exceptions of 1987, 2008 (which had a massive decline of 7 percent), and 2009. An inflation-adjusted increase of 2.1 percent in 2010 follows the trend of postrecessionary increases seen in the past. Giving USA predicts "a promising future for charitable giving in the coming years. . . . [H]owever, the slow recovery of the economy will certainly impact just how quickly charitable giving will rise to pre-recession levels" (Giving USA Foundation, 2011).

Monitoring reports such as the one produced annually by Giving USA will help you better understand the current state of affairs with regard to charitable giving and whether the private sector is a likely source for your project at any given time.

The Roles of Grant-Funded Projects in Academia

External funding can support any of higher education's missions of education, research, outreach, and economic development. The catch is that no grant award ever fully pays the cost of a project. To understand why this is the case, you have to understand how overhead costs are covered in grant awards.

Indirect, overhead, facilities, and administration—these costs are labeled differently across time and across disciplines, and all refer to the same thing. In recent years, most federal agencies have been using *facilities and administrative costs (F&A)* as the label of choice to refer to those expenses that are difficult to ascribe to a particular project but are nonetheless required for that project. A grant-funded project typically takes place in a building, for example, but does not use the whole building. It would be exceedingly time-consuming and expensive to calculate how much of the building's depreciation, maintenance, janitorial service, utilities, and grounds keeping should be apportioned to each project that takes place in that building. Similarly, the institution's libraries are available to all institutional personnel, and calculating a percentage of the library costs for each person and project is not practical.

Instead, the federal government allows institutions to negotiate a flat rate for these facilities and administrative expenses. That rate is then applied to all projects. As the name "facilities and administration" implies, calculating the F&A rate entails an extensive audit of all the institution's expenses for administration and facilities.

The administrative portion of the rate is currently capped by the government at 26 percent. This typically includes such functions as enrollment, admissions, business services, human resources, libraries, procurement, and financial management. The costs of research compliance activities—institutional review boards (IRBs) for human subjects research, animal care and use committees, biosafety committees, and such—also fall under the administrative part of the F&A rate. For many academic institutions, these administrative costs exceed 26 percent, which means that these institutions lose money on every grant award. This is also why you hear recent compliance requirements sometimes referred to as *unfunded mandates*. Once the institution's rate for administrative costs hits 26 percent, additional requirements represent costs that the institution cannot fully recover in grant-funded projects.

The facilities portion of the rate includes depreciation and maintenance of all facilities owned by the institution. For institutions predominantly housed in older, fully depreciated buildings, this portion of the rate will be lower. Once the institution calculates these costs and ties each square foot of campus space predominantly to one function—often instruction, research, or "other"—the rate for each function can be established. All this documentation is then submitted to the federal agency with which the institution does the most business, its "cognizant agency." The documentation is reviewed, and agency personnel negotiate with the institution, usually for a somewhat lower F&A rate than what seemingly could be justified based on the institution's numbers. This once again means that the institution will lose money on each grant award because it will not recover the proportionate facilities costs associated with that project.

It is also relatively common for some sponsors to limit the percentage of F&A costs that can be charged to a project. Foundation sponsors typically allow institutions to recover maybe 8–20 percent of the F&A costs of projects they fund. Federal training grants usually allow only 8 percent. The USDA's primary extramural research entity, the National Institute for Food and Agriculture (previously the Cooperative State Research, Education, and Extension Service—CSREES), currently reimburses F&A costs at 23.45 percent, regardless of the institution's negotiated rate for these costs.

So why do academic institutions support grant-funded work if the grant awards do not fully pay the cost of the work? Good question! And we believe that question gets less attention across academia than it should. This is where we circle back to the missions and priorities of the institution. If the institution's strategic plan is a dynamic, living document that is widely publicized and referenced, decisions about which grant-funded projects to pursue become much easier to make and understand. If a project is part of the institution's mission and if it represents an institutional priority, then the sponsor can be seen as a partner in achieving what the institution would otherwise be doing entirely on its own.

If the project is tangential to the institution's mission and not found among the institution's priorities, the project should be viewed solely as an expense. There may be political or other reasons for engaging in that project, but it should be viewed through a clear-eyed cost-benefit analysis to determine whether to proceed. Benefits include the chance of receiving the sponsor's money, of course, but may also include developing positive relationships with key individuals or organizations participating with you on the project, building political capital with a state agency for whom the grant work will be performed, building credibility with a new sponsor in order to position yourself for a much larger award down the line, or acquiring funding that will help your institution meet regulatory requirements. Costs can accrue from the personnel time that goes into proposal development and therefore can't be used for higher-priority pursuits; the personnel time that would be entailed in implementing the project, again draining resources from higher-priority issues; and the risks to your reputation and your institution's if lack of interest causes the project to be poorly implemented. The decision to engage in a proposal should be made with the balance of its costs and benefits in mind.

As you think about which of your ideas to pursue through grant proposals, consider these ideas against the backdrop of the expressed priorities of your institution, your division, and your department. It will be much easier to convince reviewers that your work will occur in a supportive intellectual environment if the work aligns with one or more of these institutional priorities.

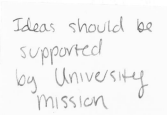

Ideas should be supported by University mission

Strategic Planning and Grant Writing

Mary Licklider

Whereas the importance of strategic planning has been a given in other sectors for many years, the concept tended to come later to higher education. Acquisition of a terminal degree traditionally means that you have been found capable of independent scholarship. The tradition of academic freedom means that you decide your own research priorities and course curricula, and tenure policies protect those individual decisions. There has been a tendency to assume that these traditions prohibit planning at the department or campus level.

There are, of course, many advantages to proceeding according to a plan rather than at random. One option for managing the planning process in higher education is to check the range of expertise on your campus. Many institutions have in-house expertise on organizational dynamics and strategic planning that could be tapped to guide campus processes. On the other hand, there is the "rule" that you can't be an expert until you are 50 miles from home. Whether or not you engage an in-house or external consultant, it seems to help to have someone without any vested interest to facilitate planning conversations. Although establishing priorities can be contentious, it is usually the easiest step in the process.

Just as there tend to be assumptions about the possibility of strategic planning in the context of higher education's traditions, there also seem to be assumptions that the development of a strategic plan is an empty exercise. The implementation of strategic priorities is sometimes actually met with surprise (or worse) by those who helped develop the priorities. Implementation has to mean that budget and hiring decisions follow priorities. Cost match is reserved for grant proposals in priority areas. Research assistants are assigned to labs in priority areas. Equipment purchases are focused in these areas. A shotgun approach will seldom, if ever, succeed in elevating the impact and stature of a department or campus. A focused approach builds upon strengths, rippling out as each area improves in turn. Some department chairs have the stomach for this, and others opt for one-size-fits-all, spreading resources evenly but so thin as to ensure mediocrity at best.

Our experience is that resources are never plentiful enough for an institution to do everything its people would like. Each choice ideally yields some benefits but also inevitably entails costs. This is especially true in grant-seeking. The National Institutes of Health (NIH) is grant-making organizations in the world, funding some $28 billion in extramural researc (NIH, Office of Budget, 2011). The programs with the highest success rates for research the NIH will *very* occasionally hit 32 percent (NIH, Office of Research Information Syst National Endowment for the Humanities, funding rates for some programs are in the (Yu, 2009). At the National Science Foundation, the average proposal is submitted just ov funding is awarded (NSF, 2010).

[handwritten margin note: 2/3's of grant proposals turned down]

In general, then, it is fair to say that in the best of conditions, at least two-thirds of grant proposals are turned down. This means that it really is not worth the effort to generate grant proposals that are written only for the money. On the other hand, if those proposals, through the detailed planning and thinking they require, help to move an outreach project, a line of research, or an instructional program forward, then the institution gains regardless of whether a given proposal is funded. And this brings us back to the need for strategic planning and its relevance to grant seeking. We need those overarching goals and priorities in order to get the best return on higher education's investment of personnel time in grant proposals.

Finally, there's the question of what happens to all the F&A dollars collected by your institution from grant sponsors. Although this answer will vary from one institution to another, the government does require that F&A dollars collected for a given purpose be spent to support that purpose, so F&A dollars collected on research projects must be spent to support the research infrastructure of the institution. This linkage is more obvious at some institutions than it is at others. Some institutions also use the amount of F&A costs recovered from sponsors to scale internal programs. At the University of Missouri, for example, the amount of F&A is used each year to determine the amount of Research Incentive Fund monies to be awarded to each department. These funds can be used to "bridge" researchers so that they can pay key lab personnel during a period without grant funds, to fund expenses entailed in securing preliminary data, or to provide matching funds for priority projects or other research-related purposes determined by the individual departments. (See the boxed piece "Motivation for Research and Collaboration at MU: Shared Credit" in Chapter 9 for a more complete description of the University of Missouri's Research Incentive Fund.)

You should be aware of your institution's and your department's policies and practices regarding F&A costs recovered from grant-funded projects. Similarly, you need to know policies related to the time you commit to grant-funded projects: What happens to the salary savings that accrue to the institution if part of your salary is paid by a grant? Awareness of institutional policies in these areas can help you plan for the next proposal and can potentially provide funding for preliminary work. If a portion of your salary is paid by a grant, does that release you from all or a portion or none of your teaching responsibilities? It is important to know where you stand on these kinds of questions to plan appropriate time commitments and staffing for the grant project in light of your other responsibilities.

Planning Your Research Agenda

When you are just starting your faculty career, it is sometimes difficult to think past tomorrow's lecture, let alone attempt to think in terms of your career as a whole, yet this way lies the road to successful proposals and grant-funded work that you will actually enjoy doing. Just as the institution must consider its goals in determining which grant funding to pursue, so must you as an individual faculty member consider your own interests and goals. It can be tempting to pursue a funding opportunity just because it is there: Tenure expectations that include receipt of grant funding probably do not specify what the funding is for; the tenure clock is ticking; the more proposals submitted, the better the chances of funding, right?

Wrong. Proposals written to chase money tend to flash neon don't-fund-me signs for reviewers, so the effort almost never pays off. Once in a blue moon, however, such a proposal is funded. Let's say you get funded for a project that does not really lie in your area of interest, although it is something you can do. Now you have to do the project, and you have to do it well. Sponsors are not fuzzy amoebic blobs; sponsors are made up of people, and people have memories. You cannot afford to be associated with a project done poorly. So now you have been diverted from your real agenda, with all the associated consequences and opportunity costs.

Stop and think. Where are your real strengths? What interests you the most? In grantsmanship workshops, we often begin with a draw-a-box exercise, asking participants to draw a box, a line in the sand, around their scholarly agendas. We ask them to list all of their scholarly strengths and interests and also to brainstorm areas that are somewhat related to but not really part of these central interests. The first list lies inside the box and represents appropriate fodder for grant proposals. The second list lies outside the box and represents opportunities for productive collaborations.

The difference between the two is extremely important and sometimes difficult to maintain. If you hold a faculty position in higher education, chances are good that you are very bright and intellectually curious. You can be lured to chase interesting questions as randomly as we chased lightning bugs as children here in the Midwest. You are good at academic work and accustomed to success. It can be hard to let go of the 10 other interesting questions intriguing you in order to systematically deal with one issue at a time. Let go you must, with the consolation of knowing that you have articulated all the interests on the list in the box and that you can come back to those interests later as time and opportunity allow.

Laying out a plan for your scholarly efforts can allow you to hang onto the whole of your interests while at the same time making your immediate effort more manageable. Having a planned agenda can also give you tremendous flexibility as to the chronology for implementing that agenda. Your plan provides a vehicle for assessing a funding opportunity that pops up unexpectedly and deciding whether it is worth your time to pursue it. It will allow you to see forward to the kinds of collaborators you are likely to need and to begin early to build relationships with them.

Some people seem to think of grants as one-time events. Get a grant, do the project, then look for another grant. It may work, but this strategy inherently assumes that your academic career will be stagnant, staying at the same level of funding (and effort) throughout your career (Figure 1).

Having a plan for your scholarly agenda will allow you to seek grant funding strategically so that each award serves as a stepping-stone to the next. We probably do not need to remind you that your time is limited, so strategy matters. Look at all the potential funders for your scholarly agenda with an eye toward which are more likely to sponsor smaller projects at the beginning of your career, which will be your "meat and potatoes" sponsors, and which will be the aspirational sponsors who fund large, collaborative projects after you have established your reputation. Think in

[handwritten margin note: Need to focus on one project at a time]

FIGURE 1

Grant-Seeking Career Strategies

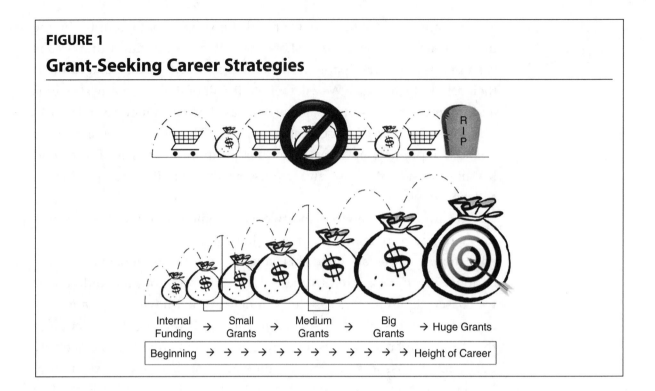

terms of using the early-stage sponsors to position yourself to grow into the next level of funding (Figure 1).

This kind of planning and prioritizing is the individual career context we mentioned at the beginning of this chapter. Just as institutions, divisions, and departments must set and manage priorities, your career will benefit if you take a strategic approach and maintain an informed awareness of the context in which you are working.

Take a strategic approach to your career

Chapter 2

The Matching Game: Finding Funders

Mary Licklider

WHEN IT COMES to identifying potential sources of funding, faculty members generally fall into one of two broad categories. Individuals in the first group know that there are well-established sources of funding for their fields of research, and for the most part they know what those sources are. An example is the basic biomedical researcher who will seek funding from "disease organizations" such as the American Heart Association or the Alzheimer's Association and from the National Institutes of Health. Faculty members in the second group either work in fields that do not have well-established sources of funding or they were never acclimated to grants culture during their graduate and postdoctoral experiences.

Funding searches for these two groups are somewhat different. For the first group, the focus is less on identifying potential sponsors than it is on understanding the current agendas and programs of the established sponsors. This is not to say, though, that faculty members in this group should not look for alternative sponsors. Your scholarly work parallels a small business in many ways, and one way to manage risk is to diversify sources of funding as much as you can in order to minimize the risk that if one category of sponsor or another cuts back, you won't go out of business. If the economy crashes and foundation endowments lose 30–40 percent of their value, as many did in the recent recession, or if Congress threatens to eliminate the Department of Education or (more recently) the Department of Agriculture and cuts the department's research budget, it is a good idea to have established relationships with multiple sponsors.

The well-established sponsors generally offer quite a bit of information online about their priorities and plans. If your primary sponsor is the National Institute of Allergies and Infectious Diseases (NIAID), for example, you would do well to make a habit of reading the NIAID Council's minutes, to subscribe to the weekly *NIH Guide for Grants and Contracts*, and to set up a funding search that specifically pulls out any NIAID announcements—all strategies for keeping up with any shifts in the interests and developing an understanding of the culture of this sponsor.

If you are a faculty member whose work does not have an obvious sponsor, this level of ongoing investment in one particular sponsor may not be worthwhile. Instead, the focus for you is on conducting the most thorough funding search possible to identify the sponsors whose agendas most closely match yours. This usually entails using more than one funding-opportunity database, examining the giving histories of potential sponsors, perhaps using Internet search engines for further information, and tapping any campus personnel and other colleagues who may have information about or relationships with a particular sponsor. The goal is to invest time on the front end so as not to waste time later with proposals that are not likely to be funded.

Funding Opportunities Databases

There are a number of these products, some more expensive than others. The industry standard for some time was the COS Funding Opportunities database, a ProQuest RefWorks product that has been recently replaced by PIVOT (http://pivot.cos.com). With over 26,000 funding opportunities, a reliable abstracting system, and an extensive, hierarchically nested thesaurus, PIVOT is probably the most comprehensive database. At this writing, RefWorks was in the process of phasing out the COS brand, incorporating the COS funding opportunities and Scholar Universe products into the new PIVOT offering that brings with it a substantial increase in subscription fees. If the traffic on the electronic mailing list of the National Organization of Research Development Professionals is any indication, this transition is causing many institutions to rethink their subscription services.

Competing funding opportunity subscription databases include IRIS (Illinois Researcher Information Service), with about 9,000 funding opportunities (http://www.library.illinois.edu/iris/), and InfoEd's SPIN (http://infoedglobal.com/solutions/grants-contracts/spin-funding-opportunities/), which tracks about 10,000 funding sources. Both PIVOT and SPIN include international opportunities. SPIN, PIVOT, and IRIS could all be categorized as comprehensive databases, including both public and private sector funding opportunities. They are organized around the individual funding opportunities rather than around the sponsor as a whole, and all are targeted to the academic consumer.

In contrast, foundation databases, such as those of the Foundation Center's Foundation Directory Online (http://www.foundationcenter.org/) and Foundation Search America (http://www.foundationsearch.com/), provide information about funding opportunities but are probably of the most value in their focus on the sponsor as a whole. Depending upon the level of your subscription, these databases can also provide access to much smaller private sponsors that operate at the state and local levels and that tend not to be included in the larger, comprehensive databases. Despite its name, Foundation Search America tracks foundations in other English-speaking countries as well as in the United States. Because private funders often place priority on specific geographic areas, both of these foundation databases offer geographic tools to enable searches of sponsors based in particular areas and of awards made in particular areas down to the county level. If your work includes localized study populations or outreach activities, these tools can be extremely valuable.

Grants.gov is the federal government's effort toward a one-stop source of information about federal funding opportunities and portal for e-submission of proposals. Whereas the search tools on Grants.gov are not nearly as sophisticated as those of the commercial products, Grants.gov usually has the information from federal agencies a little sooner than the commercial services do.

Effective Database Searches

To get the best results from these large, general databases may take a little time and experimentation, but the ability to save your searches permanently makes this investment of time worthwhile.

Start by noodling around with natural language in the main search screen to get a baseline idea of the numbers of opportunities in the disciplinary area you are researching. Then proceed to the advanced search options. Useful options in the PIVOT interface include Citizenship/ Residency, Activity Location, and Funding Type. Because PIVOT is an international database, your next step is probably to exclude opportunities that require non-US citizenship/residency and activity locations. The Funding Type category allows you to focus on research to the exclusion of awards, conference grants, and other special purposes. After you have narrowed the search through these options and perhaps others, save the search. Finally, run the same search using the database's keyword thesaurus instead of natural language, narrow it, and save the search.

At this point, compare the two (or more) sets of search results to see which yielded the most useful results and the least number of irrelevant results. If there are patterns in the results, these can sometimes help you modify one of the searches or combine the searches to create the search you will ultimately save. If, for example, many of the irrelevant results list the same keyword, exclude that keyword from the final search. If the combination of the natural language and the keyword searches together produced the most comprehensive results, combine the two sets of search terms in the final search.

If you are having trouble identifying funding opportunities, try ratcheting the level of abstraction up a few notches: instead of *oncogenesis*, try *cancer*. Try thinking of your field as an instance of a larger concept: instead of *at-risk preschoolers*, try *elementary education*. Try thinking of the broader purpose of your work: instead of *Alzheimer's*, try terms associated with elder care; instead of *fertilizer run-off*, try *water quality*. Finally, think about the populations affected by the issue you are studying: instead of *breast cancer*, try *women's issues*; instead of *food deserts*, try *urban issues* or funders focusing on a particular city.

use broader search terms if necessary

If you are having trouble establishing a good search and you have access to a grant writing consultant, see if you can schedule time for the consultant to sit with you as you work on the search criteria. I do not usually recommend that grant writing consultants spend time distributing funding opportunities to the faculty members with whom they work. As a general rule, this does not seem to me to be a good use of human expertise when there are so many electronic tools available to do this more thoroughly, more often, and with more specificity to individual interests. I do, however, think that a grant writing consultant can be a valuable asset in helping the individual faculty member establish a thorough yet focused search. As an outsider to your field but someone who probably has more experience with the funding opportunities database than you do, the grant writing consultant can often help to identify alternative search terms and approaches that will improve the results of the search.

E-mail Funding Alerts

As the name implies, e-mail funding alerts send messages directly to your e-mail account for particular kinds of funding opportunities. Your primary funding alert will probably derive from a saved search on one of the comprehensive funding opportunities databases—PIVOT, SPIN, or IRIS. The earlier you know about a funding opportunity, the more time you have to prepare a strong proposal. With that rather obvious truth in mind, you will probably want to set up alerts with more than one service. Although the weekly alert from a comprehensive database such as PIVOT, IRIS, or SPIN will be the foundation of your funding notices, you will want to consider additional options to be sure you are not missing anything and you receive notices as soon as possible. If your sponsors are likely to be federal agencies, set up an alert in Grants.gov as well. Several of the federal agencies send weekly notices of grant opportunities, although the numbers of these seem to be declining as Grants.gov matures. The NIH (http://grants.nih.gov/grants/guide/) and NASA NSPIRES (http://nspires.nasaprs.com/external/index.do) systems send weekly notices of opportunities. The NSF Update (https://service.govdelivery.com/service/multi_subscribe.html?code=USNSF&custom_id=823) allows customization so that notices are limited to your field or fields of interest. The Congressionally Directed Medical Research Programs (CDMRP; http://cdmrp.army.mil/) arm of the Department of Defense funds numerous biomedical research programs. To receive funding opportunity notifications from these programs, send an e-mail to help@cdmrp.org.

For many of us, e-mail volume is already overwhelming. It can be difficult to even think about doing anything that would make matters worse. On the other hand, many of us fail to use the tools we already have for managing e-mail. The most obvious option for managing funding opportunity alerts is to set up an e-mail rule so that all messages from a particular source (or sources) are automatically routed to a designated e-mail folder. If you plan to leave the rule turned on more or less permanently, make a recurring calendar note and block out time to scan these e-mails every couple of weeks—or at least once a month. Turn the rule off to allow these e-mails to accumulate in your in-box when you need to watch for a specific opportunity. To help clear your in-box without unsubscribing to the lists, turn the rule on when e-mail volume is high or time is especially short. With PIVOT, you can turn the e-mail alerts for each search on and off from the individual web page that comes with your PIVOT account. An archive of the most recent weeks of results is available from this web page, as is the option to run the full search rather than just seeing the new results for the week.

If you are working on a proposal for a specific funding opportunity or waiting for the agency to announce this year's guidelines for an annual funding opportunity, both PIVOT and Grants.gov will allow you to "track" the opportunity so that you are notified via e-mail if the sponsor posts any additional information or revisions to the opportunity. Use this option. Additions and revisions happen more often than you'd think.

Funder Research

At this point, I have a good news–bad news message: The funding opportunities databases are just the starting point for your funder research. The goal of this research is to run potential funders and their funding opportunities through finer and finer sieves, moving from what Brown and Brown, in *Demystifying Grant Seeking* (2001), call *leads* to *prospects* and finally to maybe three or four that are truly *matches*. Proposals are time- and labor-intensive endeavors. Most of us do not have time to just throw things at the wall and see what sticks. Similarly, sponsor personnel have little patience with proposals that are poorly matched to the sponsor's priorities or guidelines. You do not want the sponsor to associate you with a proposal that looks as though you failed to do your homework.

The database searches and weekly alerts will help you to identify a number of leads. The next step is to dig into those leads a little further. For public sector sponsors, this means reading the announcement, which may be called a Funding Opportunity Announcement (FOA), a Request for Proposals or Applications (RFP or RFA), a Program Announcement (PA), a Broad Agency Announcement (BAA), or another of any number of such terms. Technically, each of these terms has a distinct definition, but in recent years some sponsors seem to be using at least some of these terms interchangeably. Whatever the label, read the document carefully, including the text at the beginning that you will be tempted to skip. Public agencies usually include information somewhere toward the beginning of an announcement that explains the agency's view of the needs to be addressed by the funding program and the current state of work in this area. This section is extremely valuable in assessing the context, biases, assumptions, and goals of the agency. With this information as background, you will be positioned to read between the lines of the more specific proposal guidelines to decide whether or not your project looks like a match.

Research on Private Sector Sponsors

Public sector programs are just that: public. The United States is a democracy in which there is an expectation of transparency in the use of tax dollars. It is in the agency's interest to publish clear guidelines and respond to questions so as to secure as many strong proposals as possible. This in turn strengthens the agency during the budget process by demonstrating the need for its programs. If a public agency wants to fund new shoes, for example, agency personnel will have to demonstrate a need for new shoes and specify what kinds they expect to fund for what purposes.

Private sector sponsors, on the other hand, are not accountable to the taxpayer. If I as a private sponsor want to fund new shoes, I go buy some. My money, my decision. If I seek proposals from others for providing me with new shoes, I want them to tell me about the shoes, not the need for shoes or the importance or purpose of shoes. I know all that or I wouldn't have asked for shoes. I do not need or want a great many proposals that will eat up staff time for review. I want a few proposals for the right kind of shoes. And I definitely do not want proposals that attempt to talk me into boots or sandals.

So as a general rule, proposal guidelines from public sector sponsors, as well as proposals to public sponsors, include more information and more details than guidelines from and proposals to private sector sponsors. Paradoxically, private sector sponsors tend to want fewer contacts and fewer proposals. This is why many institutions of higher education place responsibility for relationships with foundation and corporate sponsors with fundraising personnel in the development office rather than leaving individual faculty members to make their own contacts, as they do with federal sponsors.

info for getting 990

Given that private sector sponsors tend to provide less information in their online materials and program guidelines, additional research is usually needed to determine whether a match exists between a given sponsor and your project. For foundations, one indispensable source is the foundation's 990, the foundation's equivalent to the individual taxpayer's 1040 tax return. If you already know the name of the sponsor, you can look up the 990 for free via the Foundation Center at http://www.foundationcenter.org/ or Guidestar at http://www2.guidestar.org/Home.aspx. Look at the total value of the foundation's assets on the first page. By law, a public foundation must pay out at least 5 percent of its assets each year, so the total assets number on the first page will give you a rough idea of the scale of the foundation's programs. Check the names of board members or trustees in Part VIII. Ask your development officer to see if any of these individuals are alums who might serve as internal advocates for your project.

Spend some time with the list of grants and contributions, usually at the end of each year's 990 document. Look for projects similar to yours: serving the same population, in the same geographic area, doing similar work. Look at the amounts of awards. If you are requesting your first award from this sponsor, do not ask for the largest amount they gave in past years; build trust gradually. Look at the past grantees and consider whether there might be opportunities to collaborate. Consider contacting past grantees to ask about their experience in working with this sponsor. Ask your sponsored programs office to run a query on your institution's grant system and see if the sponsor has made recent awards to your institution. If so, talk to the faculty members who led those projects.

Research on Public Sector Sponsors

Public sector sponsors do not file tax returns, of course, but some of them do post information that parallels the 990 data. The National Institutes of Health, with about $30 billion in extramural funding each year, is the largest research granting agency and not surprisingly devotes staff time to providing a great deal of information about its research funding. The NIH Research Portfolio Online Reporting Tools Expenditures and Results (RePORTER) at http://projectreporter.nih.gov/reporter.cfm has a powerful search interface that allows the user to search funded projects by program, funding mechanism, grantee institution, even Congressional district. Once you find a useful project, there is a "similar projects" button on the far right side of the results table that allows you to pull just that. Use this system to see who has had funding like yours—these can be seen as your competition, but they are also potential collaborators. See if the program you are considering has funded your institution in the past. If so, talk to the principal investigator to see if there is a way for your work to build on the existing relationship. Grant proposals to federal agencies are considered public information once an award is made, and these proposals can be acquired under Freedom of Information Act requests. But this takes time. Many principal investigators will share their proposals, and a phone call to ask for a copy can double as an opportunity to network with a colleague in your field.

Another source of NIH reconnaissance is the extensive data on proposal success rates at http://report.nih.gov/success_rates/index.aspx. If your work straddles several NIH institutes and centers, look up the funding mechanism (for example, R01, R21) you plan to use and compare success rates across the NIH institutes and centers. This information may tell you which aspects of the work should be emphasized in order to submit to the unit with the best success rates.

Once you know the institute or center to which you will submit your proposal, look up the descriptions and rosters of the scientific review panels for this unit at http://www.csr.nih.gov/Committees/rosterindex .asp. NIH uses both standing and ad hoc review panels. Members of the standing panels serve three-year rotating terms, so it is likely that two-thirds of the panel members you see listed will actually review your proposal. The language of the panel descriptions can be extremely useful in determining which panel would be the best target for your proposal. The cover letter template for NIH proposals (U.S. Department of Health and Human Services, Public Health Service, 2011, pp. I-92–93) includes a recommendation as to the appropriate study section to which a proposal should be directed. Use this opportunity to get the most informed peer review of your proposal. Suggest the panel you think would have the most expertise in the area of your project and use language from the panel description in the text of your cover letter to reinforce your recommendation.

Finally, each NIH institute and center has an advisory council. Minutes of these councils can give you advance notice of shifting priorities. Go to the home page of your institute or center to search for the council minutes, bookmark the council minutes' web address, and set a calendar reminder to ensure that you take time every quarter to skim through the minutes.

The National Science Foundation's award site at http://nsf.gov/awardsearch/ is another powerful tool for researching prior awards to the program or directorate you plan to target, as well as awards in your field or to your institution. A related site at http://dellweb.bfa.nsf.gov/ provides a number of reports that track funding trends and success rates. NSF does not use standing review panels, so you cannot look up panel membership as you can for the NIH, but you can look up the current list of ad hoc panels at http://www.nsf.gov/events/advisory.jsp. The NSF allows you to suggest experts who would be well-qualified to review your proposal. The NSF practice of using only ad hoc review panels means that individuals are not locked into panel service for years and that program officers must continuously identify experts to staff review panels. I have to believe that any help you can provide in identifying appropriate expertise would be appreciated.

Both the NSF and NIH also allow you to note anyone who should not be asked to review your proposal. This option may seem like questionable etiquette, but when you consider that most fields at one time or another are split into competing theoretical camps, the option to ask that those in the opposing camp be excluded from your review panel seems reasonable.

The National Science Board is the primary advisory group for the NSF, and minutes of its meetings are posted at http://www.nsf.gov/nsb/meetings/. Each directorate has an advisory committee, and you can find minutes for meetings of these groups by going to the home page of the appropriate NSF unit.

The US Department of Agriculture's grant award reporting system is the Current Research Information System (CRIS), which is expected to migrate to a new REEport system. CRIS is available at http://cris.nifa .usda.gov/aboutus.html, and summary reports are available at http:// cris.nifa.usda.gov/fsummaries.html . . . and so it goes. The agencies with the most funding for extramural research and scholarship tend to provide more details about review processes, funded projects, and success rates, but every federal agency I've checked provides at least some of this data.

· · ·

Guidelines, sponsor websites, and 990 tax returns are all organized sources of information about potential sponsors that can help you assess the match between a given sponsor and your institution, your project, and your study population. It can also be useful to run the sponsor's name and perhaps the board members' names through an Internet search engine. This kind of less-organized search can occasionally turn up very recent activities that have not made their way into the sponsor's materials yet or special interests of the sponsor's decision makers that may be relevant to your project. And remember to read the blurbs at the ends of journal articles in your field. These frequently include recognition of the entity that sponsored the research and can lead you to additional sponsors. Talk to your colleagues and professional networks. Many of the best leads will come from these sources because they are working in the same field as you.

Read blurbs at the end of journal articles for sponsors

Assessing the Match

These second-tier funding research activities will likely rule out a number of the potential sponsors that your initial database work identified. Using the "Deal or No Deal" worksheet in Section One of this book's Toolkit (Part Two) to examine a given funding opportunity in your current career and institutional context may help you determine which of several funding opportunities is most appropriate to your current circumstances.

In most cases, you will probably still be left with a handful of potential sponsors, certainly fewer than 10, that appear to be solid matches with your research agenda. These are your prospects, and your research into their guidelines and funding histories almost always leaves you with some unanswered questions that prevent you from knowing whether this prospect is truly a match. This is the time to call the sponsor's program officer.

I have found many faculty members to be reluctant to make a cold call to a program officer. If this is the case for you, it might help to consider the program officer's perspective. Most program officers are scientists or scholars—specialists in the field of grants they supervise. They built their careers actually doing the work and were then tapped to oversee the sponsor's grant program. My experience is that these folks love to talk shop, and they enjoy helping faculty callers refine their project ideas. Think of it this way: would you rather grade papers or talk shop with a colleague? This is not to say that program officers have all the time in the world. You should be well prepared, but you certainly should not hesitate to contact the sponsor.

To prepare, you'll need to do three things, and for private sector sponsors, a fourth:

- Read the sponsor's program guidelines carefully.

- Think through your project at a level of detail that allows you to boil it down to a three- to five-sentence summary.

- Make a written list of your questions for the program officer.

- If you are considering a private sector sponsor, check in with your institution's corporate and foundation relations personnel.

The rationale for the first task should be obvious. You do not want the program officer's first impression to be that you are too lazy or negligent to read the information the agency provides.

The reason for the second task is that preparing a short description of your project will allow you to move very quickly from the part of the conversation in which you are doing the talking to the part in which the program officer is doing most of the talking. In the grant world, we call this an "elevator pitch": Pretend that you are getting on an elevator on the first floor with a potential collaborator or sponsor. This person pushes the button for the third floor. Your goal is to tell this person about your work quickly and in lay language, capturing the listener's interest so that he or she will stay with you past the third floor to learn more.

The point of communicating with sponsor personnel is for you to *listen*. You want answers to your specific questions, of course, but you also want to listen for the details that were not included in the sponsor's written guidelines, for any unwritten biases, and for the language the

Use speaker phone & have someone take notes

sponsor's personnel use to describe concepts. This brings me to another recommendation for these calls: use a speakerphone and have someone with you to take notes. It's hard to simultaneously manage a meeting and take the minutes. If you have access to a grant writing consultant, ask the consultant to sit in and take notes on any calls to the program officer. If you do not have access to a grant writing consultant, consider including a graduate research assistant, a colleague who will be participating in the project, or your significant other—find someone who is willing take notes, and ask this person to read the guidelines ahead of the call for context.

Make a written list of your questions for the program officer, even if you have only two questions. These conversations can take unexpected turns. It can be ridiculously easy to forget what you wanted to ask and thoroughly embarrassing to have to call back the next day because you need the answer.

As noted earlier in this chapter, private sector sponsors may expect the grantee institution to prioritize funding requests so that the sponsor sees fewer proposals and can avoid the personnel expense entailed in managing a large volume of proposals. For some, this translates to an expectation that the grantee institutions will identify a single person to serve as the institution's liaison with the sponsor. Calls from individuals other than this liaison can be viewed as evidence that one hand does not know what the other is doing at the grantee institution. This is why corporate and foundation relations personnel serve as gatekeepers for contacts with some sponsors. In other cases, a sponsor capable of a very large award is carefully cultivated by the institution's leadership over a period of several years to build the sponsor's confidence in the grantee institution. To step in from the sidelines and ask such a sponsor to fund an unrelated project can derail the whole process. For these reasons, you will want to check in with your institution's foundation or corporate relations personnel to give them the chance to coordinate any contacts with these kinds of sponsors.

Short Deadlines

How can you possibly develop a fundable proposal in a month? The key here is to watch your potential sponsor's advisory council or board meeting minutes, study their priority areas and established programs, and note any concepts that are approved for future funding. By doing so, you can anticipate upcoming priorities the agency is interested in funding. You can anticipate a call for proposals and begin to prepare before it even comes out to the general public.

Summary

Yes, this all takes time. If you have a graduate research assistant (GRA), consider engaging him or her in this sponsor research. It's good training. I see too many young faculty members and postdocs whose mentors failed to engage them in grant work, leaving them completely unprepared to enter academic careers in which extramural funding is an expectation. Even if you do not have a GRA or a grant writing consultant who can help, funder research is very much a pay-me-now-or-pay-me-later situation. You can either do the research or do the extra work of submitting mismatched proposals that are not only doomed before they are ever submitted but also carry the additional risk of aggravating the sponsor. It is a far more efficient and effective use of the resource that your time represents to do the research. The advice in this chapter is applied to two types of research in the boxes "Funding Plan for a Young Scientist or Engineer" and "Funding Plan for a Humanities Scholar."

Funding Plan for a Young Scientist or Engineer

Shelley A. Hilton

Congratulations! After an exhausting and competitive job search, you landed your first tenure-track faculty position. Now is no time to rest on your laurels. It is time to launch your research career. As you embark on your academic career, work with your department chair or mentor to develop 1-, 5- and 10-year plans for your research.

As you develop your research plans, consider your career goal. What do you want to accomplish in this field of study? Then think in terms of chunks—steps toward your goal. If everything goes as planned, what can be achieved in one year to advance toward that goal? Five years? Ten years? The current research environment is increasingly interdisciplinary or multidisciplinary, so you will also want to consider the need for collaborators.

After developing a plan, consider possible funding sources for your work. Again, think in terms of chunks. If possible, you should seek assistance from grant personnel at your institution to learn about various funding search databases and set up electronic funding alerts. Faculty members in many disciplines know what their primary funding sources will be, whereas others must be more creative to identify sources of funding. Either way, it is wise to start small to reduce the sponsor's perception of risk—new researchers are seen as a higher risk because they lack experience with managing research projects and grants. Gradually build your research program over time. You may want to start, for example, with internal funding opportunities at your institution. These often target new researchers and are intended as seed funding to gather preliminary data which will strengthen your next proposal for external funding.

There are also several federal programs designed specifically to launch the research careers of promising new faculty. Examples include the NSF's Faculty Early Career Development (CAREER) program (http://www.nsf.gov/funding/pgm_summ.jsp?pims_id=503214), various Department of Defense Young Investigator programs, and the NIH "K" mechanisms (http://grants.nih.gov/training/careerdevelopmentawards.htm).

(Continued)

Several federal agencies have mechanisms in place to identify new or early-stage investigators, and those individuals are often given special consideration in funding decisions. Be sure you know whether your funding agency employs such a mechanism, how they define *new* or *early-stage*, what you need to do to identify yourself as such, and how this impacts the review process.

Once you get the ball rolling and submit your first proposal or receive your first award, keep going. You should continually apply for more funding so that before one project expires, your next project is funded. As your career progresses, your funding levels should increase and should keep you moving toward your career goal.

Funding Plan for a Humanities Scholar

Mary Barile

Finding funding for the arts and humanities is challenging. Although you may need to be persistent and creative to identify and pursue research funding, the good news is that most scholarship and creative work in humanities disciplines tends to be far less costly than in the life and physical sciences. One similarity, however, is that you should take the advice Shelley Hilton offers scientists: work with a mentor or more senior faculty member to look ahead at least three to five years and build your research agenda around your long-term goals. From there, I can offer several tips:

- Start local. Internal campus grants can be as large as federal support and far less competitive. Community grants often support outreach activities. State humanities and arts councils vary widely in their funding for university faculty, but most of these councils do sponsor humanities activities. You can use smaller grants to attend conferences or pay for research-related travel, and you can also use them as leverage in applying for larger grants. Two or three years of local or state funding can fill gaps in your budget and develop your grant writing skills.

- Know your potential foundation sponsors. Developing relationships with foundations takes time. Humanities funding from foundations may cover everything from planning and outreach to programming, development, and consultations. Identify your local foundations and consider inviting them to your events so that they become familiar with your work. Major national foundations may be approached through your institution's development officers, who are generally aware of contact people and current areas of interest for these foundations.

- Consider partnerships with business. Local companies may support work that contributes to the company's area of interest or the community's quality of life. It is not unusual for foundation and business partnerships to continue over the life of a project, even though initial funding may be for a single year.

- Maintain realistic expectations for federal grants. Federally funded projects in the humanities tend to have shorter terms than in the sciences. The National Endowments for the Arts and the Humanities, for example, generally fund for one or two years. These grants may be substantial and are certainly prestigious, and this sometimes—but not always—means that you should wait until your career is well established to apply. Communication with a program officer at the agency will help you make decisions about the viability of your project idea and personnel.

- Communicate with your department chair about fellowship opportunities. Fellowships provide you with time off for research, writing, and other scholarly or creative activities. This time away can complicate your chair's job by requiring that someone else be identified to cover your teaching responsibilities. Before you invest time in developing a fellowship application, discuss the timing of the fellowship and coverage of your courses with your chair. Some fellowships will fund only your salary and benefits, whereas others include funding for expenses such as travel, lodging, books, and other supplies. Some last for a semester, others for a year. Because the most common funding need for humanities faculty members is time, the concentrated effort that a fellowship allows can make a significant impact on your career.

- Finally, don't give up. Getting funded is not so much an event as it is a process, and "no" is a normal part of that process on your way to "yes."

Chapter 3

Tapping Support on Campus

Bob Glidewell and Diane Oerly

REGARDLESS OF WHETHER you work at a major research institution or a community college, all postsecondary educational institutions have at least some administrative and grant development resources that you can and should tap in support of your grant proposal. You will develop a better grant proposal package if you avail yourself of these potential resources. The trick is to find them, and you may be surprised by the resources and services that are available for the asking. It has been our experience that many faculty members who seek to develop grant proposals are unaware of the resources that may be available to them at their institutions. Although this is especially true of faculty and researchers just beginning their academic careers, it can also be true of established faculty members with plenty of previous grant experience.

Many of these resources are in the form of experienced administrators and staff who are willing to provide information you need and assist you with proposal development. Accessing these resources can allow you to be more efficient with the time you invest in developing your grant proposal, have a better understanding of what sponsors and institutions will need from you as the applicant, and reduce the stress, both professional and sometimes personal, that can plague the proposal development process. Finally, tapping these resources can help you develop proposals that will have a greater chance of being funded.

First Things First

Before you begin to search for and access campus resources, polish the "elevator pitch" that you developed for sponsors' program officers (see "Assessing the Match" in Chapter 2). You need a clear understanding of what you want to do or accomplish through the project. You can begin by asking yourself some simple questions to clarify your areas of interest and the type of work you intend to do: What problems will your work address, or what questions will it answer? What will be the outcomes of the work? Who will benefit? How much money will it take to do the work well?

Answering questions like these will allow you to provide some basic but very necessary information to administrators and support staff who can help you develop your proposal. This handbook's Toolkit includes a list of questions that can help you focus the plans for your project. (In Part Two of this book and in the online Toolkit at [see p. iv], see "Pre-writing Questions" in Section One and "Four Sentences to Focus Your Elevator Pitch" and "Developing a Concept Paper" in Section Two).

Try Not to Do Everything Yourself

In some departments, pursuing grants is seen as a distraction from the research itself. After all, the typical faculty member did not spend years acquiring an education only to "major" in grant writing. Indeed, if you do everything from finding a potential sponsor to researching and developing drafts and budgets and then submitting a finished proposal yourself, the work can seem to stretch into endless hours of effort away from what you really want to do. Even though you will need to invest significant time and effort, there are many resources that can greatly lessen the workload and allow you to focus more of your time on the elements of the proposal that actually require your expertise. The types and levels of these resources will vary from one institution to the next. Some resources will be formally part of your department's or institution's infrastructure, and others will be available more informally.

The First Grant

Mark B. Child

Stephen Sayers, associate professor in the MU School of Health Professions, studies geriatric rehabilitation in physical therapy. He received his first federal grant award from the National Institute on Aging for high-velocity resistance training in older men and women. In our interview, Sayers still recalls that moment like it was yesterday: "I remember feeling that I had arrived! The difference between feeling like a graduate student or postdoc and a real faculty member came to me the moment I received my score from the NIH reviewers. At that point, I knew that I could do this job and that I would be successful." Not only did Sayers's first grant award instill confidence that he could compete in the federal arena, it also reassured him that he could obtain future awards. "My experience obtaining my first grant award led to confidence in submitting other grants—knowing that I had done it once, I knew I could do it again."

Looking back on the proposal development process for his first federal grant, Sayers asserts, "I was very confident in my idea, so I knew that the project would be received very well if I just wrote it adequately. And the interesting thing is that writing the proposal narrative was not a struggle at all; it almost wrote itself." This is not unusual for scholars who are so immersed in the work that they develop an expansive familiarity with the subject.

However, a lack of familiarity with the other requirements of proposal development can be difficult. Sayers explains, "It was the other aspects of the grant that I struggled with: budgets, justifications, resources—things that I didn't think about much until the grant deadline got closer and I was running out of time." The obvious lesson is to give yourself adequate time to deal with the unfamiliar requirements of proposal development, but perhaps less obvious is the value of tapping institutional resources. Sayers emphasizes this in his comment that "I wish I had known more about working with grant writers, setting up deadlines, and having someone read and review my work. I did not understand the complexity of writing a full NIH grant, and because of that, spent the final few weeks before the grant was due working around the clock and operating on very little sleep." Sayers sums up his memory of the process that led to his first grant award, noting, "Perhaps no one can really know until they write that first grant what sort of time commitment it involves, but my experience was quite a wake-up call!"

Strategic Discussions with Institutional Leadership

Some faculty members can be reluctant, at least initially, to approach the department chair, school dean, or other institutional leader. The reasons for this vary. You simply may not want to "impose" upon individuals in authority, who are busy. You may be concerned that the chair will discourage you from pursuing funding because "there's no money in the humanities anyway." (Not true, by the way.) You may worry about whether your project fits with institutional priorities.

Take a deep breath and make the appointment. Institutional leaders can be a treasure trove of information. Although they are aware of short-term goals for the institution, they also look to mid- and long-term goals. There may be a new degree program being planned or a new research center in the works that aligns with your proposed project. Deans and chairs often have histories of successful grant funding in their fields and may have knowledge of new multidisciplinary projects, internal funding, or resources outside your school or department that could be available to your project. Even if such additional resources are not available, placing your chair or dean in a position to advocate for your project cannot hurt, and it will carry the certain advantage that when you finish your proposal, the internal approval process will go more smoothly because of this familiarity. This kind of conversation typically takes no more than

30 minutes, so you can lay to rest concerns about eating up too much time. Just be prepared with your elevator pitch so that you can start the meeting with a clear, concise summary that invites questions and feedback.

Support Staff

Support staff can often provide assistance specific to your situation. All resources will not be available at all institutions, and the resources available at your institution may be structured into unlikely positions. Most institutions of higher education have been around for many, many years, and positions have evolved as needs have changed. Sometimes that evolution can result in counterintuitive titles and duties. For this reason, we encourage you to ask about the tasks and expertise you need rather than asking for someone with a given job title.

Grant Writing Consultants

And speaking of counterintuitive job titles, "grant writer" is a case in point. See the Preface for an overview of the titles and typical responsibilities of grant writing consultants in higher education. Whatever the title, if your institution makes a grant writing consultant available, he or she will be one of the first people to approach for help. If you are at a larger university, a grant writing consultant may be assigned to your college or department. If you are at a smaller institution, there may be grant writing consultants available through a central administrative office, such as the office of research, to assist faculty members across campus. To find out about grant writing consultants at your institution, start by contacting your dean's or provost's office. Typical tasks with which a grant writing consultant can help include conducting funder research, becoming an expert on the sponsor's guidelines, providing a timeline for proposal development, helping to manage the proposal development process, offering professional editing and proofreading services, and drafting a budget and budget justification.

Funder Research

Once you have identified an area of interest for which you need external funding, the grant writing consultant can help you set up and fine tune the searches that generate weekly e-mail funding alerts (see "E-mail Funding Alerts" in Chapter 2 for more information on these alert services). Many of us make a practice of monitoring funding opportunities for projects in the areas in which our faculty members work and may know of sources for useful information, such as the award histories of government, corporate, and foundation sponsors and the history of a given sponsor with your institution.

Sponsor Guidelines

Every sponsor has its own guidelines and procedures for proposal submission. We sometimes wonder if this is a strategy for managing the number of grant applications they receive and "culling the herd" of applicants. Proposals can be rejected without review for failure to follow the sponsor's guidelines. At face value, this may seem harsh, but it is logical. If the applicant does not follow the guidelines in requesting the funding, how can the sponsor expect the applicant to follow the rules for managing the award?

Sponsor guidelines may be as short as 3 pages or as long as 100-plus pages. Grant writing consultants can ensure that you have the most current sponsor guidelines and track any revisions the sponsor issues. Grant writing consultants can serve as the guidelines experts on your proposal teams. They can develop checklists of required materials and supporting documents to be sure nothing is overlooked. They can create proposal outlines as described in Chapter 5 (see "Create an Outline") and ensure that all documents are formatted as required.

Proposal Development Timeline

You may be focused on completing your tasks and keeping the proposal development process moving along more or less on schedule, but your proposal may not be such a forefront concern for all of your collaborators. Teaching, research, service, and personal obligations make it easy to forget an approaching deadline, particularly if it is for a proposal you are not leading. This can stimulate a sudden rush to throw something together the week before the deadline—the Hail Mary pass of grant work.

Last-minute work usually looks and reads like last-minute work, and a grant writing consultant can help alleviate this risk by creating a proposal development timeline for your team (see "Prepare a Proposal Development Timeline" in Chapter 5 for an explanation of these timelines). This timeline will make it easier to assign tasks. The consultant can monitor the evolving proposal and the timeline, providing reminders to you and your collaborators to complete the assigned tasks. Although we sometimes feel like nags, this client's response is typical: "It just comes at us so fast sometimes that I can't overemphasize the importance of your squeaky wheel. And it's such a melodic squeak—not one of those metallic squeaks that makes you cover your ears."

Editorial Assistance

Grant writing consultants do not generally write the proposals for you. But once you have a draft of the project narrative and other text pieces, the consultant can edit to be sure your logical argument is clear and compelling. Because the grant writing consultant is not an expert in your field, it can be easier for the consultant to identify and edit passages that are too technical in order to make the proposal more readable for an educated lay reader. For grant writing consultants, length limits are a fact of life, and your consultant can also help tighten your language without losing content. Finally, the grant writing consultant can proofread the proposal for surface errors in grammar, usage, and punctuation.

Budget

The grant writing consultant can lead you through a series of questions to help develop the project budget and then incorporate your responses into a spreadsheet. If equipment bids will be needed, the grant writing consultant can help to secure those. The grant writing consultant can also help you communicate with collaborators and subcontracting institutions to develop the budgets for their contributions to the project. If the consultant is involved in developing the budget itself, he or she will then know enough to create a first draft of the budget justification for you. Although this draft will almost certainly not be acceptable as is, we have found that our faculty clients can correct our work faster than they can create a budget justification on their own from scratch, so the draft represents a strategy for saving their time. This can also be true for other proposal documents such as letters of commitment.

Other Duties as Assigned

Other assistance that you may want the grant writing consultant to provide includes coordinating tasks between the proposal development team and other institutional grants and contracts personnel, entering the proposal into your institution's grant management system, securing internal signatures approving submission of the proposal, and tracking the proposal following submission to be sure that it actually arrives and is accepted by the sponsor.

Administrative Personnel

As you seek assistance with proposal development, you may discover that your department's or school's administrative staff can assist with some tasks such as developing the budget, creating biographical sketches, entering the proposal in the institution's grant management system, or securing internal approvals for your proposal. Sometimes administrative personnel will check your budget spreadsheet to be sure that all the formulas are correct, the correct facilities and administration (F&A) rate is used, and the F&A rate is applied to the correct budget items. For some departments, administrative personnel will handle submission of your proposal to the campus sponsored-programs office.

Fiscal Officers

Developing a project budget can be time consuming. You will likely find help by contacting the fiscal person in your department or school. Your fiscal person can provide information and advice on salaries, pay scales, and fringe benefits for faculty, postdocs, research assistants, and student workers. This person will also be able to explain which items are and are not covered by your institution's F&A rate agreement. When you receive the award (note that is *when*, not *if*), your fiscal officer will help you with the accounting and reporting responsibilities for your award.

Legal and Compliance Issues

The process of developing a grant proposal involves many legal issues, even at the proposal stage. You may be surprised to realize that, as the principal investigator or project director, you are almost certainly not authorized to sign off on your own proposal on behalf of your institution. Grant awards are usually made to your institution rather than to you as an individual or even to you as a faculty member.

This is actually a good thing. It means your institution assumes legal liability for the project, rather than you as an individual. The sponsor's guidelines, along with compliance regulations for expending your award, protecting human and animal subjects, obeying export control laws, complying with the Patriot Act—it would not be a good use of your time as a faculty member to try to become an expert in all these issues, and you definitely do not want to be legally liable for all that knowledge. Keeping up with the many and changing regulations is an example of an area where you can rely upon the expertise your institution provides rather than investing your own time. You have some responsibility to be aware of the areas that apply to your work and to understand the regulations well enough to conduct your project appropriately, but you can depend upon your institution to provide you with that understanding.

More and more sponsors seem to be incorporating intellectual property issues into terms and conditions for grant proposals and grant awards. If you have selected a sponsor other than a federal agency, it is a good idea to provide the funding opportunity guidelines to your sponsored programs personnel as soon as you begin work on the proposal so that they can check for any red flags in the terms and conditions. Likewise, when your grant award comes in, be sure to read the award language carefully before you sign. We have seen instances in which the researcher would be signing away all rights to any intellectual property developed during the project, despite the fact that the project represented only one step in a 20-year career of research in a given area. Again, you do not need to be the intellectual property expert. You only need to know who the experts are at your institution so that you can tap their expertise.

Maintaining Balance

Sherri Sachdev

Carolyn Henry is a professor of veterinary oncology. She currently has seven or eight active grant-funded projects, mostly in clinical research. She also teaches professional and graduate students and facilitates campus-wide collaborative efforts in health and medicine. Though she became tenured nine years ago, Henry remembers the challenges of being a new faculty member. "It definitely helps to find a mentor who has already been through it. It's important to know what 'counts' toward tenure. Expectations can be a moving target with changes in administration," warns Henry. For example, some departments do not consider grants from pharmaceutical companies as "real" funding. "Issues like this need to be outlined in the letter of offer," she advises, "as well as every time you have an annual review. Keep rigorous files that document your success and contributions."

Henry agrees that it is important to write grants throughout your career: "The proposal helps clarify the study design and provides an element of quality control. Grant success helps to build your research program, increase the numbers of trainees, and ultimately increase the stature of your institution." When asked about the secret to grant success, Henry replied, "Have someone who is not immersed in your area read your proposal. Your science may be fine, but if you don't convey the message, then it really doesn't matter. Start out with internal funding opportunities and then use the data from those projects to apply for external funding."

Henry spends approximately a third of her professional time on teaching. "The tenure decision process tries to reward teaching excellence, but the metrics are difficult to define," she says. "In my opinion, teaching success is revealed by the effectiveness of the end product—how prepared the students are for their careers—but this is difficult to document after the students are gone." New faculty members need to spend much more time on teaching preparations, but Henry now devotes more time to her research. "By now, I'm very comfortable with what I teach. I could get called out of bed and teach with one eye open if necessary," she laughs.

Balancing teaching, research, and scholarly activity is only part of the equation for Henry. She is also the mother of five children and three stepchildren and has been functioning as a single parent for the past 2 1/2 years following the death of her husband. Although departments often are willing to stop the tenure clock for major life events such as childbirth, she did not take advantage of this option. Instead, she used maternity leave as a time to write papers and grants. She says it helped that her husband was also an academic in her area and that they shared the parenting responsibilities. She recalls a day when her pager failed and her husband ended up taking their 10-day-old infant with him to perform a C-section on a cow.

I wondered how Henry manages to cope with relentless stress and avoid burnout. "There are a few things that I need to stay happy as a person," she replies. "I need time for exercise. I need time for faith and family, and I need social interaction that does not involve talking about work. I will usually sacrifice sleep before anything else. . . . Staying physically fit helps too," she adds. "Running gives me a chance to de-clutter my mind. No matter what, you need to schedule some time to unplug. Go to the most remote place you can find and turn on your out-of-office reply."

When asked about the best advice she received as a new faculty member, Henry replied, "Focus your efforts. Don't try to do everything. Do a few things well and establish your area. Most importantly, learn to say no."

Faculty Mentors

Most departments and programs include established faculty members who are both experienced and successful in garnering external funding. Successful scholars and scientists have valuable experience and will often share advice on potential funding opportunities and areas of special sponsor interest to which they are privy because of their relationships with program officers. Consider asking one or two experienced faculty members to serve as a friendly reviewer of your grant proposal, offering comments as to how the proposal can be improved. If the experienced faculty member is truly interested in the proposed project, he or she might be willing to participate as a co-investigator on your project team. Adding such an experienced and successful member to the team will almost always strengthen your proposal.

Other Faculty and Disciplines

Many funding sponsors are looking for ways to get a bigger bang for their money. As Sherri Sachdev explains in Chapter 4, many sponsors are increasingly interested in project teams that incorporate more than one discipline. For instance, a project that brings together research about business entrepreneurship with research about biofuel development would be more interesting to some sponsors than a proposal from either of these disciplines alone. At MU, we have seen relationships with faculty members from other departments develop very readily.

Internal Funding Programs

Although most faculty members focus their attention on external funding sources, there may also be internal programs at your institution that can provide funding to get your project started. Contact your dean's office and your institution's research office to learn about internal funding sources, submission processes, and any support that might be available for soliciting these funds.

Your institution may also have a research incentive program that distributes funding to you or your department in some proportion to the external funding garnered in a given year (see the boxed piece, "Motivation for Research and Collaboration at MU: Shared Credit" in Chapter 9 for a description of MU's Research Incentive Fund). If so, your department chair may be able to provide pilot funding to enable you to strengthen the preliminary work you present in your proposal.

Summary

Proposal development is only one facet of a successful academic career. It can be difficult sometimes to figure out the best balance among developing your professional expertise, conducting research or scholarship, securing tenure and promotions, teaching courses, mentoring students, and attending to your personal life. Especially for new faculty members who were accustomed in graduate school to doing everything themselves, it can be difficult to make the transition to letting go of tasks that do not require their particular expertise. We see this ability to delegate and manage as one of the most important skills for new faculty members to learn. As Mary Licklider noted at the beginning of Chapter 2, a faculty member's scholarly agenda is essentially a small business. To grow and thrive, you cannot continue to be your business's only employee. If you take the opportunity to identify and avail yourself of the resources your institution offers, we believe you will find the challenge of securing grant funding to be less stressful and more productive.

Chapter 4

Collaboration: The New Frontier

Sherri Sachdev

THE TERM *COLLABORATION* is certainly a buzzword these days, but what does it really mean? The standard definition involves people working together on a common endeavor. This seems simple enough, but the language of collaboration has become increasingly complex as different types of collaboration have begun to evolve. In a "multidisciplinary collaboration," people from different disciplines work independently or sequentially on a common goal. In an "interdisciplinary collaboration," people from different disciplines work jointly on a common goal. In "transdisciplinary collaboration," individual bring perspectives from different disciplines together to transform ideas and generate comprehensive answers that can be put to practical use.

There are also different geographic levels of collaboration: local, domestic, and international. The geographic continuum ranges from a couple of individuals working together at the same institution to an international team consisting of individual researchers, corporate partners, policy makers, and stakeholders.

Why Collaborate? What Good Does It Do?

Collaboration is not necessarily easy. It takes time to build relationships, communicate with the other individuals on your team, and agree on common goals. So, what makes collaboration worth all of the effort? The idea of *collective wisdom* explains many of the benefits of collaboration. Curiosity and the ability to ask compelling questions are the essence of good science and scholarship, but a single individual simply cannot know enough to answer today's complex questions. A case in point is the field of biosensors. Chemical and engineering experts are needed to develop sensing technologies that can translate biological elements into detectable signals, and biological experts are needed to understand the phenomena that are being measured. The health-care industry is another example: collaborative efforts have improved patient outcomes when teams include not only physicians but also physical and occupational therapists, psychologists, social workers, and other professionals. The reality is that today's problems often require diverse sets of experts to provide a wider range of potential solutions.

In addition to the direct benefits that collaboration can provide to you and your stakeholders, it also has potential benefits for your students. In today's job market, a critical combination of expertise and experience is more important than ever. Students and postdocs who have already worked in a team environment will have a competitive edge over those coming out of siloed disciplines.

Your own career will also benefit from involvement with collaborative teams. Collaboration involves a certain amount of networking, meaning that more people will know who you are and what you bring to the table. Collaborative teams can also offer access to the other members' expertise, instruments, funds, and prestige. Collaborative efforts lead to enhanced productivity: more publications and more funding. Citation rates suggest that collaborative papers tend to be more significant and that it is increasingly difficult for a sole author to produce highly cited research (Guimerà, Uzzi, Spiro, & Amaral, 2005; Wuchty, Jones, & Uzzi, 2007; Jones, Wuchty, & Uzzi, 2008).

Why Is Collaboration So Important Now?

During tough economic times, science policy tends to focus more on practical outcomes. The new National Center for Advancing Translational Sciences within the National Institutes of Health (NIH), for example, is focused on moving new discoveries from labs into clinical trials. Funding agencies recognize that *team science* is necessary to achieve their goals and often stipulate a collaborative team as a condition for funding. Agencies seek to stimulate interinstitutional and interdisciplinary synergies to address complex problems. A partnership between at least two institutions may be an eligibility requirement, or applicants may be encouraged to establish international collaborations or to form partnerships with industry. For example, a funding opportunity from NIH states that "research teams may include basic genomic and genetic scientists, clinical and social scientists, and researchers from law, bioethics, and the humanities" (NIH, National Human Genome Research Institute, 2006).

When you choose team members for a collaborative grant proposal, it is important to read the sponsor guidelines carefully. Sometimes only new collaborations will be considered. Sometimes, sponsors allow more than one principal investigator (see "Key Personnel" in Chapter 8). For some sponsors, this is a deliberate effort to catalyze and provide formal recognition for collaborative work with an eye toward higher education's promotion and tenure processes, which have traditionally worked against collaboration—and at least to some extent still do. Schools have begun to modify their policies to emphasize collaboration, but the contributions of individual team members can be unclear without proper documentation (Bunton & Mallon, 2007). Letters and evaluations that show the significance, impact, extent, and form of your contributions to the work will help you build a convincing case for promotion and tenure.

Timing

The art of forming a collaborative team raises a chicken-or-egg set of questions. The traditional sequence of events usually begins when a faculty member becomes aware of a particular funding opportunity, develops a research strategy, and then identifies potential collaborators based on the needs of the project (Figure 2).

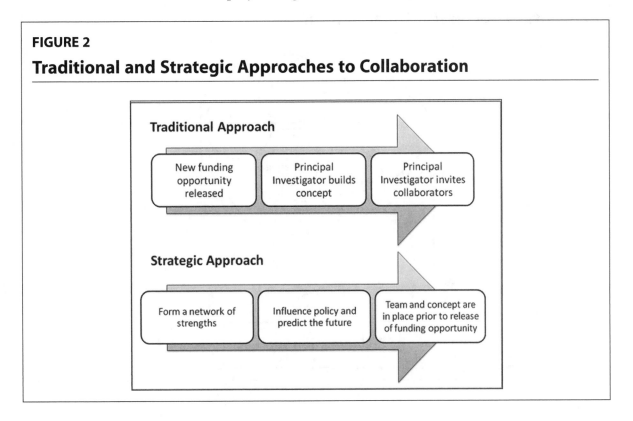

FIGURE 2

Traditional and Strategic Approaches to Collaboration

Traditional Approach

New funding opportunity released → Principal Investigator builds concept → Principal Investigator invites collaborators

Strategic Approach

Form a network of strengths → Influence policy and predict the future → Team and concept are in place prior to release of funding opportunity

It takes time to bring the other collaborators up to speed on the project, engage their interest, earn their trust, and come to agreement on project roles. All the while, valuable time is being lost that could be spent developing and writing a competitive proposal.

A more strategic approach is to build a network of experts based on individual strengths and then anticipate upcoming funding opportunities based on the political climate and the priorities of state and federal government and other sponsors. Even better is to serve on advisory boards and actually become involved in forming the policies and outlines of funding announcements before they are released. The optimal situation is to have a strong and competitive network of collaborators already in place and ready to act quickly when major opportunities are announced.

Requirements for Successful Collaboration

Although no two collaborative teams will be exactly alike, certain characteristics do seem to be shared by most successful partnerships (Figure 3).

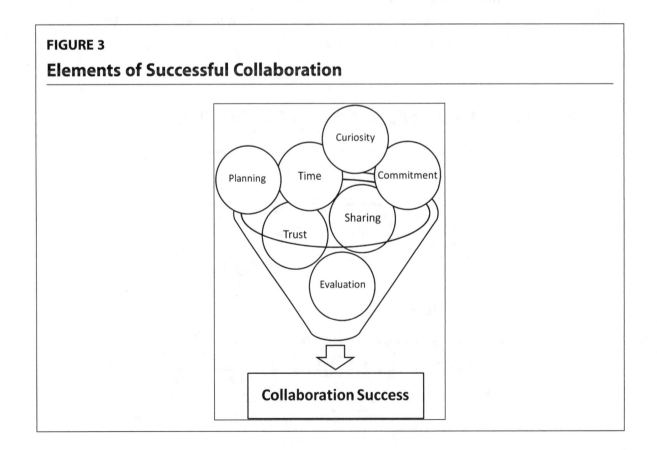

FIGURE 3

Elements of Successful Collaboration

The members of your team should share a common goal and vision for what they hope to accomplish. Although there may be one or more leaders in the group, the decision making, rewards, and responsibilities should be distributed among all members of your group. Each member of the team should bring a specific set of knowledge and skills to the group and should have a distinct role so that the group is interdependent. Individual expertise should be respected. If individuals feel neglected or used, they will be more likely to leave your team. Individual experts should be appropriately assertive when making suggestions that relate to their potential contributions to the project.

Communication is essential for successful teams. Communication becomes more difficult with distance, but face-to-face communication is not always practical, particularly if members are located in separate buildings, institutions, time zones, or countries. It is tempting to think of the meetings, phone calls, and e-mails that keep everyone on the same page as time away from the "work" of the project. Realize that to reap the synergies and other benefits of collaboration, these communications are a big part of the work of the project, not a distraction from the work.

One of the reasons to include individuals from different disciplines on your team is that people from different disciplines think differently. They approach problems from distinctly different perspectives. They speak "languages" that are specific to their own fields. Their priorities are different. The rich diversity of viewpoints and techniques that this brings to your project can be an enormous advantage. It can also mean that your team members will need to invest a significant amount of time to understand each other's perspectives, clarify vocabulary, and realize the potential of the team as a whole (Strober, 2011).

Make every effort to keep communication within your team open and the expectations for each member clear. This is one way to build the trust that will move your team members from a willingness to cooperate to being able to benefit fully from the partnership. Communication among the group as a whole is a critical component. E-mail is convenient and provides a record of requests and discussions, but try also to tap the value of face-to-face meetings. They will make collaborations go more smoothly, and the value of face time among team members is also often appreciated by sponsors and reviewers. Whenever you can, arrange for all members of the team to visit the institutions and departments of other team members to gain a full cross-disciplinary perspective.

Challenges to Successful Collaboration

The benefits of collaboration are becoming clearer and sponsors are encouraging this kind of work, so why are so many faculty members either reluctant to participate or discouraged from participating in interdisciplinary research? Some assume that collaborative work will be less rewarding. After all, the success must be shared with the other members of the team. The order of the authors must be negotiated for publications. The balance of power can be tricky to orchestrate so that everyone is heard and everyone benefits from the partnership. Academic rewards such as hiring, promotion, and tenure are largely controlled by single departments. Individual contributions to interdisciplinary efforts can be difficult to evaluate and can cause conflict between departments. Prestigious prizes are typically given to outstanding individuals rather than outstanding teams, and this can make individuals reluctant to share their ideas with others. Logistical issues like sharing samples or data require commitments from all involved to maintain the quality of the materials or data. Money and management issues are always more complex in a group setting.

And the list goes on. Certainly, there are challenges entailed in collaborative work, and some of these challenges can be difficult to resolve. The key is to have a plan in place before issues arise. Rather than avoiding questions of shared credit, intellectual property, and project management, incorporate these issues into the team's discussions just as questions about the methods and timeline of the project are collaboratively planned. Particularly for longer-term projects, it is also worthwhile to have a plan for removing team members who do not meet the expectations of the group.

A Senior Faculty Perspective on Collaboration

Sherri Sachdev

Judy Wall, MU professor of biochemistry, is fascinated by sulfate-reducing bacteria and their ability to convert toxic metals into less dangerous forms. This may sound like a lonely field, but our conversation illustrated that this research niche is rife with collaboration.

Wall began collaborating when she was approached by another team: "They needed someone who could handle genetics of recalcitrant microbes," Wall said, "but collaboration is a give and take. We made the mutant strains, and they sent back the tagged transposons that allowed us to identify which genes disappear when certain types of stress are applied. This would have been a huge investment to attempt on our own." One way that Wall gives back to the collaboration is by listing all of the mutants on a website. People can then request the strains they need.

Successful collaboration requires communication and trust. "There is nothing more effective than face-to-face meetings, but I simply cannot travel to California on a quarterly basis," said Wall. She often uses technology to connect with collaborators. "Unfortunately, when there are 50 people on a conference call, some individuals are hesitant to share their insights," she cautions. "Likewise, one must be careful not to lose credibility. For example, if you share an exciting research result too quickly, before you have had a chance to repeat the experiment and confirm the results, you might end up in an uncomfortable situation later, when you must make a retraction."

It is very difficult for one person to lead multiple collaborative efforts. Wall solves this problem by delegating leadership of certain projects to her research staff, who travel to meetings and report back. Wall has observed that when early-career scientists engage in collaborative leadership, they often continue to engage in the partnership after moving on to their own independent labs. She notes that collaboration really pays off when job seekers need letters of recommendation.

For Wall, the benefits of collaboration are numerous: "The more people you know, the more people know you." These partnerships have opened the door to new applications of techniques that were previously unavailable, and she has made good friends in the process. Collaboration is not without challenges, though. "Individuals will undoubtedly have different personalities. Some people are not as helpful as others. Don't come into the partnership with a lot of ego."

Another problem is that collaborative journal articles may have 20 different authors. "Someone needs to take responsibility for questioning the science and checking for accuracy," said Wall. "If people haven't been careful with the references in an article, then you can't believe that they have been careful with the data. It's important to take ownership when something has your name on it."

When considering very large collaborations, Wall shudders. She serves on the advisory board for a large research center. "For me, obtaining a grant of $25 million would be my worst nightmare," said Wall. "A grant of this size changes your life. The responsibility to spend all that money in an effective way in such a short time is incredible. Academia is often not set up for administrating these large awards. The hiring effort to bring in more than 100 new people, many of whom are nonresidents, would be overwhelming. When the PI [Principal Investigator] has to take care of these things, there is no time left to prepare all of the required reports and presentations, not to mention teach and conduct research."

Wall describes her collaborative work as a delightful experience. "I have been very lucky," she said. "It's been fun." When asked about future collaborative directions, she smiled. "I'm interested in environmental microbes," she said, "but pathogens relevant to the medical field are likely to share some commonalities. It's important to always see the broader impacts of your work in order to begin to answer new questions."

Traits That Influence Interdisciplinary Collaboration

Although you will clearly look for particular areas of expertise as you put your collaborative team together, potential team members' personalities and other traits may be equally important. Faculty members with higher academic ranks and those who have held positions at multiple institutions may be more accustomed to collaborative arrangements than faculty members who are at earlier stages of their careers (van Rijnsoever

& Hessels, 2011). Likewise, faculty members in applied fields (engineering and social work, for example) who are more often engaged in strategic relationships with partners outside academia may be more amenable to collaboration than those accustomed to basic research in very specialized fields.

Seek collaborators who can keep open minds when unfamiliar ideas are presented. Rather than reacting with doubt and criticism, team members who respond with intellectual curiosity, probing questions, and informed discussion will keep the group moving ahead. Be patient, though. Group dynamics can take a little time to settle with a new team.

Once you have a collaborative team in place, the group will look to you to strengthen the relationships and sustain the momentum over time. Although a balance of power is important, this does not eliminate the need for leadership in facilitating conversations, merging personalities and work styles, and managing power dynamics among team members. A common focal point such as a grant proposal can help to cement your network. As you learn about each other's disciplines, encourage your team members to cite each other's publications when they publish their own work.

Finding and Cultivating Partnerships

The collaborators you need for your next project may be waiting right on your desktop, available through online databases such as PIVOT and InfoEd (see "Funding Opportunities Databases" in Chapter 2). Newer and more specific collaboration websites are also being introduced. The NIH-funded Clinical and Translational Science Awards consortium has launched a new Collaboration Opportunities web page (https://www.ctsacentral.org/content/collaboration-opportunities), and the National Health Council has launched a Health Research Funding website (http://healthresearchfunding.org/) that serves as a new second-chance pathway for projects that are reviewed but not funded. Potential collaborators can also be found by searching federal agency funded projects databases such as the NIH Research Portfolio Online Reporting Tools (RePORT; http://report.nih.gov/), the National Science Foundation (NSF) Award Search page (http://www.nsf.gov/awardsearch/), or the US Department of Agriculture (USDA) Current Research Information System (CRIS; http://cris.nifa.usda.gov/).

Face-to-face meetings are also wonderful opportunities for making collaborative connections. Think of social events, seminars, and conferences as networking opportunities. Most of us are comfortable attending events in our own fields, but to build interdisciplinary bridges, try attending events at which the majority of attendees have a different perspective than your own. The idea here is not necessarily to have a specific agenda in mind but rather to set yourself up for serendipity by putting yourself in a position where connections can form. You may also want to consider inviting individuals from other fields to attend events within your discipline.

In any of these networking situations, be ready for people to ask about your expertise and research interests. Have an elevator pitch ready (see "Assessing the Match" in Chapter 2).

Stakeholders and potential partners can be found at meetings of associations and civic and business groups and at press conferences and ribbon cuttings. To ensure that conversations with new contacts are productive, try to identify common ground between your own goals and the needs of potential partners and stakeholders. Even if you think you understand their needs, it is still important to listen and ask questions rather than assuming that you already know. To build trust from the start, keep conversations transparent. Put your agenda and needs out in the open, and make it clear that you are willing to share knowledge and resources. As Judy Wall says in the boxed text "A Senior Faculty Perspective on Collaboration," collaboration involves give and take. It also may require some patience. As the complexity of Figure 4 illustrates, collaborative relationships typically do not happen instantly, but rather develop along a continuum that begins with communication, then moves to coordinated efforts, and finally grows into genuine collaboration.

Stakeholders should not simply be token partners on a project; they should be truly involved in its leadership, planning, and implementation. Imagine how the faculty at your institution would receive an expert who comes in from another field, announces that he or she has received a grant to improve the situation of faculty members at your institution, and asks for volunteers to serve on the advisory board of the project. Stakeholders want to be respected as full members of the team, and it is reasonable to expect that this means inclusion in the planning rather than being brought in as an afterthought. There should be an agreement regarding expectations and desired outcomes. In addition to the goals of the project, funding and sustainability strategies should represent shared aspirations.

An advisory board is a valuable project component. It can help to evaluate the project and the team and ensure that the project contributes to the needs of the community targeted by the project, whether a scholarly

FIGURE 4

Collaborative Relationships

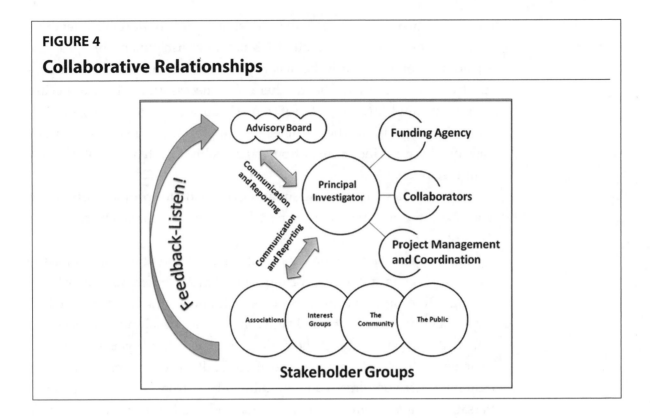

or a lay community. To make advisory positions worthwhile for those who accept them, these individuals will want to see that the time and thought they devote to your project makes a difference. Feedback from stakeholders and partners should be taken seriously and acted upon, and evaluation reports should be made widely available so that others can learn from your work. The theme here is that the costs of being a partner should not outweigh the benefits.

As the project progresses, you may need to add or remove members from your team. You will need to fill gaps that emerge in the collective knowledge and expertise of the group and replace partners who are no longer needed or do not fulfill expectations. This translates to an ongoing effort to identify, involve, and support new partners. Specific group members should be assigned as liaisons for particular contacts so that the group's initial contact makes a good impression and duplicate requests are avoided.

Managing Collaborators

Once a collaborative group is formed, it takes consistent effort to manage the group and keep progress on track. A leadership plan should be developed early during the collaboration; this is a formal requirement for some grant applications. The leadership plan should include roles and responsibilities of team members, how fiscal matters will be coordinated, how decisions will be made, policies for publications and intellectual property that come out of the project, and procedures for resolving conflicts. Whether or not the sponsor requires a collaborative team, the sponsor will want to know how your team's expertise and other resources will be managed and how your team represents a novel approach to the problem you plan to address.

Similarly, data management plans are increasingly required for competitive grant applications. Depending on your project, the team may need to share a substantial number of documents and data. Documents can be shared and managed by web applications such as Microsoft SharePoint, Basecamp, and Wiki. Some options are more secure and reliable than others, so you may want to engage your information technology professional to help select an appropriate solution for your team's needs.

Frequent project meetings and ongoing communication will allow you to measure progress, clarify expectations, and navigate pitfalls. When face-to-face meetings are not possible, virtual meetings and conference calls can be used. Tools such as Adobe Connect and Skype can be used for videoconferencing to facilitate collaboration from a distance and minimize travel costs.

The National Cancer Institute (NCI)'s teamscience.net (https://www.teamsciencetoolkit.cancer.gov/public/TSResourceTool.aspx?tid=1&rid=395) is a new tool that helps researchers develop skills relevant to forming, leading, and evaluating teams. This site provides self-guided learning modules with real-world scenarios that are unique to cross-disciplinary, team-based research. The NCI's Team Science Toolkit (http://www.teamsciencetoolkit.cancer.gov) is a user-generated collection of resources, including measures to study or evaluate team science, an expert directory, blog, and listserv. The Collaboration Success Wizard (http://hana.ics.uci.edu/wizard/index.php) is a diagnostic survey that probes factors that may strengthen or weaken your collaboration and then provides a personalized report that contains feedback.

Summary

Collaboration is indeed a new frontier for higher education. Many of us were trained under the traditional paradigm of the individual, independent scholar. It can be a challenge to navigate the new terrain of collaborative work, but this work can be richly rewarding, as some of nature's and society's thorniest problems begin to yield to the synergies of collective wisdom.

Chapter 5

Preparing to Write

Joann Messbarger, Shelley A. Hilton, and Bondi Wood

AFTER YOU HAVE found a funding opportunity that seems to match your research or programmatic agenda and started to round up campus support for your project, there are several activities and approaches that will help to make the proposal development process go more smoothly. This chapter will focus on what to look for in the sponsor's guidelines, how to organize the proposal development process with a proposal timeline and outline, and how to approach the writing itself.

Note Key Elements of the Sponsor's Guidelines

Begin by looking carefully at the funding opportunity guidelines. To ensure that the opportunity is a good fit, that you do not waste time or run into a last-minute issue, and to help plan your proposal preparation process, check the items we highlight below:

General Proposal Guides

Some funders, particularly the large federal agencies, have established guidelines that apply across all of the agency's funding programs. Examples of these are the National Science Foundation's *Grant Proposal Guide* (2011) and the U.S. Department of Health and Human Services' *SF424 (R&R) Application Guide for NIH and Other PHS Agencies* (U.S. DHHS, Public Health Service, 2011). When the agency has a general guidelines document as these agencies do, its funding announcements will reference that document rather than repeating the information, and any exceptions will be noted in the funding announcement.

Agency-Dictated Goals and Objectives

Funding opportunities sometimes address a specific topic or certain goals and objectives of importance to the agency. These will be outlined in the funding opportunity announcement and must be addressed if your proposal is to be competitive. Recall Mary Licklider's discussion of shoes in Chapter 2 (see "Research on Private Sector Sponsors")—if the sponsor's goal is to buy shoes, it will not be productive to try to convince the sponsor to buy sandals or boots.

Eligibility

Double-check eligibility language to be sure that you as the principal investigator (PI) or project director (PD) and your institution are both eligible to apply. There are often very specific requirements for a PI or a PD. Career development programs, for example, often specify such PI/PD characteristics as the number of years since your last degree, tenure-track or non-tenure-track position, number of years in a tenure-track position, and field of expertise. Funding opportunities sometimes limit institutional eligibility according to the level of degrees granted (for example, only those that grant PhDs), student population, geographic location, or other criteria. If these criteria are not met, the proposal will almost certainly be rejected without review.

Number of Applications Allowed

More and more funding agencies are limiting the number of applications allowed per institution or per PI/PD in an attempt to reduce the burden of reviewing applications. These are usually referred to as "limited submission" opportunities. Many larger institutions have systems in place to inform faculty members of and manage applications to limited submission opportunities. These systems allow institutions to make decisions as to priorities, to send the strongest proposals forward, and to prevent multiple investigators from spending time on proposals that ultimately will not be submitted.

Occasionally, there are also limits on the number of applications in which a given individual may participate. If you are considering seeking funding for more than one project from the same funder for the same deadline, be sure to check the guidelines for possible limitations. These limits may also apply to any co-investigators with whom you are collaborating.

Single-Stage or Multistage Processes

For some programs, only a full proposal is required, whereas for others, there are more steps. An increasing number of programs require a letter of intent before a full proposal may be submitted. Letters of intent serve two purposes: (1) to provide the agency with enough information about your project to begin to recruit reviewers with appropriate expertise, and (2) to give agency personnel an idea of the number of proposals to expect, again to help with planning the review process. Letters of intent are generally short and simple, and the funding opportunity announcement almost always specifies what to include.

Instead of a letter of intent, a preliminary proposal, or preproposal, may be required. This is a much more detailed description of your project to enable agency personnel or review panels to decide which proposals they want to see in full. Preliminary proposals require just as much planning and thought as full proposals, and typically they have guidelines that parallel those for the full proposal in terms of complexity. Preliminary proposals can be even more difficult to write than full proposals due to their shorter page limits. Be sure to think through your project fully and to communicate regularly with collaborators as you develop a preproposal.

The submission process for a preproposal may or may not be different from submission of the full proposal. Check with your sponsored programs office to find out how your institution handles preliminary proposals. Some require all proposals to flow through that office, and others allow some preproposals to be submitted to the agency by the investigator or departmental personnel.

Key Dates

Look at the due date with an eye toward the amount of time you will need to put together a well-formulated and well-written proposal. If you will have collaborators or subcontract arrangements with other institutions, is there time for those folks to complete their pieces? When a subcontract is proposed, your collaborator at the subcontracting institution will need to submit the plans to that institution's sponsored programs office for approval so that you can submit that approval along with the full proposal to your own institution's sponsored programs personnel. You will need to ask collaborators how much time to allow for this.

Funding Restrictions and Limits

Check the guidelines before you start writing to find the limits on the total amount of funding and allowable uses of sponsor funds. You want to avoid getting deeply involved in proposal preparation only to discover that the amount of money the funder will allow is not enough to do the work. If the project has a critical expense that the guidelines do not allow, you will want time to see if you can cover that expense through some other means, perhaps through your department, your institution, a collaborator, or a third party. This may also be a sign that this funding opportunity is not the best match for your project.

Watch for requirements or restrictions regarding cost sharing or cost matching. This means that the sponsor dollars must be matched by dollars from your institution or partners in specific proportions. A program may require 50 percent of the amount you request from the sponsor, for example. In addition to the proportion of matching dollars, there may also be restrictions as to the source of cost matches. Cash matches represent new commitments, such as equipment purchases or new personnel positions. In-kind matches represent the dedication of ongoing investments to a specific project—a portion of an existing faculty member's time or a portion of the facilities and administrative expenses, for example.

In contrast, other programs will return proposals without review if cost match is included in the budget in order to avoid the administrative burden of tracking cost-matched funds or to level the playing field for all institutions. These policies vary from sponsor to sponsor and even from program to program at the same agency.

Submission Methods

There are a variety of methods for submitting proposals, though electronic submission has become the most common. Most federal agencies now require submission through the Grants.gov system, but some, including the NSF, the Department of Defense, and NASA, have their own electronic proposal-submission systems. Some agencies not only want certain pieces of information included in the application but also ask you to label them in a particular way or to separate the pieces and attach them to the online system individually.

If your proposal will be submitted via an online system that you have not used before, be sure to register with the system and log in well before the deadline. We have had the disconcerting experience of finding requirements in online submission systems that did not appear in the funding announcements. In one case, those surprises set off a last-minute scramble when we thought we were nearly finished with the proposal. This kind of disconnect seems to happen more frequently for small funding agencies and private foundations where staffing can be thinner than at larger organizations.

Some sponsors require proposals to be submitted via e-mail from a certain contact person or position within your institution, such as the vice chancellor for research, or directly from you as the principal investigator or project director. The majority require submission from your institution's sponsored programs office.

Some sponsors still require paper submission, including an original and multiple copies. It is typical with paper submissions for the sponsor to request that the proposal not be bound with anything but rubber bands. When this is the case, be very cautious about including color or half-tone images in your proposal. Unbound paper submissions usually mean the sponsor will at some point place the proposal in the document feeder of a photocopy machine. The resulting copies will lose detail that you present in color. In all submission situations, communicate with your institution's sponsored programs office to be sure all sponsor requirements are met.

Formatting

Note formatting requirements, such as margins, font size and type, and spacing. These guidelines are in place to enforce equity of text space for all applicants. Failure to follow the sponsor's formatting rules can result in your proposal being rejected by online submission systems or, in the case of paper submission, returned without review. Agencies that provide a general set of guidelines in addition to the funding opportunity announcement will typically include the formatting rules within the general guidelines document.

Required Elements

Different funders and different types of programs within a funding agency require different elements. The general guidelines or the funding opportunity announcement, or both, will tell you which elements are required. The Project Summary section of an NSF proposal, for example, must include separate statements addressing the intellectual merit and the broader impacts of the proposed work. If those two items are not there, your proposal will not be reviewed. A training grant application to the NIH requires data tables that document graduate student applications and progress in the relevant departments, but different institutes and programs within the NIH require different portions of those tables. Making a table of contents for the whole proposal can help you keep track of all the required elements at a glance. Many online systems generate the table of contents automatically, so the table of contents you create during proposal development is often strictly an internal document.

Review Criteria

Funding opportunity announcements usually provide information about the review and selection processes. This section of the announcement will give you a sense of what the reviewers will be looking for and what they will be expected to comment upon. In addition to the questions to be answered or content to be covered, the review criteria may include information as to the weight assigned to each criterion. If you use the guidelines to create an outline to guide the writing of the proposal, you will want to incorporate the review criteria into that outline so that you can keep these criteria in mind and highlight them as you write your proposal.

What If There Are No Guidelines?

Elizabeth D. Miller

Even the experienced researcher can make mistakes when sponsor guidelines are nonexistent or nearly so. Experienced researchers are so accustomed to following detailed guidelines that they may strictly follow poor guidelines, even when they are not as detailed as they should be. So what can you do?

Begin by calling or e-mailing the program officer or sponsor contact for more details. If that produces only limited help, look to the premier sponsor in your field of study (for example, the NIH for biomedical fields, the NSF for engineering and social science disciplines, the Department of Education for education, the USDA for agriculture and rural development fields). Because the reviewers are likely to be funded by these dominant sponsors, using their guidelines and review criteria will produce a proposal that seems familiar and meets reviewer expectations as to the level of detail and organizational structure.

Use the freedom that the sponsor's lack of guidelines gives you to provide details that you know a reviewer will appreciate. Be sure to include the who, what, when, where, why, and how of the work: what the project activities will be; when the work will be accomplished; why it is important to do the work now; and how you plan to go about the work. You might also want to include a section on how your project will help the agency meet its mission.

Finally, try to obtain an example of a funded proposal. Although this will give you some sense of the sponsor's past expectations, be careful not to take a previous proposal's success too literally. Guidelines change, and the previously funded proposal may not reflect recent changes. Occasionally, proposals are funded based on demographics, specific annual funding guidelines, or the principal investigator's or project director's relationship with the sponsor and not because of what is written in the proposal; there is no way to know this by simply reading the funded proposal.

Typical Perpetrators
- Professional foundations and associations may use forms similar to or modified from those of the dominant sponsor in the field of study, yet their guidelines are only two or three pages long and do not include review criteria.

- Some family foundations only want letter proposals, and the reviewers are members of the family that funded the foundation. In this case, be sure to cover the basics in lay language. They probably do not have expertise in your field of study, let alone doctorates in the field.

- New grant makers often do not yet know what they want. The personnel may not have had any grant experience before setting up shop.

Folks in these categories often have convoluted guidelines and restrictions that vary from the norm. These atypical requirements might include, for instance, a limit on the number of active grants an organization may receive from the agency in order to better distribute funds to various grant seekers.

Create an Outline

Creating an outline is one of the most helpful things you can do for yourself, especially when the timeline is tight and you must pull things together quickly. For proposals that will be electronically submitted as one document or as a paper copy, we recommend an outline that includes *all* pieces of the proposal—everything from the cover page through the appendices. For proposals that are submitted electronically and uploaded as separate documents, we recommend an outline of the sections that describe the meat of the project, such as the Research Plan or Project Description, and a cheat sheet listing every element of the proposal to be used as a checklist.

Organize Sections according to the Guidelines

Your program guidelines and the agency's proposal guides will almost always tell you what should and should not be included in the proposal. If the sponsor's materials do provide an outline structure, incorporate the review criteria into this structure. This is not the place for creative license. Save your creativity for the project itself. Use the sponsor's terminology, especially in the headings and subheadings, to make it easy for reviewers to find the review criteria they need to score your proposal. Sometimes the funder will be quite specific about the sections and headings; an example is this guidance for the Research Strategy section from the *SF424 R&R Application Guide for NIH and Other PHS Agencies*: "Organize the Research Strategy in the specified order and using the instructions provided below. Start each section with the appropriate section heading— Significance, Innovation, Approach" (U.S. DHHS, Public Health Service, 2011, p. I-111).

In other cases, the funder will list a litany of items in a single sentence, and it will be up to you to sort them into headings and subheadings. An example is the following section from the NIH *Recovery Act Limited Competition: Core Facility Renovation, Repair, and Improvement* (NIH, National Center for Research Resources, 2009):

Engineering Criteria: Provide information about the mechanical, electrical, plumbing systems and utilities in each component. Include information about the number of air changes per hour, electrical power, light levels, hot and cold water, steam, MEP requirements, fire protection requirements, biohazard and radiation safety requirements, chemicals used, major scientific equipment to be installed including environmental rooms, density of fume hoods, building population, number of workstations, security/surveillance and building automation systems. (Sect. IV, 6)

For this situation, because there is quite a lot of detail implied in the list, the main heading would be "Engineering Criteria," and subheadings would use the NIH's terms for each item listed. If each component is easy to locate, this makes life easier for reviewers than a proposal that runs everything together in one long section.

Include Instructions and Review Criteria

As you read through the funding opportunity announcement and create headings and subheadings, copy and paste into your outline any information about what should be covered in each section. The Toolkit includes an example of a proposal outline (see "Sample Proposal Outline: Engineering Information Foundation" in Section Three of Part Two). Include details as to the review criteria and scoring system as well as information from the general application guide, if the sponsor has one. This puts all of the reference information in one place, making it hard to miss something important and easy to assign sections to collaborators. We recommend that you use different colors to differentiate guidelines information from the text of your proposal.

When you get to a point at which you need to check the length of your text, you can transfer the information you copied from the guidelines into Comments to keep it accessible but remove it from the document's page count. Once you are certain all the issues have been addressed in each section, delete the comments so that you submit a clean narrative to the sponsor.

Prepare a Proposal Development Timeline

Preparing a timeline for the development of your proposal serves three purposes. First, it gets you organized and sets goals for completing each piece. Second, it serves as a tool for managing collaborations. Finally, the proposal timeline can serve as a checklist as you pull the entire proposal together. The process of creating the timeline puts the project in perspective and grounds the tasks in the realities of your calendar.

As you work through the dates for each of the items below, be cognizant of holidays, breaks, and vacations when people might be unavailable. If the sponsor deadline falls on January 2, for example, you may want to plan to have signatures in before December 15 in order to catch people before they leave for holiday trips, and this would ripple back through all your other deadlines.

As you focus on coordinating with your collaborators, remember to keep your own schedule in mind. Watch for the timing of your classes, when grades are due, when you will be away at a conference, and when other projects or collaborations might interfere with writing this proposal.

The easiest way to assign due dates for each element of your proposal is to work backward from the sponsor's deadline. Samples of completed timelines are included in the Toolkit (see "Narrative Timeline for Proposal Development," "Table 9: Timeline for Proposal Development," and "Table 10: Proposal Timeline: Engineering Information Foundation" in Section Two of Part Two).

A grant proposal is a project in itself and one that will proceed more smoothly if you treat it as such. The following tasks are in reverse order of when they would appear on a proposal development timeline because proposal development timelines are usually constructed in this way, working backward from the submission deadline.

Internal Review

When does the complete proposal need to be submitted to your sponsored programs office? Two working days prior to the external due date? Five days? Does your department or college need to review it before it goes to the campus sponsored programs office?

Signatures

Check with your department's fiscal or grants personnel to find out when and from whom you need signatures to document approval of your involvement and that of others in the proposed work. At many institutions, you will need to collect signatures from your chair and dean as well as from some or all co-investigators, their department chairs, their deans, and fiscal personnel.

Data Entry

Find out if there are internal deadlines for completing the electronic (or paper) application packet with all the associated documents uploaded to it. Besides the sponsor's application packet, your institution may have a local grant management system into which your proposal information or packet must be entered before you can seek approval signatures.

Subcontract Information

If your project will include subcontracts, find out what documents your institution requires from the subcontractors at the proposal submission stage. Find out when and to whom those documents must be submitted. As you build your proposal development timeline, allow three or four weeks for the subcontractor to go through its internal processes for approving the proposal and gathering institutional signatures. Many times, this will drive the deadline for a final budget because your subcontractor will need final budget numbers, sometimes for the entire project as well as the subcontract, in order to initiate the approval process on that end.

Final Polishing

Almost all grant proposals these days entail collaborative teams, and this means that there will probably be several people engaged in writing the various parts of your proposal. At some point, all these pieces must be brought together and made to look like and read as a coherent whole. Think about who will do this for your proposal, and then consider when this individual will need the final drafts in order to proofread the proposal from beginning to end to give it one voice, proofread for surface errors, format for readability, and assemble the application packet. For the average federal proposal, allow two or three days for this work, although the amount of time can vary quite a bit based on the complexity and length of the proposal.

Final Budget and Budget Justification

Sheryl Koenig and Susan Hazelwood cover construction of budget documents in Chapter 9. As you incorporate this work into your proposal development timeline, plan to finalize the budget earlier if there are subcontractors who need the information to initiate institutional approvals on their end. If there are no subcontracts, the budget deadline will be whenever you need to enter proposal data into your institution's grant management system and seek internal approvals for the proposal.

Supporting Documents

Biographical sketches and letters of commitment or support can be completed earlier than the project narrative and should be finalized as early as possible. Note that this means you will also need to determine the project title early on so that it can be used in these letters.

In your timeline, include deadlines for your team to complete draft letters, to send the draft letters out as part of your requests for letters of commitment or support, and to receive letters back. Include deadlines for sending requests for biographical sketches to all key personnel on the project, for receiving biosketches from the team, and for formatting all the biosketches with the same fonts, headings, and margins so that they give the reviewer the appearance of a real team. Be sure to provide enough time for people to respond while you continue to work on other sections of your proposal.

Friendly Review

This is where you submit a close-to-final draft of the proposal to a colleague for review. We highly recommend that you do everything you can to build this step into your proposal development timeline. One way to include this review without losing much time is to schedule it well ahead of time. Arrange a mutually agreeable date when you will submit the draft to the reviewer and a date three or four days later when you will receive the review comments. Scheduling well ahead allows the reviewer to block calendar time for the work.

Many faculty members will do this review for free, but consider offering a small honorarium if the reviewer is from outside your institution. Whether the offer is accepted or not, you will have conveyed a strong message about how seriously you take the review. As a result, you are much more likely to receive a quick and thorough response and lose relatively little preparation time. Even if you are only able to provide a draft rather than a nearly final version by the agreed-upon date, the review will still give your proposal an advantage.

Review by Collaborators

Issues of trust can work against collaborative proposals in surprising ways. We have seen investigators who were reluctant to share proposal documents with collaborators. Consider whether you would engage in another collaboration with someone who did not trust you enough to see the full scope of the work in which you were asked to participate. On the other hand, we have also seen investigators who use tools such as SharePoint or

Google Docs to make all proposal drafts and finished documents available to all members of the team throughout the process. Consider here whether you would take time to read every draft once you understood the project and trusted the team.

In either of these scenarios, it would be possible that no member of the team—the individuals who know the project best—gives the proposal a critical review before it is submitted. We have had the best response by scheduling specific days on which everyone on the proposal team is asked to read a close-to-final draft and provide comments and corrections. Besides strengthening the logic and presentation of the proposal, running a polished draft by your collaborators will ensure that everyone is on the same page about the project and each person's role.

Proposal Data and Images

Collecting proposal data can be very time-consuming, especially for training grants. Incorporate into your timeline generous deadlines for requesting the data, for follow-up questions, and for final data. Organizational charts, supporting graphics, and data images take time to put together. Putting these things on the timeline helps to ensure that they are not overlooked.

Drafts

Including dates in your timeline for tasks to be done along the way, such as distributing drafts to the team, returning comments to you, and sending requests for materials, will help keep your project moving.

Get Organized, Stay Organized

Starting with the timeline and outline are great ways to really think through the project as a whole. Once you make them, *use them*. You may fall off of your deadline dates, but your timeline will still provide a chronology and a task checklist so that you don't have to rely on memory alone. If you have a large team, include a column that specifies the responsible party or parties for each task. Check tasks off as they are completed.

Another way to stay organized is to make a list of required elements for the application. This will tell you at a glance which documents still need to be completed. You can identify the required elements by looking through the electronic application package, the funding announcement, and the agency's general proposal application guidelines (if applicable). This list will save you time and worry as the proposal deadline draws near.

Establish a naming convention for files that includes the PI's last name, program, proposal component, date, and initials of the last person to work on the file. For example, for a project summary, the file name might be "LastName_NSF_Summary_062310_jbs." Alternatively, for a biographical sketch, include the individual's name, the agency, the date, and the initials of the last person to work on the file. For example, "Expert_John_NSF _Biosketch_072211_sah." Using a method such as this will allow you to easily identify the latest version of any given component. When a component is truly final and ready for submission, the file name should include the word "Final."

We set up an electronic file folder for each proposal component (for example, biographical sketches, current and pending support, project description). You may also want to have subfolders for drafts and final versions of these smaller pieces. When a component is ready for submission, it should be moved or copied to a "Final" folder.

Summary

After you have identified a sponsor and funding opportunity that match your project and tapped support on campus for your project, the next step is to organize your proposal development. Prewriting activities can save a great deal of time and aggravation later in the process. Reading the sponsor's guidelines carefully and pulling the key points into a proposal outline can facilitate your own writing because the outline will make it easier to pick up manageable parts of the proposal during your daily writing time. A proposal outline will also make it easier to assign portions of the writing to other members of your team. Similarly, developing and sharing a proposal development timeline with your team will keep the process moving forward and help to ensure that none of the many bits and pieces of the proposal falls by the wayside.

Section Two

Developing Your Proposal

Chapter 6

The Writing

Bondi Wood

OVER THE YEARS, composition theorists have developed distinct stages of the writing process; however, not all writers produce writing in a linear fashion, often rejecting writing strategies that are segmented into prewriting or postwriting activities. Some composition theorists of the 1980s (for example, Elbow, 1981; Horton, 1982; Kennedy, 1985) were even cynical of prewriting activities, particularly anything as confining as a plan or outline. But these critics still agreed that if the type of writing you are producing requires structure—as all grant proposals do—that you should engage in certain prewriting activities.

For proposal development, you will be gathering, assessing, and organizing your personal research or scholarly endeavors, but you will be generating very little new information. Your task is to report your existing ideas or research within the context and framework of the funder's guidelines rather than to invent or create new information. Therefore, it is crucial that you first examine your ideas and information.

First, look at your proposed project globally; examine it from all angles. Get together with trusted colleagues, friends, or a grant writing consultant and discuss your idea, your approaches, your goals, and any anticipated outcomes. This is not the time to seek praise; rather, you want honest, critical feedback. With your team, walk through the logistics of the project. Will it work on your campus? What are the potential pitfalls? Does it align with the sponsor's funding goals? Can the project be accomplished within the time frame and budget allowed by the sponsor? If not, how could the project be changed? Should it be changed?

Taking time for this prewriting discussion will improve your first draft and, by clarifying your thinking, it will be easier to write that first draft. Unclear writing is nearly always the result of unclear thinking, so analyzing your proposal up front will save time on later revisions. Once you are satisfied that your concept and approach are strong, you can begin the writing process.

Finding Time

We all seem to struggle to find time for everything we would like to be able to do. Producing grant proposals and other academic writing can certainly be part of this struggle. There is, however, research that can help you raise the odds of producing what you need. As far back as the early 1970s, Peter Elbow was observing and publishing on writing as a form of thinking (1973). Elbow encouraged "free writing"—writing continuously without criticism, focusing solely on creating; developing automaticity; and finding the sound, texture, and rhythm of the uncensored voice.

Elbow's work was primarily qualitative, though, and in the 1980s Robert Boice tested some of these principles via quantitative studies with university academics as his subjects (1983, 1989). In classic Skinnerian style, Boice used a control group in addition to three experimental conditions: (1) those who wrote only when they felt like it, (2) those who wrote for an hour a day, five days a week, and (3) those who were expected to produce three pages per day to avoid "punishment" for failure to produce the target quantity of writing. (The punishment entailed subjects making donations to detested organizations.) Boice found, as Elbow had, that regularly scheduled writing seemed to be the most productive approach.

More recently, Stephen Krashen (2002) reexamined Boice's findings and looked particularly at the difference between the latter two conditions. By distinguishing between the number of *pages* produced and the number of *ideas* produced, Krashen's work makes an important distinction between productivity and efficiency (see Table 2).

If we consider *productivity* as the number of pages, that is, the volume of writing, and *efficiency* as the density of ideas and a placeholder for the

---

TABLE 2

Writing Productivity and Efficiency under Three Conditions

Condition	Pages per Day	Ideas per Page
Spontaneous	0.35	0.8
Regular	0.9	0.7
Forced	3.2	0.43

Source: Krashen, 2002.

amount of usable writing, it is immediately obvious that your best bet is to schedule a regular block of time and treat it as you would a class or meeting commitment. As highlighted in Table 2, the efficiency of regular writing (0.7 ideas per page) approaches that of spontaneous writing (0.8 ideas per page), and it generates well over twice the productivity (0.9 versus only 0.35 pages per day). We have probably all done "binge" writing at some point: the all-nighter to get a paper finished and turned in the next morning. What we know about binge writing is that over time, these authors will produce less than those who write very regularly. The reason is that following a binge, these authors will usually stop writing for a period of time before the pressure mounts and results in another binge. For academics who need to maintain a steady flow of productivity, binge writing is simply inefficient.

So schedule your writing time as you do other commitments, then either close the door or hide at the local coffee shop, and write. One final recommendation, if you need more detailed advice, is to read *How to Write a Lot* (2007). Written by Paul Silvia, this is a quick read and combines solid advice with a wonderful sense of humor.

Successful Communication

Historically, communication has been viewed as a three-legged stool: the speaker, the message, and the audience. In the study of rhetoric, successful communication is traditionally expected to address all three equally. The speaker, or in this case, the principal investigator or project director, needs to establish credibility so that the audience will bother to read the message. Equally important, the speaker must analyze the audience—in this case the reviewers—to tailor the message specifically for them. In proposal development, the proposal is your message, and the sponsor's personnel and reviewers are your audience.

Despite this traditional wisdom, certain types of communication require more emphasis on one leg of the stool than another. For example, instructions about how to file your taxes are heavy on message and weak on speaker and audience. Similarly, a curriculum vita focuses primarily on the speaker because the purpose of the document is to establish credibility. Grant proposals are heavy on message, but you still need to keep yourself and your audience in mind. The following sections of this chapter will address speaker and audience, and the central part of your message, the project description or "narrative," will be covered in detail in Chapter 8. In that chapter, you will find the most common components of proposal narratives, the information to include in each of these components, and effective approaches for these components.

Establishing Credibility: The Speaker

Most sponsors conveniently offer distinct sections of the proposal to allow you to establish your credibility and that of your team: the biographical sketch, a list of your current and pending research, previous collaborations, publications lists, and letters of support. Chapter 10 provides advice on these elements of the proposal.

Beyond the facts that these documents contain, there are additional ways to establish credibility. You want to infuse your writing with authority, writing from a position of strength rather than need. Read the two examples below:

> *The country of Georgia is experiencing a demographic catastrophe, with the entire population suffering the effects of postconflict trauma, displacement, and interruption of services. This network of 22 soup kitchens will fill the void left by the demise of Georgia's economy.*

• • •

> *Using the existing and highly effective government-operated network of 22 soup kitchens, we will serve two nutritious meals per day for a 12-month period to 11,100 Georgian people, resulting in 7.3 million meals served.*

The first is needy and weak; the second specific and strong. Use active rather than passive voice, and avoid subjunctive mood to make your message more direct and powerful.

Subjunctive mood makes your voice sound unconvinced: "this *would* be wonderful"; "this *could* revolutionize the field." If you as the writer are not convinced you will do the work, you can't expect to convince the reviewer. Drop back to what you *can* promise, and use future tense: "We *will* serve 7.3 million meals."

With passive voice, the subject of the sentence is being acted upon ("The ball was thrown"), whereas with active voice, the subject of the sentence is the actor ("I threw the ball"). Piling passive constructions one upon the other throughout a grant proposal conveys a cumulative effect of avoiding accountability. If we don't know who's doing what, we have no way to assess their competence or our own confidence that the work will be done.

These days, it is perfectly appropriate to use first person in a grant proposal, and this will help you avoid passive voice. See the two examples below. The first is passive; the second is active. You can easily see that the second example is more dynamic and confident. The second also flows better, making it easier for your reviewers to follow.

> *Quantitative data analysis, particularly logistic regression, will be used to examine the medical home and transition services component. Qualitative data will be analyzed for themes derived from the literature and previous analysis. Study findings will expand our understanding of medical home and transition services for youth with Autism Spectrum Disorder (ASD). This information will be used to develop interventions and new service models.*

• • •

> *Our team will employ quantitative data analysis, particularly logistic regression, to examine medical home and transition services. In addition, we will analyze the data for emerging themes from the literature and other previous analyses. These findings will expand our understanding of medical home and transition services for youth with Autism Spectrum Disorder (ASD), ultimately allowing us to develop interventions and new service models.*

Find opportunities to make your proposal memorable. Certain words are so overused that they have nearly been drained of meaning—words like *unique, significant, important, meaningful, innovative,* and *novel.* These words convey no detail about the project. Unless you draw comparisons with topics or approaches that are less important and less meaningful, the reader has no context for placing your project on a scale of importance. See the two sample sentences below. Because the vague word *important* is changed to *workhorses*, the reader gets a distinct image of how this method will impact microbiology labs. More importantly, the reader will be more likely to remember the word *workhorse.*

> *We expect our method to retain the advantages of the current automated culture systems, making these systems important to the microbiology labs of hospitals and food- and water-quality testing facilities.*

• • •

> *We expect our method to retain the advantages of the current automated culture systems, making these systems the workhorses of the microbiology labs of hospitals and food- and water-quality testing facilities.*

You will further establish your credibility by submitting an error-free proposal. You can cite all the accolades you want, but a misspelled word or grammatical error leaves the reviewer with the impression that you are sloppy. Funders do not give money to sloppy people. Allow time for frequent and thorough proofreading by someone other than yourself. Computer-based spelling and grammar checks are helpful but far from foolproof. They should be used as tools, not rules. Read the text, take a break, and read it again hours later. We also recommend that you print a hard copy of the final draft. Set it on a table and turn the pages. This hard copy review allows you to catch overlooked errors in spacing and format.

Remember, there is a flip side to credibility. To keep the three-legged stool stable, you do not want to overemphasize your expertise at the expense of your message. This is particularly true for proposals with short page-length requirements. Mentioning your NSF CAREER award five times in a six-page proposal is probably overkill. The strongest proposals mention relevant past accomplishments as they relate to the current project.

Finally, you do not elevate your credibility by elevating your vocabulary and expanding your sentence structure. For years, academicians incorrectly believed that a lack of clarity in writing somehow implied prestige. Intricate sentences and baroque vocabulary somehow implied knowledge beyond the ordinary. Today's grant review processes call for clear and often jargon-free writing. The more a reader has to concentrate on how something is being said, the less he or she is concentrating on *what* is being said. Do not lose your reviewer in a thicket of profound thoughts or a maze of jargon and acronyms. If you must use jargon, define the jargon and acronyms for the readers, and then refresh their memories later in the narrative.

Truly good writing does not show off; it obliges. Your reviewers should be so engrossed in the reading that they fail to notice the writing.

Grant Proposals and Other Forms of Academic Writing

Shelley A. Hilton

Grant proposals require that you write with a different conception of your audience than you have for other forms of academic writing. This is because the purposes of grant proposals are different from those of journal articles and other scholarly writing. In most forms of academic writing—a journal article, for example—the readers want something from the writers: information to further their work, validate their theory, or understand something new. The writers want to further their work, build their professional reputations, and build their curriculum vitae. There is a relative balance between what readers and writers want and have to gain.

With a grant proposal, in contrast, the reader is often fulfilling a service and may not receive much for the effort. The writer obviously wants something: funding. Here, the equation is more one-sided, and this implies a different stance as you write. Although academic writing and grant proposals are both forms of persuasive writing, they are differently persuasive. In academic writing, the writer's primary focus is to persuade the reader of the validity, reliability, and significance of work that has already been done. In proposal writing, the writer's focus is prospective—the work has not yet been carried out. The reader must be persuaded of the value of the work without the evidence of project results. Because of these differences, you need to understand and approach the readers of grant proposals differently than the readers of other forms of academic writing. Even for grant proposals, there are several types of readers, and understanding the differences between these types of readers will help you craft your proposal to convey key ideas to each type.

First and foremost, however, grant reviewers tend to share the following characteristics: they are in a hurry; they are not being paid much or at all for their services; they have regular jobs; and they do a lot of reading. At most agencies, all reviewers on the panel, regardless of their levels of expertise in your field, will help determine the fate of your proposal. Generally, these readers can be placed into one of three groups: critical readers, search readers, and skimmers.

Critical readers are those reviewers who read every word on every page of your proposal and think critically about the information. These readers are usually what some agencies refer to as the primary reviewers. They are assigned to write the most comprehensive review and lead the review panel's discussion about a proposal. The critical reader is considered the easiest reader to capture, and your goal is to make it easy for this reader to follow your logic and argue on your behalf. These strategies will help the critical reader:

- Use an organizational scheme that ties the major proposal sections together.

- Use topic sentences to preview each concept and step.

- Keep paragraphs short to move the reader through the text.

Search readers are often the secondary reviewers. These readers will also write a relatively detailed critique of the proposal, so they will search the text for responses to review criteria. They need to acquire the main points of the proposal, but they will not necessarily read every word. Think of a person who reads through a document very quickly, trying to hit the high points. These strategies will help the search reader:

- Follow the agency format for major headings.

- Use review criteria in subheadings to make it easier to fill out the sponsor's reviewer form.

- Use bold or underlined text sparingly so that the two or three most critical points on each page are obvious.

- Use graphics to capture attention and convey important ideas.

The rest of the review panel typically comprises skimmers. These reviewers have the option of reading your proposal in detail, but they probably will not do so if time is short because they have other proposals to which they are assigned as critical readers. These reviewers skim the proposal. Despite this, they have a vote in funding decisions and will help determine the fate of your proposal, so it is important to write in such a way that even skimmers can take away important points. These strategies will help the skimmer:

- Make subheadings descriptive, perhaps beginning with a required label such as "Preliminary Studies," and then following it with a colon and a phrase that pulls language from the review criteria that are covered in this section.

- Underline only one or two key phrases per page, again so that the most critical points are obvious.

(Continued)

- Put the goals, objectives, and impact of the project on the first page to make these critical pieces more difficult to miss.

- Devote significant time to crafting your title and abstract/summary, as these may be the only pieces of the proposal that skimmers read carefully.

As you hone your grantsmanship skills, you will become increasingly accomplished at writing for the various readers. Next time you serve as a reviewer, pay attention to your own reading. Consider which type of reader you are for any given proposal, what you look for, and what you need to make an informed vote. And if you have not yet served as a reviewer, consider doing so. (See the boxed text, "Becoming a Reviewer: Selected Funding Agencies" in Chapter 11 for information about volunteering to serve as a grant reviewer at a number of federal agencies.) We consider review work to be the very best grantsmanship training there is, and this is perhaps the most important personal benefit of contributing your services to the review process.

Accommodating Your Audience: The Reviewers

You cannot sell vinyl siding to a person living in a brick home. Many communications fail because they do not bother to analyze or accommodate the audience. Although you may not be able to identify your reviewers by name or area of expertise, two general rules will help you avoid irritating your reviewers right off the bat.

- *Follow the guidelines.* You have already seen lots of "read the guidelines" advice in this handbook. Reviewers quickly develop an eye for proposals that have fudged on margins and font size. Don't fudge. Doing so gives the reviewers a reason to dislike your proposal immediately; it also speaks to your credibility. Instead, you want to accommodate your audience, making it as painless as possible to read your proposal.

- *Use transitions.* Your ultimate goal is to get the reviewers to read every word. So help them along by connecting your thoughts. Transitions are not limited to the traditional *however, consequently, furthermore, thus,* and the like that you learned in high school English class. A transition is any strategy that links one idea to another. This can mean repeating a word or phrase from the previous sentence at the beginning of the following sentence, a strategy than can be especially helpful if your subject matter is dense or complicated. Despite what you may have been taught, purposeful repetition can be highly effective. In the sample below, the italicized text highlights how the writer has picked up the final thought of the first paragraph and repeated it at the beginning of the next paragraph, weaving the information together and assisting the reader in moving from one idea to the next:

The eIRB desktop software is designed for IRB office staff to manage information related to each project. With the requested funding, we will add extensive reporting and quality assurance functionality. IRB staff will be able to track project-related actions such as amendments, adverse events, and continuing reviews. Through a system of customized fields and web access, investigators will be able to access the review status of the project and obtain information on IRB requirements and issues related to particular studies.

Although a customized system can support the vast majority of needs, there are always unpredictable information needs. Extensive ad hoc query capacity in eIRB will enable staff queries without programmer support.

You can further accommodate your audience by placing your ideas in relation to each other. Emphasizing main ideas and subordinating less important ideas allows readers to understand the appropriate relationship among ideas. Even a lay person can often understand the essence of an unfamiliar, complex process if the writer describing the concept has mastered the use of emphasis and subordination.

Your audience will appreciate it if you describe for them why your ideas or research are important. In fact, many funders are requiring explanations of the significance, broader impact, or innovation of potential projects. We often refer to this as the *So what?* or the *Why should I care?* aspect of the writing. You need to make your readers care about your project rather than assuming that they do.

Finally, you are more likely to keep your reader's attention if you use a variety of sentence structures, but do so sparingly and thoughtfully. Readers are accustomed to the traditional subject-verb-object pattern of most sentences. They rely on this structure to receive and interpret information. Research has shown that most people prefer poems that rhyme, pictures or objects that are symmetrical, and sentences that are subject-verb-object because they can subconsciously predict the outcome. Such structures provide a sense of familiarity and satisfaction. Still, the surprise of an occasional sentence that breaks with the traditional format can be highly effective in keeping the reader interested in what you have to say and can avoid a monotonous, sleep-inducing rhythm.

Summary

In the composition classrooms of the 1970s, any task that preceded actual writing was referred to as prewriting and considered optional or supplemental, much as revision was considered a bonus, a task to be completed as time allowed or if your instructor required it. In the last 40 years, we have come to realize that preparing to write will save time, heartache, and unwelcome surprises. With this realization, the definition of *writing* has expanded to include both prewriting and revision tasks. Most of us today would not consider submitting a piece of writing that has not been reviewed and proofed.

Despite this knowledge, we still sometimes find ourselves tempted to dive into a complex writing task like a grant proposal without taking the essential preliminary measures included here. Scheduling regular daily writing time will keep your proposals and other academic writing moving forward as efficiently as possible. That's not to say, however, that your proposal development will always follow the plan you lay out for it. Sometimes a first draft may not become a second draft; it may become trash. And you'll see in our discussion of abstracts in Chapter 7 that writing can be recursive and regressive. Still, our experience in proposal development has shown that engaging in the recommended prewriting tasks and scheduling regular writing time will save time in the long run.

The writing itself is, of course, the core task of proposal development. As with any writing task, it is critically important to balance the audience, speaker, and message.

Chapter 7

The Abstract

Susan Hazelwood and Bondi Wood

MOST OF US have mothers who coached us on the importance of first and last impressions. Appearance, manners, behavior, and language were all expected to be appropriate. The abstract for your grant application, sometimes called the executive summary or project summary, serves as the first, often the lingering or last, and sometimes the only impression of you and your proposed work. For readers who are not the primary or secondary reviewers of your proposal, time is sometimes so short that the title and abstract are the only portions of the proposal that they read carefully. We cannot overemphasize the need for your abstract to be clean, crisp, and easily understandable.

The abstract must hold the attention of the expert reader and still be clear to the lay reader. The main audience for this piece of your proposal will be the peer reviewers and staff at the sponsoring organization, but your audience may also include members of the lay public who read the sponsor's website, members of Congress who fund the sponsoring agency, and voters who put those elected officials into office. For these latter groups, the value of the project will rest on what they glean from the abstract as a stand-alone document. Once submitted to a sponsor, the abstract will probably not be updated after the award is made, so you should allow yourself enough preparation time to write an abstract that will stand the test of time and that will be a publication of which your mother would be proud.

A bit of a debate persists as to whether the abstract should be written at the beginning of your proposal development timeline or the end. Our answer is "both." You may have read advice urging you to write the abstract at the end of your proposal development work when all the details have been settled. We have found that, although the abstract will ultimately sum up your proposal, it can also serve as a guiding document as you develop your proposal. We recommend that you consider it a dynamic document that begins with the elevator pitch described earlier (see "Assessing the Match" in Chapter 2). You will use this pitch to describe your project to others, including the program officer, as noted in Mark Child's interview of former NSF program officer Cerry Klein (see boxed text, "The Program Officer's Perspective"); the questions others ask and the comments they make about your successive drafts will help you focus the content of the abstract. That content will likely change frequently as you fine-tune the details of your project plans.

The abstract functions as the synopsis of your entire grant application. It should highlight for the reader the importance of the work you propose to do, emphasizing the significance of the work and the innovation it represents for your field. The goals for any proposal abstract should be to build interest in and excitement about the proposed project.

The content of the abstract should include summaries of the work that will be done, the way it will be done (such as methods, approaches, activities, and project design), and the point of the work (goal or goals and objectives). The abstract states how the project's accomplishments will be evaluated and disseminated, occasionally including a high-level timeline of action steps. The abstract should convey why you are the perfect or perhaps the only person or group with the expertise and experience to do the proposed work. Some abstracts also include the amount of funding requested for the project, and some will detail institutional contributions that increase the value of selecting your organization for funding.

This often-short piece of writing will be for some readers the sole representation of your credibility, the novelty of your idea, and the soundness of your plan. This is the one document from which most people will determine their opinions as to the value of your project.

As you close in on the final version of the proposal as a whole, space limitations for the abstract will often require several iterations to pack as much information as you can into the fewest possible words. Most sponsors limit the length of the abstract to about 150 to 250 words—a half-page to a page. This is a lot of information for a small box or a limited number of words. Every word must add value to the abstract's content. Put another way, any word or sentence that does not contribute to the goals of building interest and excitement should be cut.

As a consequence of the difficulty of providing the required content and meeting the goals of the writing in very limited space, most abstracts are written and rewritten. They are passed to other team members, including graduate or undergraduate students, for their review and input. They are shared with spouses and nonacademic friends, all to determine what the readers understand. Missed or misunderstood points mean additional revisions are in order. This level of friendly review cannot occur at the last minute, which brings us back to our initial recommendation that, to achieve a strong abstract, the writing should happen throughout the proposal development process.

The Program Officer's Perspective

Mark B. Child

Cerry Klein, a professor in the MU College of Engineering, recently returned to MU after serving as a program officer for the National Science Foundation. This experience has given him an inside understanding of the grant-funding process. In our interview, Klein stated that "the purpose of the grant-funding process is to advance knowledge to the benefit of mankind. The desire is to always try to fund the best and most innovative ideas." Although a number of ideas that get funded fail, Klein explains that "program officers are cognizant that they are spending taxpayers' money and want the best return on that investment they can get. To that end, it is critical that research ideas be vetted by the best and brightest."

Looking back at his service, Klein gives his perspective of what grant seekers should do before contacting the program officer. He emphatically asserts, "They simply need to be prepared. The last thing you want to do is waste a program officer's time!" Although there are many ways that grant seekers can prepare, Klein offers three suggestions:

First, prepare a project summary that includes the intellectual merits and broader impacts of your research. Then e-mail the program officer and ask him or her to look at your project summary and let you know if it fits his or her program. Ask if you can call and talk for about 15 minutes.

Second, prepare an elevator pitch for the phone call that lucidly and briefly explains your idea. If you cannot concisely present your idea, then the program officer may conclude that you don't understand it well. A program officer will generally assume that the better you know your subject, the better you can explain it.

Finally, prepare a list of questions you wish to ask. Make them short and direct. Allow the program officer to also ask questions that expand your idea. Do not ask questions that can be answered by reading the RFP [request for proposal] or guidelines because program officers will assume you are not serious and want them to do your leg work.

Although preparation is essential before contacting program officers, Klein asserts that a well-written proposal that fits a program's criteria is the greatest way to get their attention. He warns,

Do not submit proposals that are not ready or do not fit the program. Make sure your ideas fit the program you are interested in by seeing what has been funded in the past. If they tell you not to submit, then do not submit! Most importantly, do not submit a poorly written proposal or one that was put together at the last minute. It is not difficult to tell who has just thrown something together and who has actually put the time and effort into the process. It should take you a good three to six months to write a concise, cogent, well-written proposal. These are the ones that always get funded.

Perhaps this sentiment is summed up best when Klein concludes that "what makes program officers' jobs easy and also thrills them is a well-written proposal about a great idea they have vetted that meets all the criteria of the program and has high intellectual merit and true broader impacts."

Putting It All Together

Begin the abstract by setting the context for your work. Give a broad statement about why your proposal is important now. If you can, cite dramatic and significant statistics that illustrate the compelling reasons to fund your project. Think of this opening line as a hook to engage your readers' curiosity. If your project involves studying a small but crucial link in a larger chain that impacts society, explain that broader significance.

The two examples below are opening lines of an abstract. The first example explains the gist of the project but not its significance to a broad audience. The second example sets up the importance of the work before getting into the nitty-gritty of the project.

> *We posit that estrogens improve over-nutrition and/or angiotensin II (Ang II)-induced INS resistance in skeletal muscle and cardiovascular tissue via decreased S6K1-mediated Ser (P) of IRSs.*

• • •

> *More than 17 million Americans suffer from type 2 diabetes, the seventh leading cause of death, with premenopausal obese and diabetic women at particular risk. Preliminary data from our laboratory show that in different animal models of obesity, female rodents are protected when compared with same strain male rodents. We posit that estrogens improve over-nutrition and/or angiotensin II (Ang II)-induced INS resistance in skeletal muscle and cardiovascular tissue via decreased S6K1-mediated Ser (P) of IRSs.*

We see a dramatic difference between the two abstracts and find that the second example propels the reader forward, creating a sense of importance and urgency.

Once you have set the stage with the why—the importance of the work—move quickly to the who, what, where, when, and how, just as journalists do. To further your thinking, consider these questions:

- Who will do the work?
- What will be done?
- Where will the work be done?
- When will the activities be accomplished?
- How will the results be evaluated and disseminated?

Even though your abstract should make the reader want to know more about the project, it must also provide a clear overview of the work to be done and how the sponsor's money will be spent because it is the first and sometimes the only part of the grant application that readers will see. It is the page most often turned to by the peer reviewers and sponsor personnel. After the award is made, the abstract will usually be published to summarize the work you are paid to accomplish. Because the abstract is nearly always separated at some time from the rest of the proposal package, it should be written as a stand-alone document. Avoid references that rely on the rest of the proposal for clarification.

500-Word Abstract

In the example paragraphs below, we review what we consider to be a successful 500-word abstract, written by MU investigator Steven Sayers. Sayers opens with dramatic and significant statistics to support the universal need for his proposal. We would expect reviewers to see the relevance and urgency of the project based on these three opening sentences:

> *America is rapidly aging, with more than 33 million individuals age 65 years or older, and this number is expected to double in the next 30 years. Approximately 20 percent of men and women 65 years of age and older possess chronic disabilities, and the number one medical condition in the US contributing to chronic disability in older adults is knee osteoarthritis (OA). With the increasing age and number of older adults in our population, functional limitations and disablement resulting from knee OA will likely rise.*

The next three sentences describe more specifically how OA affects those over 65. More importantly, these sentences paint a picture of how current medical practices are not meeting needs and circle back to the broader significance by noting how the entire country suffers as a result:

> *Older adults suffering from knee OA are often caught in a downward spiral of reduced physical activity, loss of muscle mass, reduced function and mobility, and increased physical disability. In most cases, impairments progress slowly, so that by the time they are noticed by health-care professionals, the mounting deficits have resulted in the inability to perform activities of daily living or function meaningfully in the community. We believe it is essential to find ways to improve quality of life, maintain functional independence, and reduce physical disability in older adults with knee OA to lessen the ever-increasing health-care burden in our country.*

The next three sentences prove Sayers has done his homework and contextualize the project by acknowledging existing research and methods of treatment for OA:

A primary focus of rehabilitation in older adults with knee OA has been strength training using moderate to heavy resistance. This traditional approach has been shown to improve functioning in only some studies, and these effects have been small to moderate. Currently, there is little consensus on the most effective method of training to alleviate the symptoms of knee OA.

The remainder of the abstract tells how the project will be carried out. The second sentence in the paragraph below conveys the team's prior experience in this field. The italicized sentence is the nutshell sentence that captures the essence of the project. The sentences that follow it explain the anticipated outcomes and benefits of the proposed project for the patient, the health-care community, and ultimately the entire country.

We will explore a unique weight-training program for men and women 65 years or older that stresses high-speed training using moderate resistance. Several of our studies suggest that the speed at which muscles move is more important to performing functional tasks than how strong the muscles are. *We will compare high-speed weight training with traditional strength training in 53 older men and women with knee OA to determine which method has greater effects on muscle strength, speed of movement, functional performance, physical disability, and joint pain and stiffness* [emphasis added]. We believe that higher-speed training will improve these physical measures to a greater degree than simply training for increased muscle strength. Further, we believe there is a critical need to investigate alternatives to traditional strength training and identify the best strategy to improve the health of our older knee OA population. If, indeed, higher-speed training is a viable alternative to traditional strength training, this project will help improve quality of life and maintain independence of older adults with knee OA in the community and also provide health-care professionals with the most appropriate strategies to help knee OA patients in the clinic. We believe that high-speed training may change the way weight training exercise is practiced in the community, as well as how it is prescribed in the clinic for older adults with knee OA.

Note that Sayers does not explicitly give the reviewer the where and when of the project. We recommend that you do so if space permits. Proposal writing is very much the art of the possible, and there will always be trade-offs entailed in producing the best proposal you can within the time and space you have available.

250-Word Abstract

MU professor of biological engineering John Viator wrote an effective 250-word abstract for his project on improving the detection of tumor cells via a photoacoustic detection system. With less than half the length of the previous example, Viator does not have the luxury of using many adjectives, adverbs, or transitions to enhance his writing, yet he has to explain a fairly complex process to a lay audience, which we think he does successfully. The first paragraph of the abstract has only three sentences, and in them, Viator efficiently moves from the broader significance of the work to the need for his project and then the weaknesses of current solutions as he presents the importance of detecting circulating tumor cells (CTCs), three specific health outcomes related to improved detection, and the lack of existing technology for CTC detection.

> *Detection of circulating tumor cells (CTCs) in human blood and lymph systems has the potential to aid clinical decision making in the treatment of cancer. The presence of CTCs may signify metastasis, indicate relapse, or serve to monitor disease progression. Although other methods exist to detect CTCs, they require expensive instrumentation and complex procedures that necessarily introduce human error.*

In the second paragraph, Viator describes the technique this project will employ to improve detection of CTCs. He is able to describe the complex procedure clearly and closes this paragraph with the greatest challenge facing the proposed project. Including this potential challenge in the abstract provides reviewers with an early signal that this will be a thoughtful proposal from a team that has considered potential pitfalls and is cognizant of them. Although this strategy may not be appropriate in all abstracts, we think it works well here.

> *We propose to use photoacoustic waves, conceptually described as laser-induced ultrasonic waves, for rapid, accurate detection of circulating melanoma cells which absorb low-energy, nanosecond-duration laser pulses and thereby generate photoacoustic waves. To implement this concept, we will obtain a cell block derived from spinning a blood sample from a melanoma patient in a centrifuge. The resulting cell block will be mixed with approximately 20 milliliters of normal saline and injected into a detection system consisting of a peristaltic pump, a fluid receiver, a transparent flow cell with an integrated acoustic detector, and a laser system capable of generating acoustic waves. The most challenging aspect of this concept is detecting photoacoustic waves from small sources such as single melanoma cells.*

As is often the case in shorter abstracts, Viator has had to sacrifice some details in order to explain the multistage technique that is the core of this proposal's innovation. He does not identify his team or where they hail from, but he has cleverly built credibility for his team and their work into the last sentences of the abstract by describing the previous successes of the technique and, by inference, the team. The reader tacitly understands that those who developed and used the technique must be well qualified, even if they are not explicitly mentioned.

Currently, our photoacoustic detection system has been tested on 7-micron diameter black latex microspheres from a maximum of 10A 6/ milliliters to simulate melanoma cells. We found the detection limit to be approximately 10 spheres in the laser beam path. We obtained cultured human melanoma cells and tested them on the same system, with a detection limit of approximately 30 to 50 melanoma cells at a time.

160-Word Abstract

Now, let's take a look at a much shorter abstract. The successful abstract below is from MU professor of Greek art and archaeology Sue Langdon:

Excavations in the 1960s at ancient Corinth in Greece revealed a sanctuary dedicated to the goddesses Demeter and Kore. The abundant finds included 24,000 terracotta figurines made as offerings from the 7th c BCE to the Roman conquest of the city. I have been invited by the excavators to publish the figurines that date from the earliest worship to the end of the Archaic period, 700–480 BCE. I have created a database for 500 well-preserved figurines and 1,800 for quantification purposes. Next summer I will work in the Corinth museum, analyzing the terracottas by date, source, fabric, and type based partly on comparison with figurines from other Greek sites and museums. My study is critical in determining precisely when worship began and what influences may have led to the establishment of the cult at this site. Moreover, it contributes to understanding how early communities created ritual activities and beliefs to serve a growing population within a complex regional setting.

This abstract very clearly presents the who (Sue Langdon and the Corinth museum), what (analyzing the terracottas), when (next summer), where (ancient Corinth in Greece), and how (by date, source, fabric, and type using databases) of the proposed work. The global importance of the work—the why—is presented in the last two sentences of this abstract rather than at the beginning, as we typically recommend. Although we think that the abstract could have been strengthened by leading off with the importance of the work, this is of lesser importance in such a short abstract than it might have been in a longer abstract such as Sayers's 500-word abstract above.

Note, too, that this 160-word abstract fails to mention that this work will ultimately result in a monograph. The importance of the work rests on furthering understanding of this site and of early communities more broadly, so publication is critical to making these understandings available to others. Mention of the monograph would therefore strengthen the abstract. The invitation to publish the figurines will allow others to engage in analysis of the finds from the site, though the abstract leaves the reader to draw this conclusion (or not).

Summary

Along with the title, the abstract is one of the two most-read sections of any grant proposal. Because it will be the only part of the proposal that many readers will see, it must be written as a stand-alone document. Your goals in writing the abstract are to generate interest in and excitement about the project. The content of the abstract is often specified by the sponsor. In general, readers will seek a clear sense of the project from the abstract. This can be achieved by treating the abstract as a journalist would treat the lead of a story, by addressing the reader's questions about why the work matters, what will be done, how the work will be done, who will do the work, and where and when it will be done. Because it is difficult to cover so much information in very little space and because the abstract is so critically important, we recommend starting the abstract early in the proposal development process and subjecting draft versions to review by many readers to be sure that the final version is as cogent and compelling as possible.

Chapter 8

The Heart of the Matter: The Proposal Narrative

Bondi Wood, Mary Barile, Chris Montgomery, and Sara Vassmer

THE NARRATIVE IS the heart of the proposal. It is a form of persuasive writing and not unlike a sales pitch. This is where you put forward your reasons for doing your research and make an argument for the need, impact, and timeliness of your work. The narrative needs to be clear, lively, and persuasive. More and more funders are also requiring that it be free from jargon and technical language and, for some sponsors, appropriate for general readers rather than academic audiences.

At this point you have surveyed the literature on your subject; learned about the work currently being conducted in the field; discussed your idea with trusted colleagues and team members; assessed the feasibility of the work relative to your time, resources, and available expertise; and formulated your approach to the work. You have researched various funding agencies to determine which grant program is most closely suited to your needs. You have read the relevant guidelines and understand the funder's criteria. You have contacted the program officer to verify that your proposal is aligned with the sponsor's interests, and you have completed your prewriting analyses of your project, as outlined in Chapter 5. At last you are ready to write.

Different funders require different information in the proposal narrative, but most want you to tell them the basics: who, what, when, where, why, and how, just as you do in the proposal's abstract. The difference is that in the narrative, you get to elaborate. Some funders provide an outline. Others provide a brief description of the areas to be covered and allow the applicant to determine the organizational structure. Either way, it is good practice to adopt the funder's language.

In addition to the proposal requirements, some funders also list their methods for evaluating submitted proposals. This section will often provide some hints as to the sponsor's language for relevant concepts as well as the order in which the reviewers' evaluation form may present the sections of the proposal. Although the language may differ from discipline to discipline and the order of requested information may vary from sponsor to sponsor, any funder wants to know that you have a workable plan and the resources to complete the proposed work.

As you finalize an outline based on the required components of the proposal and tie it into your timeline for grant preparation (see Chapter 5 for guidance on outlines and proposal development timelines), you may want to estimate the writing time you will need for each section of the narrative and set target dates for completing each piece rather than treating the narrative as one large assignment. Almost all sponsors impose page limits, and these can range from 6 to more than 30 pages for the narrative section of the proposal. Most will allow 10 to 12 pages, including tables, figures, and graphs. Be prepared to tailor your story to the length requirements. Regardless of the length, your intent will be to make a convincing case for the potential impact of the work and to demonstrate that your team has the ideal qualifications and environment to do the proposed project. Again, requirements vary by funder, but most proposal narratives include the following:

- need for and significance of the work,
- goals and objectives to be accomplished,
- preliminary studies or pilots related to the proposed work,
- methods and approaches to be used to do work,
- key personnel and their expertise,
- expected outcomes and evaluation strategies, and
- plans for disseminating the results of the project.

Proposal Logic

An effective proposal narrative presents a sales pitch, a logical argument for your project. This is why so many sponsors require logic models as part of the proposal narrative. The narrative begins with a problem. Regardless of whether this is a proposal for research, instruction, outreach, the arts, or some other endeavor, you should think about the larger significance of the project. This will usually lead you to a societal problem or need on some level. The work may relate to a public health issue such as the rate of obesity in the US population; to a safety issue such as the need for faster, more cost-effective methods to identify contaminants in the food supply; to the need for more qualified workers in science and engineering fields; or to a quality-of-life issue such as rural access to arts programming. Whatever it is, this societal problem is the *so-what* that provides the fundamental justification for your project.

Such a broad problem, however, will not be solved by a year or two or five of grant funding, so your argument should move very quickly from this root issue to establish the portion of this larger issue that your project will address. For research projects, this is usually a gap in knowledge that keeps the field from moving ahead. For instructional projects, it is typically a recruiting or curriculum need in a specific area of study. Outreach projects often focus on the needs of a particular population, whereas arts projects may focus on access or on better understanding something about ourselves as humans. Addressing this portion of the larger problem becomes the overall goal of your project.

Having narrowed the problem, the next part of the proposal argument looks at what has been done to date and which of these efforts have and have not worked. The idea here is to create a logical "funnel" that leads the reader to the objectives for your project. Although the goal may be a longer-term effort that will not be completed within the time frame of your project, the objectives should define the work of the project itself.

Defining your goal and objectives leads logically to the methods or activities section, in which you describe how the objectives will be accomplished, and from there to the results of the work. Finally, these outcomes are tied back to their importance in addressing the broad societal need to remind the reader of the reason for funding the work, the so-what (Figure 5).

Need for the Work

This section of the proposal narrative is variously called the Problem Statement, Needs Assessment, Background, Significance, or Broader Impacts. Whatever the label, this is where you directly address the so-what that justifies your project. Why should the reviewer care about your project? A sponsor will rarely put hand in pocket for dollars to support someone else's personal curiosity. This section must convince your audience, the grant reviewers, that your project will serve the greater good of humanity and, more specifically, the sponsor's constituency.

FIGURE 5

Proposal Logic

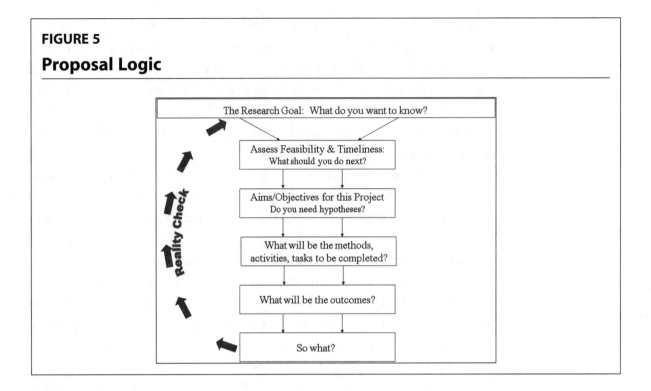

Begin with a broad problem statement, one that is global in nature and closely aligned with the funding agency's goals or criteria. Provide accurate and up-to-date background information on the current state of the problem. This should flow logically into the problem or question you want to address: Why is this work necessary and whom will it serve? The two examples below contain identical information; only the order of presentation is different. The first example launches into the science and methodology of the proposal, whereas the second sets up the project's importance to a wide audience.

> *This research project will accomplish two objectives: first, we will develop the first-ever search tool for retrieving information from diverse human services databases; and second, we will use the search tool to assist investigators of child abuse. To date, there are no advanced information retrieval tools available in the human services despite the broad use of database management systems throughout the United States. This situation is especially problematic for Child Protective Services workers who investigate over 10 million allegations of child abuse each year.*

• • •

Despite the broad use of database management systems throughout the United States, there are to date no advanced information retrieval tools available in the human services. This situation is especially problematic for Child Protective Services workers who investigate more than 10 million allegations of abuse each year. Importantly, this research project will develop the first-ever search tool for retrieving information from diverse human services databases and will use this search tool to assist investigators.

The second example funnels from a global statement of need to the specifics of this project and then describes how it will meet that need and who will benefit.

After you explain the global importance of your project, you will want to review the relevant literature, noting how others have addressed aspects of this problem or need and any problems with or gaps in those efforts. Be careful not to allow facts to hang in isolation. Tie these needs into the stated goals of the sponsor, and describe why your project will move beyond the past efforts to solve a specific problem. As you give your reviewers a clear picture of how your work fits into the larger landscape, be very clear about what will be done and why it needs to be done.

As you wrap up the needs section, explain why this project needs to be done now and, especially if it is a research project, why it is innovative. It helps to create a sense of urgency to note that, unless you do X by the end of two years, more than Y might change. It might be as simple as saying that you must interview World War II veterans immediately because more than 1,000 die each day, and soon their stories will be lost. You need to provide the funder with specific supporting documentation, avoiding vague word choices and ambiguous claims. As a general rule, the more people impacted by the work, the more seriously a sponsor will take the need for the project.

Innovation is a broad term and can relate to your entire project or just certain aspects of it. In the broadest sense, your project would be innovative if it questioned accepted research or sought to shift existing paradigms. Aspects of your project may be innovative in terms of the concepts, approaches, methodologies, interventions, or instrumentation employed. You may be proposing to apply a method that is traditional in one field of study in an innovative way in an unrelated field of study. Typically, it is not considered innovative enough just to be the only person proposing this type of project.

Goals and Objectives

Having funneled the narrative from the broad societal issue to the portion of that issue your project will address and from there to the best way to go about that, the next step in the narrative process is to succinctly summarize the purpose of the project in one or two goals and then lay out the project's three or four primary objectives. Even if the funder does not specifically ask for goals and objectives, you will want to incorporate them to lend cohesion and focus to your argument.

What is the difference between goals and objectives? A goal tends to be abstract and conceptual. It presents the big picture and should also be tied to the goals of your funder. If the problem highlighted in your needs statement is that children are going hungry, your goal is probably to feed children. Your goal points the reader to the larger societal issue that is the main purpose of the project, such as alleviating hunger, tackling illiteracy, or curing diabetes. A goal is similar to a thesis statement, encapsulating in a sentence the broad scope of what you hope to accomplish or learn. If you have difficulty stating your goal in one or two simple sentences, this could be a signal that you need to refine your project. Having more than one or two goals per project is seldom recommended. The three examples below show how the broader societal issue that anchors the proposal logic can be focused in a single project goal.

Need Statement: *More than 10 million allegations of child abuse are reported each year. Child Protective Services workers must investigate each case without adequate information retrieval tools.*

Goal: *Provide Child Protective Services workers with better tools to investigate child abuse cases.*

• • •

Need Statement: *Approximately one in every six adults—16.3 percent of the US adult population—has high total cholesterol. People with high total cholesterol have approximately twice the risk of heart disease.*

Goal: *Reduce illness and death from coronary heart disease (CHD) in the United States by reducing the percentage of Americans with high total cholesterol.*

• • •

Problem/Need: *Melanoma is the most rapidly growing cancer by type, with an incidence rate that more than doubles every 10 to 20 years. Early detection of melanoma is essential for improving treatment outcomes.*

Goal: *Improve the potential to monitor therapy, detect relapse, and guide clinical management of melanoma treatment.*

To reach your goal, you plan to take certain steps. We will refer to these steps as objectives here, but they can be expressed as objectives, specific aims, research questions, or hypotheses, depending upon the conventions of your discipline or the specifications of the sponsor. Regardless of the label, they convey the specific, measurable, and shorter-term steps you will take to accomplish your goal. They lead to the data or the product that will impact the final evaluation of your project. Objectives outline *how* you will design a project to successfully achieve your goal.

Objectives can define products to be created, processes to be conducted, behaviors to be initiated or changed, products to be created or refined, or performance benchmarks to be researched (Hall & Howlett, 2011). The four examples below show how the longer-term goal of a project can be further narrowed into specific objectives that delineate the work of the project. The first objective in the first example illustrates a product objective. The second objective is a process objective. The work entails the development of search tools but not their incorporation into a software product. In the next example, the first objective sets a performance benchmark, and the second aspires to change physician behaviors.

Goal: *Provide Child Protective Services workers with better tools to investigate child abuse cases.*

Objectives:

1. *Create a database for diverse human services cases of child abuse.* [Product: The database will be completed.]

2. *Develop search tools to assist investigators.* [Process: The search tools will be in development.]

• • •

Goal: *Reduce illness and death from coronary heart disease (CHD) in the United States by reducing the percentage of Americans with high blood cholesterol.*

Objectives:

1. *Increase the percentage of the public who have ever had their blood cholesterol checked from 35 to 50 percent within two years.* [Performance]

2. *Encourage physicians to initiate dietary changes before cholesterol levels require medication.* [Behavior]

• • •

Goal: *Improve potential to monitor therapy, detect relapse, and guide clinical management of melanoma treatment.*

Objectives:

Aim 1: *Improve the early detection system.* [Product]

Aim 2: *Improve the specificity of the test within the system.* [Performance]

Aim 3: *Study the time course of metastasis.* [Process]

• • •

Goal: *This seminar will demonstrate that significant new insights can be realized about Jane Austen by reading her closely alongside the now-understudied—but once well-known—writers of her own time.*

Objectives:

1. *Undertake collective close reading and discussion of primary texts by Austen in tandem with those of her once-celebrated contemporaries.* [Process]

2. *Provide tools for pursuing advanced study of Austen using both emerging digital and traditional archival research techniques.* [Product]

Your objectives should be numbered so that reviewers can find and refer to them quickly and easily. Mary Licklider and Bob Glidewell outline below some of their observations of the way in which they approach proposals when they serve on review panels (see boxed text, "The Reviewer's Perspective"). Limit yourself to three or four realistic objectives that are concrete, narrow in focus, and achievable within the project period. The results of your objectives will serve as the foundation of your final project report to your funder. If your funder makes the final report requirements available, awareness of those requirements at the proposal stage may help you write your objectives in a way that will facilitate completing the report.

Preliminary Studies

Sponsors often require that you begin with pilot data that you and your team have already collected from previous work related to this project and explain the implications of this work for future projects. In other words, the proposed project is expected to serve as a link between previous and future work. The National Institutes of Health (NIH) now allows you to resubmit the same proposal only once. Particularly for sponsors with resubmission limits such as this, strong, relevant pilot data is crucial to convincing the reviewers that the proposed work can be done.

The preliminary studies section of your proposal can also be used to demonstrate your experience with the methods to be employed in the proposed work. Think carefully about the areas of expertise a reviewer might consider necessary to your proposed project. You may want to consider collaborating with a more seasoned investigator whose research you could then tap as part of this section.

The Reviewer's Perspective

Mary Licklider and Bob Glidewell

Between the two of us, we have reviewed grant proposals for multiple federal and state agencies as well as for internal grant programs here at MU. The observations we share below are both ours and those of other individuals who served with us on review panels:

- All reviewers read the title and abstract, whether they are assigned to be the primary reviewer for the proposal or not. Be sure to write these for more general audiences than the body of the proposal.

- Some reviewers go from the abstract to the project description, and others go to the budget. Both groups are seeking a more detailed glimpse of the project. Be sure these two pieces convey a consistent message.

- If the budget is too low, reviewers question whether the work can be done. If the budget is too high, reviewers may suspect that the applicant is treating the sponsor's funding as play money. In worst-case scenarios, reviewers will question whether the project personnel know what they are doing and consequently recommend against funding the project.

- Reviewers tend to be experienced professionals, which usually means they have accumulated a certain number of birthdays too. Proposals with tiny print and no white space tend to make negative first impressions.

- Reviewers almost always struggle to get all the proposals read before the agency deadline. We are often reading proposals late at night or on the plane on the way to the review meeting.

Our motivation for serving on panels is to learn more about the grant process and to contribute to our professions. Neither of us has ever served on a panel with someone who did not take the work seriously. But we have served with individuals who carried particular biases, who were assigned proposals outside their areas of expertise, or whose personal circumstances allowed them to spend less time on the proposals than they would have liked. The primary reviewer has a tremendous influence on the outcome of the proposals to which he or she is assigned. If the luck of the draw assigns your proposal to someone who has a bias against its approach or who does not understand the importance of the innovation you are proposing, the odds of your getting funding will suffer.

What this means first of all is that having a proposal declined is not the end of the world or even the end of the proposal. It means that it is very important to request the reviewer comments and to attempt

(Continued)

to discuss the review with the sponsor's program officer. These two sources of information will tell you how close you are, where the review panel's concerns were, and how to proceed toward the next round of funding.

One final observation is that quality will put your proposal in the running for an award; luck gets you funded. Understanding and accepting this can go a long way toward helping you get past a negative review to try again.

Work Plan

Your work plan, sometimes called the research strategy or methods section, is essentially the road map of your project. It describes in detail what will be done, who will do it, and how and when the work will be accomplished. This section tells your reviewers that you have thought through the logistics of how your idea will play out in real time. Many sponsors specify exactly what to cover in your work plan, but others do not. The sponsor may ask for a Gantt chart or timeline for the project which shows who does what and when. Even if the sponsor does not require a timeline, you may want to create one for your own use. It can help, too, with developing your budget.

Many physical and life science proposals organize the methods section around the objectives, using the objectives as the main headings for this section. This works well when the objectives of the project will be addressed sequentially. In the social sciences and humanities, however, this is often not the case. In the example goal/objectives above that target CHD rates and cholesterol levels, activities associated with both objectives are likely to happen simultaneously. Similarly, a curriculum improvement project with objectives to improve the quality of students' writing and reasoning skills on lab reports and improve the quality of essay responses on exams may engage in writing exercises or peer review activities that simultaneously serve both objectives. For these kinds of projects, the methods section might be organized chronologically by month or quarter. A table with columns for Objectives Addressed, Target Date, Activity, and Responsible Parties can help to make the relationships of time, objectives, and activities clearer. See the Toolkit in Part Two of this handbook and online for examples of project timelines.

The sponsor's evaluation criteria may differ slightly from the required content and headings for the work plan section, so it can be easy to omit critical information that reviewers will be required to evaluate. For example, the Engineering Information Foundation indicates on its "How to Apply" web page (http://www.eifgrants.org/info/apply.html) that proposals should include a problem statement, the significance of the problem, and the approach to solving the problem along with a cover letter and some supporting information. Selection criteria include the overall quality of the project, the potential of the project to contribute new knowledge in the relevant area, and the potential of the project to be sustained beyond the period of foundation funding. It would seem that everything needed is included on this page.

However, additional information and proposal requirements are found within each of the programmatic descriptions. The Enhancing Communications and Use of Information in Engineering program (http://www .eifgrants.org/info/progareas.html), for example, specifically requires applications to describe the proposed project's innovative approaches, emphasis on effective teamwork, and emphasis on information-seeking as a lifelong skill and to include a matrix of instructional programs and materials. Similarly, the Women in Engineering and the Developing Countries programs carry their own unique requirements. Finally, the "What We Fund" web page (http://www.eifgrants.org/info/index.html) articulates additional foundation-wide priorities for projects that promote significant and lasting change and can be successfully replicated and for methods that are specific, well-defined, and cost-effective. The sample proposal outline for the Engineering Information Foundation provided in the Toolkit (see Section Three in this handbook and online) offers a model for pulling together requirements and priorities from multiple places in the sponsor's guidelines to help guide proposal development and distribute writing assignments among team members.

As you finalize the work plan section, engage your team to help predict and address potential weaknesses, objections, or fallacies in your proposed methods. These can be discussed under a subheading at the end of the description for each objective or time period or under a final heading at the end of the methods section. Either way, you will want to take control of these potential weaknesses. Including these issues in your proposal will rob your reviewers of the opportunity to point them out to you. There is no such thing as a perfect project. These are human creations. Addressing these issues demonstrates your awareness of weaknesses and potential problems and allows you to articulate again your rationale for the choices you have made.

Key Personnel

For many sponsors, this is a separate section of the narrative. If this is not the case, you will still want to create an opportunity to make the case that you are the ideal leader and the team you have put together is the ideal team to do this work. If a key personnel section is not part of your sponsor's narrative outline, you will want to include some of this information in the work plan. This information can also be included in the budget justification as part of the description of each key person's role in the project.

Think about what your team brings to this work that no one else can offer. Think about the various areas of expertise that a reviewer might consider necessary to accomplish each aspect of the work and who on your team can claim each of those areas of expertise. Consider what kinds of facilities and equipment a reviewer might consider necessary to do this work well. You will especially want to highlight any specialized equipment, facilities, study populations, and the like that will be important to the success of the project, to which your team has access, and that are not generally available.

Be aware that for many sponsors, *principal investigator* or *PI* denotes the one individual who will be the sponsor's point of contact for the project and who will ultimately be responsible for all the requirements of the grant award. Other key personnel to be involved in the scientific development or execution of a project are usually referred to as *co-investigators* rather than *co-PIs* (U.S. Department of Health and Human Services, Public Health Service, 2011, pp. I-89, III-31). Many sponsors will not accept a proposal with multiple PIs. The NIH allows this but requires a leadership plan that describes how the PI responsibilities will be divided and coordinated, including the decision-making process for scientific direction, resource allocation, and disputes. There is no "lead" PI, and each PI is responsible and accountable for all components of the project. There is a contact PI, but this does not imply special authority or responsibility.

Even if the sponsor does not require a formal leadership plan, it is always a good idea to include a general management plan. With it, your reviewers will know how the key personnel plan to work together, who will be accountable for which aspects of the project, and who will provide leadership to the team.

Sustainability

Sustainability in the grant world refers to your ability to sustain the work of the project after the sponsor's money is gone. Getting money from a sponsor, then, is only the beginning of your work. You may receive funding a single time, or you may be able to renew your grant several times. No matter where the money comes from, the sponsor will expect a plan for sustaining your project. Funders do not want to give you money only to see the work come to a dead stop when the grant period ends. They want to see a plan which projects one, five, or more years into the future and includes strategies for continuing the work, generating income, applying to other sponsors, or approaching your institution for support beyond the program period.

For research proposals, a description of institutional support for your area of research often provides evidence of sustainability. Reviewers are often willing to believe that if an institution has invested in you today, it will continue to support you tomorrow. Examples of institutional support are not limited to direct funding for your research but can also include such investments as the following:

- Offering you specialized training
- Buying specific equipment
- Providing lab space
- Supporting your professional travel
- Waiving tuition for your graduate students
- Cultivating campus-wide programs or initiatives that speak to your academic endeavors
- Providing a mentor
- Adding faculty positions in the same area of research as yours
- Releasing you from other duties to pursue this project

Evaluation of Outcomes and Impact

Whether it is a multi-million-dollar research project or a small arts program, sponsors expect organizations and investigators to measure the impact of their work. Sponsors want to know, up front, how you are going to determine if your project was a success or not. This is why most narratives include a section about how you intend to evaluate your project. In fact, many sponsors expect that at least 5 to 10 percent of your budget be devoted to project evaluation.

The evaluation section is tied directly to your objectives. If your objectives say you are going to perform specific activities, your evaluation section should explain how you will evaluate those activities. If, during the development of the evaluation section, you determine that your objectives are not measurable, then you should revise your objectives.

There are typically two types of evaluation in grant-funded projects: formative and summative:

- Formative evaluation occurs from the start of the project, is ongoing throughout the project, and is used to evaluate progress. Formative evaluation monitors the process and interim benchmarks to allow you to adjust your course as you go along.

- Summative evaluation happens near the end of a project to examine end products.

A third type of evaluation, impact evaluation, focuses on the broader societal goal of your work; this cannot typically be assessed during the term of your grant award because this type of effect usually occurs over the long term. You will most likely want to incorporate both formative and summative evaluation into your plan, and both should be structured and analytical to answer specific questions. Section Three of the Toolkit in this handbook and online includes a sample list of evaluation questions to help stimulate your thinking.

Next, consider whether you should hire an internal or external evaluator or some combination of the two. There are advantages and disadvantages to both kinds of evaluators, and written (and unwritten) sponsor expectations may also influence your decision. External experts have the advantage of an objective viewpoint that carries credibility with the sponsor and other external audiences. External experts can also bring specialized evaluation expertise to the tasks. External expertise can be costly, however, as you build travel, communication, and subcontract costs into your project budget.

Internal evaluators also offer several advantages. Their in-house knowledge carries credibility with project personnel and perhaps also with the study or outreach population. They have firsthand knowledge of internal culture, and they cost less than bringing in external consultants. Although project personnel may be able to perform many aspects of formative evaluation, sponsors often expect someone outside the project to perform mid- and end-of-project evaluations. The latter can be costly, and one way to minimize expense is to have the external expert create the evaluation design, use project personnel to collect at least some of the evaluation data, and then hand the data off for analysis to the external expert.

As you consider the kinds of evidence that will document the extent to which you have achieved each of the project objectives, the nature of this evidence will probably lead you to qualitative or quantitative evaluation methods or both. Currently, many funders like to see a combination of qualitative and quantitative, or *mixed methods* in data collection and analysis. Just as your methods section lays out a timeline for the activities of the project, the evaluation section should provide a timeline for evaluation activities that are well coordinated with the project's methods. One of the greatest weaknesses of project evaluation is a failure to plan evaluation activities at the same level of detail and with the same care as planning the rest of the project.

The National Science Foundation (NSF) offers this list of common problems with evaluation plans (Westat, 2002), problems that are certainly not specific to NSF-funded projects:

- Lack of funding in the budget for the evaluation

- Unclear outcomes, which make it impossible to know whether they have been achieved

- Use of only quantitative methods, ignoring qualitative techniques

- Lack of knowledge about different evaluation techniques

- Failure to look at other projects and the evaluation techniques that worked for those projects

- Failure to collect evaluative data over time, resulting in snapshots rather than a panorama

- Short-circuited evaluation process; an evaluation may have to follow a project for a year or so after the end of the program

Numerous methods of evaluation are at your disposal, including surveys, interviews, focus groups, observations, tests, document studies, key informants, and case studies. Most faculty members have had some training in statistics, and many incorrectly assume that this training makes it unnecessary to include a statistician on the project team. Most scientific review panels now include a statistician. Statisticians at MU who serve on federal agency review panels agree that one of the most common problems they see is a mismatch between the scientific question to be answered and the statistical methods proposed. If your project entails quantitative work, at least consult with a statistician before you decide whether or not to include this expertise in the project.

Finally, a word about evaluation in research proposals: Many of us do not think about the data analysis of research projects as *evaluation*. These analyses are generally covered in the methods section rather than a separate evaluation section, and many scientists tend to think of these analyses as part of the methods rather than as evaluation. We would argue for a shift in thinking. Whereas the work will probably be easiest to follow if the analysis of data remains in the methods section, a separate section for "Expected Results" that explicitly describes what will and will not be considered successful outcomes, what would be implied by various possible outcomes, and what would be considered appropriate next steps will subject research activities to project evaluation questions. Taking these questions and answers into your own hands, just as with the "Potential Problems" section, allows you to set the bar for success rather than leaving the reviewer to decide what might be "good enough" and what your results may or may not mean.

Dissemination Plans

Dissemination plans show funders how you will share the results of your work with others and, especially for private sector sponsors, ensure that your sponsor receives credit for supporting your project. Sharing information about your project makes the public and other potential sponsors aware of your work, as well as contributing to the knowledge base in your discipline. Your dissemination plan shows a sponsor that you are savvy regarding the audiences for and impact of your project and the sponsor's grant dollars. The flip side of this coin is that if you fail to share the information the sponsor helped you develop, this sponsor may be less likely to consider you for future funding.

It is important to remember the truism that sponsors do not fund research or institutions of higher education. Sponsors pay others to advance their own agendas, and these agendas often have to do with advancing practice or knowledge in particular fields. Sponsors ask grantees to disseminate their work to help achieve these ends. Sponsors benefit from your good work, and you benefit from the sponsor's dollars. This does not mean that you must give your work away. Commercializing your work is one way of disseminating it, by getting it into the marketplace so that it can improve people's lives.

Dissemination plans typically take into account the audiences for your information, the scope of the information to be shared, and the methods for sharing that information. Knowing with whom you will share information will help you determine methods for sharing that information in order to reach the target audiences. A good dissemination plan identifies groups that can benefit from your work and data, including local, regional, and global stakeholders such as researchers, community members, politicians, business owners or managers, and other grant sponsors. Besides identifying the target audiences, explain why you will share your work with these target groups and what impact this sharing might have beyond just general information. Will your research help a community solve a problem or doctors prescribe more effective drugs? Each audience has different needs and uses for your information, and these should be identified, along with a short discussion about how your work (and by extension, your funder's dollars) will benefit each group.

A strong dissemination plan will typically include a variety of methods for sharing information as well as a timeline for implementing the plan. List conferences, workshops, site visits, and other outreach events at which you will share the results of your project. Your research may yield a great deal of data, not all of which may be suitable for or useful to all of your audiences. The dissemination plan should identify the information you will share with each group and why: what good will the information do those audiences?

Active dissemination entails proactively reaching out to the target audience. Consider the information style or format. Technical reports, journal articles, media press releases, and web pages, for example, all require different styles and methods of presentation. Examples of active dissemination include going to a conference that you know the target audience routinely attends; bringing members of the target audience to workshops or courses; spending time in high school classes to share your findings; and providing articles for the newsletters of relevant trade, disease, or community groups. Active dissemination strategies allow you to monitor the response to your work and ensure timely dissemination of the information.

Passive dissemination methods rely upon the target audience to seek out the information. Examples of passive dissemination include books, websites and, to some extent, journal articles. These methods may be longer-lived and more accessible to large audiences than active dissemination methods, but their success can vary widely. You may be able to count hits on a website, but it is difficult to determine whether anyone actually read your materials, let alone understood or was affected by them.

A strong dissemination plan often combines both active and passive methods for moving information out of the project and into the hands of those who can benefit from it. Some NIH proposals must now include data sharing plans that outline how you will share your final data with the larger scientific community. The NIH defines final data as "the recorded factual materials commonly accepted by the scientific community as necessary to document, support, and validate research findings" (NIH, National

Institute of Allergy and Infectious Diseases, 2011b). NIH data sharing plans may include such activities as the following: presentations at national meetings, sponsored lectureships, newsletters, websites, a disease awareness week, storage of large datasets in public databases, and distribution to online libraries.

Be sure to budget dissemination costs for compiling, preparing, archiving, storing, and disseminating data.

Diversity Plans

Not all funding programs require diversity plans, but many do. Historically, proposals that include or address aims for achieving diversity are received favorably by reviewers. Diversity plans should demonstrate that your office, workplace, and institution recognize and embrace inclusiveness in such areas as race and ethnicity, gender, religion, or socioeconomic status. Developing a diversity plan for a proposal may mean that your team will be diverse or that your university encourages and supports a diverse campus.

To begin, your institution has invaluable demographic information that can strengthen your diversity statement, including longitudinal data that documents historical or recent trends in faculty, staff, and student recruitment. Check with your institutional research office to see what reports they generate routinely and whether they can generate specialized reports to support your proposal. Other campus services may include offices and outreach groups attuned to the needs and goals of groups specific to your campus or geographic area.

Most universities have diversity plans in place. Utilize your campus diversity statement to bring home to reviewers the message that your institution fosters a rich culture of academic diversity. That being said, the diversity of your campus or department is beyond your immediate control and, with rare exception, beyond the scope of your project. Capitalize on your department's successes, and meld shortcomings with the efforts that have been made to improve its standing. For instance, if your department has a proven track record of recruiting and retaining diverse faculty members, emphasize it. Highlight your department's or your institution's recent research, grant funding, or other efforts aimed at diversity, and be sure to mention the integration of this work into the community at large.

What *is* within your grasp is the diversity of your own project. Details of how you plan to involve stakeholders or recruit staff, subjects, and audiences should be included in the diversity section. Be sure to emphasize any dissemination efforts to underrepresented groups. Highlight how diversity within your project contributes to your ability to recruit special populations if this is relevant.

You may also have opportunities to use outreach activities to expand your project's diversity efforts. Community or external partnerships may benefit from your dissemination activities. Increasing community awareness and building relationships with community services create opportunities to use your findings beyond the direct scope of the academic community, and this should be stated in your proposal.

Some funding sources use administrative supplements as financial incentives to enhance the diversity of their funded projects. For instance, NIH awards administrative supplements to grant recipients who recruit underrepresented postdoctoral and faculty collaborators. This may be an invaluable opportunity for expanding your project to include additional researchers in the future.

Summary

The project narrative is indeed the heart of your grant proposal. It lays out your core argument for the proposal. The project narrative usually opens with a need statement and functions as a logical funnel that begins with a broad societal issue and quickly narrows to the aspect of this issue to be addressed in your proposal. The activities of the project are outlined in the goal and objectives and then fleshed out in the work plan or methods section. Plans for evaluating the success of your project may appear in a separate section or as part of the methods section. The expertise of your project team can be highlighted in a key personnel section and also in the budget narrative. Diversity issues are increasingly being allowed a separate section, especially as this relates to subjects for research projects and participants for training projects. Dissemination of your project results must take into account the full range of audiences for your work and represents a key goal for many sponsors. Taken as a whole, the sections of the project narrative constitute the meat and potatoes of the proposal. As you create your proposal development timeline, you will probably want to reserve a substantial portion of your own time for the development of this section.

Chapter 9

Budgets

Sheryl Koenig and Susan Hazelwood

YOUR PROJECT SHAPES the budget, and the budget shapes the project. Your project's activities determine what should be included in the budget. Request enough to cover the expenses for those activities; otherwise, you will have to find other funds in order to meet your project's objectives. Frequently, however, sponsors limit the amount you can request from a given funding program. In these cases, the budget will shape the project. If the cost to cover your needs exceeds the sponsor's limit, you will need to look for ways to cut back the scope of your project or look for additional funding to augment the sponsor's.

The National Institutes of Health (NIH) recommends that "the best strategy is to request a reasonable amount of money to do the work, not more and not less because reviewers look for reasonable costs and will judge whether your request is justified by your aims and methods" (NIH, Office of Extramural Research, 2010). The NIH site goes on to warn that "significant over- or under-estimating suggests you may not understand the scope of the work." The National Science Foundation (NSF) has a similar perspective: "Proposals that do not adequately match the budget to the scope of the project" will fail the review process (Phelps, 2008). Although some sponsors will expect you to request only a portion of the actual cost of your project, the majority have policies similar to those of the NIH and NSF on this matter.

The time period of the project also shapes your budget. Be realistic in estimating how long the project will take, and budget accordingly. Because the largest portion of most research project budgets is personnel (salaries and fringe benefits), consider who will be doing what for each of the project's activities and how long it will take each person to fulfill those responsibilities.

What Does the Budget Reveal about the Project?

The budget comes into play well before an award is made. It is an important part of the proposal review process. Reviewers might examine your budget to see how carefully you plan, how much attention you pay to details, how thoroughly you document and explain, and how realistic you are. A reviewer may assume that you will manage time and personnel resources the same way you plan to manage the grant money.

You have read in previous chapters about the internal logic and persuasive goals of a grant proposal. The budget and budget justification are integral parts of your sales pitch and should tell a clear, consistent story. You have three opportunities to tell your tale in a grant application: in the project narrative, the letters of support and commitment, and the budget numbers and justification.

We have observed that reviewers seem to fall into two groups: the "numbers people" and the "word people." Word people tend to read a proposal's abstract and then the project narrative. Numbers people also start with the abstract but tend to turn from there to the budget and the budget justification. Both groups are looking for the same thing. They want a feel for what the project is about. If the budget and justification are done well, the numbers people will understand the work you propose almost as well as the word people do after reading the project narrative.

Provide enough detail in your budget justification for reviewers to understand how you arrived at the figures. Most sponsors do not limit the number of pages that can be used to justify the funds you are requesting, and thorough explanations of your anticipated costs will make it more difficult to cut your budget at the time of the award. If you explain how you calculated the travel costs, for example, and the purpose of each trip, then cutting your travel budget would reduce the scope of the work you can do. The sponsor's program officer may not be willing to do that.

One mistake we see occasionally is for the principal investigator or project director to equate the project narrative with the proposal as a whole and consequently spend nearly all of the proposal development time on the narrative, leaving everything else for the last minute. The proposal development timeline you read about in Chapter 5 will help you avoid this error. Because the narrative and the budget are two versions of the same story, they are best developed concurrently, in an iterative process in which each version of the story informs the development of the other. As you work through the details of your budget, you will likely realize the need to clarify points in the narrative that you otherwise may have missed.

As you develop the narrative, you will catch activities or other costs that you missed in the budget.

Campus Resources

If you are inexperienced with budget building, there is probably someone on your campus who can help. Your department or division may have access to a grant writing consultant. Your department's fiscal manager may be able to give you an idea of typical expenses for a project in your field. The sponsored programs or research office may have personnel who can help. Most institutions of higher education have established rates for costs that change regularly, such as mileage, per diem, and facilities and administration rates. There may also be unwritten rules. Keep looking until you find someone who knows your institution's policies and procedures well enough to help you learn the ropes. If you engage this person early in the process, you will have time to incorporate budget changes into the narrative so that the story your proposal tells is completely consistent.

Getting Started

Use a spreadsheet template if you have one available. We have provided an Excel budget template in the online Toolkit for this book (see p. iv). Some sponsors also provide budget templates that will help you set up the spreadsheet for your project's budget.

One way to begin is to list everything and everyone you can think of that will be needed to do the work of the project. It can help to build a timeline because so many costs depend upon how long the activities take to accomplish. Some things might not be needed during the first year of the project. Evaluation costs may occur only at certain benchmarks.

Sponsor guidelines often limit the kinds of expenses that will be allowed for a particular program. Some programs, for example, will not fund equipment costs. If you need a specialized piece of equipment that your institution does not have, you can consider finding a collaborator who has access to this equipment or look for a funding opportunity that allows equipment costs. Many funding opportunities specify a maximum amount that can be requested, and some also specify a minimum amount that can be requested. If your total is outside the allowable range, consider adjusting your project objectives to expand or reduce the scale of the project.

Federal guidelines require that expenses you include in your project budget be allowable, allocable, reasonable, and necessary. As discussed above, there may be expenses that the sponsor will not allow for a given funding opportunity. Expenses that are allocable can be traced directly to your project. They are not general overhead costs that also support other activities at your institution. Reasonable costs are budgeted at the going rate for similar goods or services in your area. No $15,000 screwdrivers, please. Necessary costs are those required to do the project. Even if you have $2,500 left in the budget a month before the project ends, a new computer and printer for your office are probably not necessary to finish your project.

We are often asked in workshops whether it is better to budget high so that there will be enough money left if the budget is cut, or to budget low so that it looks as though the sponsor is getting a good deal. The answer is neither. Reviewers usually have at least some expertise in your field. They will know about what your project should cost. If you budget high, you look greedy and careless with the sponsor's money. If you budget low, you appear naive. Budget what you think it will cost to do the project well—no more and no less.

Assembling the Framework

Budget categories can serve as a framework to help you think through your project in detail, and this detail will play back into the narrative to benefit the proposal as a whole. This is why it is risky to leave the budget until the very end or to hand it off to someone else to do it for you. As with the narrative, assistance and editing help are great, but you will almost certainly lose consistency across the proposal as a whole if you hand off whole sections entirely to someone else.

The categories that follow are not exhaustive, but they are the most common cost categories we see on budgets for grant proposals. If these categories do not match those on your sponsor's template, use the sponsor's template. Just as with the language of your narrative, your goal is to speak to the sponsor's personnel in language they will find familiar. One way to do this is to use the budget categories (and forms) that they provide.

Personnel Costs

For many projects, salaries and fringe benefits total 60 to 80 percent of the budget. To get a handle on these costs, begin by thinking about the project's activities. What activities are required to achieve your objectives? Who will be involved in getting those project activities done? Do you have all the expertise you need at your own institution, or will you need to bring in outside help? Will students be involved? Who will be involved in which activities?

How long will each person's responsibilities take? Many of your budget variables, such as personnel salaries, depend on time, and making educated guesses as to how long each task will take can help you decide how much of each person's time you will need. This is where gathering preliminary data or conducting pilot projects will help. If it takes 30 minutes to conduct one interview, two hours to transcribe it, and another hour to code it, all you need to know is the number of interviews, and you can calculate the total number of hours to conduct and process interviews in your project.

Another way to think about time is as a proportion of a typical work-week. If 40 hours is one full-time equivalent (FTE), how many hours a week would this person likely spend on the project? A half day each week would be 10 percent FTE; one day each month would be about 5 percent FTE.

Once you have an idea of the amount of time you will need from each individual involved in your project, your departmental or divisional fiscal person can probably help you get exact salary information for existing employees and make reasonable estimates for new employees you will hire. It may be tempting to just get the salary numbers from your collaborators, but we recommend against that. It may be hard to believe, but many people in higher education do not know their actual salaries. This makes a little more sense when you think about how many different sources contribute to the salaries of some faculty members: there may be proportions of time on two or three different grant projects, contributions from a couple of different departments for joint appointments, incentive income, extra compensation for teaching summer school—you get the idea.

Keep in mind as you set up your budget spreadsheet that most sponsors will take six to nine months to make an award after your proposal is submitted. By the time your project is actually under way, you will probably be into the next fiscal year. Most sponsors expect to see an inflation factor of about 3 percent each year. It is a good idea to inflate current salaries to account for the possibility of raises between submission of your proposal and award of your grant. Do this even if you do not expect those raises to happen. Even if you do not have everyone involved immediately on Day 1 and do not need a full first-year salary for everyone and even if the raises do not happen, there *will* be unexpected expenses. Although there are usually limits on how much money you can move from one category to another, most sponsors will allow some of these adjustments. The first-year salaries for your project personnel represent an opportunity to give yourself a little wiggle room to accommodate those unexpected costs so that they do not spiral into disasters for your project.

The people who are employed by your institution are considered *personnel*. Costs for individuals from outside your institution fall into the consulting or subcontract categories. This can sometimes cause confusion if you plan to use a faculty member from your own institution on a consulting basis. In lay terms, this person's role may be that of a consultant, but the cost for compensating that person will fall under the personnel category.

Fringe Benefits

Fringe benefits usually include medical insurance, retirement, Social Security, and Medicare contributions—those types of things. Many universities have a fringe benefit rate that is negotiated with the federal government as part of the negotiation for the institution's facilities and administration (F&A) rate. Whether it is federally negotiated or institutionally assigned, you can expect changes in the fringe benefits rates for your institution from year to year, largely because medical insurance costs have been volatile in recent years.

Many institutions have multiple fringe benefits rates. Some have a rate that applies to proposals for federal sponsors and another rate for other sponsors. Some have a single rate for all employees, but at other institutions, the fringe benefits rates vary with the employee's job classification. Most institutions do not provide the same benefits for part-time or temporary employees as they do for full-time employees. The employer contribution to Social Security and Medicare totals 7.65 percent, and this is often the rate for employees who do not qualify for the institution's full benefits package.

Students represent yet another category of employee for fringe benefits calculations. Students who are washing glassware in the lab or doing routine clerical work in the office may be handled as other part-time employees for benefits purposes. Students whose work on your project can be seen as part of their training experience and those who are using their training to fulfill their roles on your project may be handled differently. Some institutions, for example, include tuition or medical insurance or both as fringe benefits for some student positions. Check with your campus resources to determine the university's policies for students who are included or hired as personnel on a grant-funded project.

Consultants

As noted above, consultants are individuals or small organizations not employed at your institution. To qualify as consulting, the work to be performed should be a small part of your project and should be work routinely provided for the general public, not unique to the project, and involving little discretionary judgment.

If a collaborator asks you to serve as a consultant, we recommend that you think carefully about taking on grant-funded work as an individual rather than running the income through a subcontract with your institution. Consulting fees paid to you as an individual are taxable income, and the liability for the work accrues to you as an individual rather than to your institution.

If an individual or group from another institution with whom you collaborate will use their home institution's labs, offices, supplies, or other resources, their work should be budgeted under the subcontract line rather than as a consulting expense. In our experience, institutions of higher education tend to gravitate toward subcontracts rather than consulting agreements for arrangements through which their faculty members will collaborate with other institutions. Once you know you will have a partner at another institution, it is a good idea to talk to your sponsored programs personnel about what the partner's role will be and whether you should handle the partnership through a consulting agreement or a subcontract.

Travel

Budgeting for travel can help you think through how the project will work. Where do the project personnel need to go? How many people will be going? How often will these trips occur? How long will they need to stay each time? To budget appropriately for travel, you have to think through each person's role in the project at a level of detail that can only help to clarify your proposal narrative.

The cheat sheet "Calculating Travel Expenses" in Section Three of the Toolkit will help you think through travel from doorstep to doorstep. Remember ground transportation to and from airports and at the destination. Find out what your institution's guidelines are for meal allowances. Visa costs and other special costs of international travel should be included. The US Department of State has a website (http://aoprals.state.gov/web920/per_diem.asp) that offers government-approved per diem costs in foreign countries. You might use an Internet travel site such as Travelocity or Expedia to estimate airfares and hotel costs. If you do not know when during the year or the week the travel will happen, try different seasons and different days of the week to account for seasonal variations and variations between "tourist" and "business" travel days. Budget a high average for airfares, hotels, and shuttle services.

Equipment

The federal government defines *equipment* as anything that has a unit cost of more than $5,000, has a useful life of more than one year, and is not software. Any software, regardless of cost, falls into the supplies category. This is a specialized definition that varies from our day-to-day language, where we might consider a computer or a desk as equipment. For budgeting purposes, though, these items should be listed in the supplies line if they cost less than $5,000 each.

This definition of equipment implies that qualifying items will be infrastructure items, and as such, they will probably serve multiple projects. Sponsors want to pay only for their own projects and sometimes not even all of that. A sponsor does not want to pay the full cost of a piece of equipment that will benefit other projects as well as the one the sponsor is funding. It follows that reviewers will look very carefully at any equipment requests in your proposal budget. That said, you can sometimes leverage institutional cost match to pay for part of a piece of equipment and then ask the sponsor for the balance. This can be a win-win strategy in that it will help to build the institution's infrastructure at a reduced cost and at the same time demonstrate that the institution is investing in the long-term success of your work.

Supplies

The supplies budget represents another opportunity to think about the people who will be involved in your project and what, exactly, they will be doing. What resources will they need? What supplies will each activity require? Do you need extra computer resources? Is there a place for each person to work? Do you need to purchase mice or other research animals and provide for their care? Glassware for the lab, chemicals, other consumables, and animal purchases are all classified as supplies.

If your institution has a negotiated facilities and administration (F&A) rate, this rate will include routine office supplies and other overhead items. If this is the case, these items should not be itemized in your proposal budget. If they are already part of the F&A charges, including such items in another cost category such as the supplies line would amount to charging for them twice.

Costs charged to a grant project should be trackable and specific to the project. Although normal photocopying costs would not be eligible, copies for a large mailing or a survey that is part of your project would be allowable. If you are not sure about a particular cost item, talk to your sponsored programs personnel.

If your project team includes a statistician, this person may be another source of advice on the supplies budget. The numbers of subjects, tests, surveys, or other data that you collect may be driven by the level of statistical significance you need to achieve. If your project includes human subjects, the statistician may also have experience with the attrition rates you can expect for particular subject populations, and this information can affect the amount of supplies you will need. Incentives for human subjects also typically fall into the supplies category.

The supplies budget can be a bit of a pain because it tends to involve lots of small items. Our advice is to try to get reasonably close on these costs rather than just pulling numbers from the air. It is a bit ironic that, the more experienced you are with the type of work your project entails, the more you may be tempted to budget ballpark numbers for supplies: You have been doing this kind of work for a long time, and you know what these costs are likely to be. Why do the math to calculate food and care for X number of days for Y number of mice? The answer is that the reviewer does not know that you know unless you demonstrate it.

Providing the math for numbers of procedures, copying and postage for surveys, and the like serves you well with two audiences. The first audience is the reviewer, who looks to the proposal for evidence of the kind of work you will do if you are funded. Attention to detail in the budget is one way to communicate the care with which you will implement the project. The second audience for budget details is the sponsor's program officer. The main reason grant proposals are not funded is that there is not enough money to fund all the worthwhile proposals. Program officers will sometimes cut the budgets of selected proposals in order to fund more proposals. If your calculations are all clear and tied tightly to the proposal narrative, it will be obvious that cutting the budget will reduce the scope of work that you can do. The program officer may be reluctant to lose the portions of the work that drop off as a result of reducing your budget. In addition, you yourself may be a third audience for the supplies budget; a detailed supplies budget can be a tremendous help when the proposal is funded and you must recall exactly what you planned to do when you wrote the proposal, often nearly a year earlier.

Participant and Trainee Support

Participants are people who receive services or training during a workshop, conference, seminar, or other short-term sharing activity. They are not required to provide you with any deliverables, nor are they employees of your institution. Participants may include students, national scholars and scientists, private sector representatives, agency personnel, K–12 teachers, and others. Participant support costs include such items as stipends, subsistence allowances (room and meals), travel costs, and registration fees paid to or on behalf of participants or trainees. Because all members of a given category of participants—graduate students or K–12 teachers, for example—are usually treated alike, you can calculate a cost per participant and then simply multiply by the estimated number of participants.

Be sure to consult the sponsor's guidelines for any restrictions regarding participant or trainee support. This category often comes with a number of ifs, ands, and buts. If your project will have trainees or other participants, give some thought to how you will go about recruiting them and who will do that recruiting. There may be travel, personnel, and supplies costs to include in your budget for this recruiting.

Subcontracts

In contrast to a consultant, a subcontractor performs work that will have a significant impact on your project as a whole, work that is unique to the project and designed specifically to enhance your scholarly goals and objectives. The subcontract organization will be identified in your proposal, and the subcontract personnel will be free to a certain extent to determine how to carry out the activities of their share of the program. The individual who will lead the work at your partner institution is considered the principal investigator for the subcontract and is usually designated as a co-investigator for your overall project.

It will help to give this person an estimate of the amount of money you have in mind for the subcontract as early in the proposal development process as you can. This will give your collaborator an idea as to the scope of the work you expect and help you avoid the inevitably uncomfortable conversations that happen when a subcontract budget comes in at two or three times what your budget will allow.

Knowing the target amount will also allow your collaborator to create a budget for the subcontract work. Our experience is that subcontract personnel cannot be expected to be as invested in the total project as you are, and this means that you may need to point out any restrictions the sponsor imposes on project expenses rather than assuming your collaborator will read the sponsor's guidelines. If educational expenses for participants must be budgeted at $10,500, regardless of what the "real" cost is at your partner institution, you should probably let your collaborator know this. Subcontract budgets are subject to all sponsor guidelines, just as yours is.

The subcontract budget will probably be submitted to the sponsor on a separate copy of the sponsor's budget form with its own budget justification. The total for each subcontract for each year will also be included on your institution's budget, which will reflect the total cost of the project. This means that the subcontract budgets become part of your institution's budget when it is submitted to the sponsor, so your institution's sponsored programs office will want to know that the partner institution has approved the subcontract budget and will stand behind it. To get that approval, your collaborator will submit the subcontract work and budget to his or her sponsored programs office for approval before sending it to you, just as a proposal to another sponsor would be processed. In this case, your institution is the sponsor for the proposed subcontract. Processing times vary from one institution to the next, but you will want to allow a week or two for the partner institution to process the subcontract materials and provide your institution with an authorized signature to document the partner institution's intent to enter into a subcontract with your institution if your project is funded.

Other Direct Costs

This is the catchall category for expenses that do not fit elsewhere in your budget, such as research computing resources, radioactive waste disposal, human subject stipends, publication fees, research animal per diem costs, and service fees. If the project includes graduate research assistants (GRA) and your institution's policy is to request tuition costs as a benefit for the students, some sponsors require that those tuition costs be listed in the other direct costs category rather than with fringe benefits. The sponsor's guidelines will say so if this is the case.

Facilities and Administration Costs

Facilities and administration costs, also known as F&A or indirect or overhead costs, cover items that you need to do your project but that would be difficult to budget because they are part of the institutional environment. These include such shared resources as buildings, air conditioning, libraries, and required annual audits. (See "The Roles of Grant-Funded

Projects in Academia" in Chapter 1, for an explanation of F&A costs.) Each institution's F&A rate agreement is particular to that institution, so you should check most of what we write about budgeting these costs with your local grant writing consultant, fiscal manager, or sponsored programs personnel.

With that as a caveat, we can say that most institutions have more than one F&A rate. The rate that applies to your proposal will be determined by the type of activity—usually research, instruction, or other sponsored activity—and by whether your project will be conducted on or off campus. If your institution is sponsored by your state, you may need to consider whether your sponsor is an entity of state government as you select the appropriate F&A rate for your project. MU is a state-sponsored institution, for example, and some of our overhead costs are covered by the funding provided by the State of Missouri. Because the State supports some of our overhead costs, we reduce our usual F&A rates to take out the proportion of those expenses supported by the State for sponsors that are part of state government.

Once you determine the F&A rate for your project, the next step is to figure out how to apply this rate to your budget. For many institutions, the F&A rate is applied to *modified total direct costs*. *Direct costs* refers to everything in your budget except the F&A costs. *Modified total direct costs* means that you subtract some costs and then multiply the balance by the appropriate F&A rate. Typical exclusions include equipment and other capital expenditures, patient care costs, subcontract amounts over $25,000, tuition, rental costs, animal care per diem costs, and student support costs. Again, your local grant writing consultant, fiscal manager, or sponsored programs personnel will be able to tell you which costs should be excluded from the F&A calculation for your institution.

In addition to the exclusions that are routine for your institution, some sponsors limit the amount of F&A they are willing to fund. If this is the case for your project, check your sponsored programs office to see what your institution's policy is for these sponsors. As discussed in Chapter 1, these are real costs, and accepting an award from a sponsor that does not reimburse the institution's F&A costs means that the project is a net expense for the institution. Some institutions have elected not to accept such awards. Others may require an additional layer of approval in order to submit proposals with less than the institution's full F&A rate.

Accepting awards from sponsors that do not fully reimburse F&A costs can sometimes affect your department and you as an individual faculty member as well. As Sheryl Koenig explains below, MU has a research incentive program that scales according to the amounts of F&A reimbursed in the previous year. You will want to know whether the amount of reimbursed F&A is considered for similar programs at your institution.

Motivation for Research and Collaboration at MU: Shared Credit

Sheryl Koenig

Why, after all, should you invest time in writing grant proposals? First, there is the opportunity to get grant dollars to pursue work that can advance your academic field. There is the opportunity to fund the salaries and research of your graduate students. There is the fact that writing fundable proposals keeps you current in your field of study. There is also the "fame and glory" that comes with receipt of external funding. A grant award represents a vote of confidence from your peers in the timeliness and significance of your work. Your institution basks in the reflected fame and glory that your award brings to your campus. An active research enterprise makes it easier to recruit the best students and postdocs.

At MU, the Research Incentive Fund (RIF) encourages grant applications and provides successful faculty members and their departments with funds for research and scholarship. An amount equal to 25 percent of the F&A collected from grant sponsors is allocated to the departments of key personnel on grant-funded projects. The amount for each grant-funded project is distributed according to shared credit percentages negotiated among the project's key personnel at the proposal stage of the project.

RIF funds are used for a wide variety of purposes: to hire someone to assist with grant preparation, to purchase or maintain shared equipment, to provide cost share on a project that requires it, or to bridge a gap in grant support for a particular faculty member. The shared credit percentages, which are recorded in the MU grants database, are used by some departments to track the contributions of their faculty members to grant projects for consideration when decisions are made regarding merit raises and promotion and tenure.

RIF funds are distributed to departments, and each department has its own policy as to how these funds will be used. In some cases, 100 percent of RIF funding received for a given project is passed on to the principal investigator or project director to use as he or she sees fit. In other departments, 100 percent of RIF funding is held at the departmental level and used for equipment purchases, seed funding, and other department-level priorities. Still others share RIF funding between the department and PI or PD.

The important point is not so much what the departments do with the money. Perhaps the most influential aspect of MU's RIF distribution is the fact that the contributions of every faculty member on the project are recognized. By allowing these incentive monies to be shared, MU conveys an institutional expectation about collaborative work: it is not only recognized but also rewarded.

Cost Share or Cost Match

Any portion of the budget for your project that the sponsor does not pay is considered cost match or cost share. Some sponsors require cost sharing: *mandatory cost share*. Cost sharing that is not required is *voluntary cost share*. Some sponsors do not allow voluntary cost sharing as a way to level the playing field for institutions that have limited funds available.

If you mention anywhere in your proposal, whether in the narrative, the budget, or elsewhere, that a quantifiable cost share will be made to support your project, this is considered committed cost share. Any committed cost share must be tracked by your institution and reported to the sponsor as part of the financial reporting. If the committed cost share is not spent on your project or not appropriately documented, the sponsor will require repayment of a portion of the grant funds, or the grant could even be terminated. Finally, if you spend money on your project but do not mention those funds anywhere in your proposal, those funds are considered an uncommitted cost share and do not need to be tracked or reported.

The sponsor's guidelines will give you a sense of its stance on cost sharing. Some sponsors, particularly foundations, expect to fund projects in partnership with institutions of higher education. For these sponsors, an expectation of some level of cost sharing will be the norm. Keep in mind that you can spend a given dollar only one time. If you designate the cost of new lighting in the campus theatre as cost share for one project, these costs cannot be used for another project.

The Grand Total

If you end up with a total that is too high for the limits of the funding opportunity you have targeted, one way to reduce the budget is to eliminate one of the project objectives and the activities associated with it. Another possibility is to reduce the number of data cells and simplify the analysis you will be able to do. Reduction of the work scope is generally a better strategy than looking for funding from your institution to make up the difference. Unnecessary cost sharing drives your institution's F&A rate down because it is added to the denominator of the rate calculation. Dollars committed as cost share to one project will then be tied up and may not be available for another project for which the sponsor actually requires cost sharing.

Even if your total falls within the sponsor's guidelines, it is a good idea to think about how you might reduce the scope of the project if the sponsor were to award 10 or 15 percent less than the amount your budget requests. If you are engaged in budget negotiations for an award for your project and agree to do the whole project even though the budget is reduced, it will send one of two messages to the sponsor: either you do not really know what the project will cost, which calls your competence into question, or you knowingly budgeted more than the actual cost of the budget, which suggests you were treating the sponsor's funding carelessly. Neither is an attractive first impression as the sponsor considers funding your project. Better to think ahead about which aspects of the project could be dropped and still leave a worthwhile and doable project that moves the sponsor's agenda forward.

The Budget Justification

The budget justification or budget narrative explains your budget to the reviewers and, in the process, offers a more complete picture of your project. (See Section Three of the Toolkit for a sample budget justification, "Budget Justification for Terrytoons University." The online Toolkit also includes an Excel template for building your budget.) Begin by creating a heading for each of the sponsor's budget categories. List the categories in the same order as they appear on the budget form to make it easy for reviewers to go back and forth between the budget and budget justification.

Salaries

Beginning with the principal investigator or project director, for each person listed in the personnel section, provide at least two or three sentences pointing to the individual's key qualifications and tying those to the individual's role in your project. Explain how much time each individual will devote to the project and how that time will be used. This is also a chance to provide information about the team members you may not have had room for in the project narrative.

Fringe Benefits

Explain how fringe benefits have been calculated for each category of employee. Because these rates vary by category of employee rather than by individual employee, you can usually just explain the benefits rate for each category rather than repeating the listing of individuals from the salaries section.

Consultants

Consultants are handled in much the same way as personnel are: with a short summary of each individual's most relevant qualifications and the relationship of those qualifications to the tasks the individual will be assigned in your project. Explain how much time the consultant will devote to the project, how you arrived at this time estimate, and how your project will be billed for this time. Consultants typically bill by the hour or by the day. Travel expenses can be covered in the travel category of your budget, or they can be incorporated into the consultant's fees. Either is fine as long as you explain how you got the numbers in your budget.

Travel

Like equipment, travel seems to be a category that reviewers may approach with a certain amount of suspicion. To counter this, be sure to explain the purpose of each trip and how it supports your project's objectives. Explain how many individuals will participate in each trip and why their participation is important to accomplishing their roles in the project. Finally, detail your calculations for arriving at the travel budget, listing the amounts you used for each component, such as airfare, lodging, mileage, and per diem expenses.

Equipment

As discussed earlier in the equipment budget section, sponsors must be convinced that any requests for equipment funding are absolutely essential for the success of your project. Confirm prices with vendors and, for large equipment purchases over about $10,000, provide vendor quotes as part of your budget justification. Explain very carefully why the equipment is necessary and whether it will be used exclusively for your project. If not, you will probably need to provide some cost match to convince the sponsor to approve part of the funding.

Supplies

After salaries, the supplies line is the largest line item for many projects. This can make your supplies budget an attractive target for a sponsor seeking to cut your budget. For this reason, you will want to avoid the assumption that the supplies to be used will be obvious to expert reviewers. Avoid phrases such as "based on recent experience in running our laboratory" as justification for your supplies budget. Instead, list the types of supplies you will need to do your project. For larger projects, you can sometimes lump together subcategories that total less than $1,000. If a category of supplies is very large, consider breaking it into subcategories. For example, instead of requesting $20,000 for lab supplies, break that down into separate amounts for glassware, consumable kits, chemicals, and animals. For multiples of small items like meals for a conference or workshop, research animals, or incentives for research subjects, explain your calculations just as you do for travel expenses. Explain the number needed, what the item is for, and the cost per item.

Unusual items need to be explained in more detail. This is not a reason, however, to take an expense out of the budget. We once helped the scientist who led the first Western-style clinical trial of native plant therapies in South Africa, working with native healers to deliver the treatments. As we planned the project, we learned that the respectful way to compensate the native healers most integral to the project would be to provide them each with a heifer. We researched the cost of cows in South Africa, explained the expense in the budget justification, and budgeted to purchase cows. The NIH approved the budget.

Other Direct Costs

This category by definition will include expenses which fall outside the traditional budget categories, so explain each item and its relevance to the project activities. Again, as your junior high math teacher may have said, "Show your work." Explain how you calculated any expenses where multiples are involved. For example, if you have two graduate research assistants working during the academic year, and each needs a computer work station, show the monthly cost for network ports times nine months times two GRAs.

F&A Costs

As with fringe benefits, this is a rate that applies across the board, so there is no need to show the math for each item to which the rate applies. Simply provide your institution's negotiated F&A rate and, if the rate is to be applied to modified total direct costs, list the categories or items to which the F&A rate is not applied.

Summary

The budget and budget justification should tell the story of your project in parallel with your project narrative. Any discrepancies among the budget, budget justification, and proposed activities may confuse reviewers. If you mention in the narrative that you will use 100 mice, and 150 mice are listed in the budget, reviewers may begin to wonder if your statistical power analysis and cell sizes are appropriate. If you indicate that a particular individual will be involved in only two years of the project, but the budget shows salary and fringe benefits for this person for all five years of the project, reviewers will begin to question your attention to detail. This brings us to a caution: always double-check your math, making sure the numbers listed in the budget justification match the numbers in your budget and match the numbers and activities in the project narrative. It is all too easy as drafts evolve for inconsistencies to creep in. If you arrange for a friendly review of your proposal, as recommended in Chapter 5 ("Friendly Review"), be sure to include the budget and budget narrative in the materials you provide to the reviewer. It is far easier for someone unfamiliar with your project to catch these kinds of inconsistencies than it is for a member of your team.

The logical justification that you provide for the budget expenses is part of the logical argument that the proposal presents. If expenses are justified relative to the aims and methods of the project, this bolsters your argument. If, on the other hand, there is another way to accomplish your aims without spending nearly as much, this weakens your argument.

Besides reading the budget and budget justification for the story of your project, reviewers will look at these parts of your proposal as samples of your work. If the budgeted amounts are realistic and reasonable, if the budget represents a sufficient amount of funding to do the work well but without extravagance, the reviewers and sponsor personnel are more likely to believe you will do the work conscientiously and respect the sponsor's investment. If you have a very large project, consider doing a budget by activity if this will make the budget easier for the reviewer to comprehend.

A grant award is about more than just the project that the award will fund. Grant awards are about moving the sponsor's agenda forward and can represent the first step in building a long-term relationship with a given sponsor. A solid budget and budget justification will not be enough to land a grant award, but they are vital factors in the total proposal package that will land you that award.

Chapter 10

Making It Shine: The Proposal Package

Cynthia Haydon and Mary Licklider

IF YOU ARE a faculty member at an institution of higher education, odds are good that you have had the experience of grading papers. And if you have ever graded papers late into the night or for too long on a weekend, you may at some point have paused between papers and then paged through those remaining to be graded, looking for a "good one." This chapter is about making your proposal one of the good ones that the reviewer enjoys reading and approaches with the positive attitude that makes it easy to support the content of the proposal. It is about managing first impressions and about creating a reader-centered, rather than a writer-centered, document.

Most grant proposals incorporate many pieces of information beyond the narrative description of the project. These supporting documents, such as the cover letter, the budget justification, and the resources statement, are usually not page-limited and therefore offer you the opportunity to elaborate on specific points that you did not have the space to address in the narrative. This chapter will cover these supporting documents and how to maximize your use of these elements to be certain that you do so appropriately and with attention to the guidelines so that they will not be viewed by reviewers as circumventing the page limits.

Cover Letters and Transmittal Letters

Many funding agencies allow or even request a cover letter. If one is not required, your institution may include a very simple transmittal letter to officially convey your proposal to the sponsor. If a cover letter *is* suggested or required, this represents an opportunity to introduce yourself.

The purpose of the cover letter differs by sponsor. Federal funders in the sciences often prescribe a memo format and are generally looking only for basic information about the subject of your proposal so it can be routed to the appropriate review committee. In these cases, you should describe the type of expertise that will be needed to properly review your proposal. If you know the name of the most appropriate review panel (or *study section* at the NIH) for your proposal, list it, but avoid naming specific individuals unless this is requested by the sponsor.

Nonscience agencies and private foundations may allow or expect a more conversational letter in which you introduce yourself as the project director or principal investigator, your organization or research group, your project, and the amount requested. Use this as an opportunity to make a good first impression by crafting the cover letter to capture reviewers' attention and draw them into your project.

Biographical Sketches and Résumés

Almost all sponsors will request some type of biographical sketch or résumé for the principal investigator or program director as well as for all personnel who have key roles in your project. Sponsors often specify the format for these biographical sketches; they typically include sections for education, work history, awards and honors, publications, and research funding. Sometimes a list of collaborators or a description of your research is also part of the sponsor's format. Most sponsors limit biographical sketches to two to four pages. If the sponsor does not request a particular format, it is a good idea to use the format required by the largest funder in your discipline, as Elizabeth Miller recommends in Chapter 5 (see boxed text, "What If There Are No Guidelines"). Reviewers are likely to be experts in your discipline and to be familiar with this sponsor, so this format will make your proposal seem familiar to them. In the biomedical sciences, for example, the NIH biographical sketch is often used by other smaller funders. This format has the advantage of including a personal statement which allows all the key personnel involved in your project the space to describe the focus of their research, convey professional accomplishments, and explain why they are the right individuals to perform their roles in your project.

Occasionally, a sponsor will allow or request a résumé instead of a biographical sketch. In most of these cases, it is better not to use a general résumé or a full curriculum vita. Adapt the résumé to the project so that reviewers do not have to sort through the many details that are irrelevant to the work you will do in this project. Tailor the résumé just as if you were applying for a specific job—in essence, you are.

Resources, Facilities, and Organization Description

Just as reviewers will want to know that you and the other key personnel are the best people to do your project, they will also want to know that your team has the appropriate resources and institutional environment to do your project well. We find these descriptions of resources and facilities to be less and less about square footage of labs and offices and long lists of equipment. More and more, these descriptions are expected to be about access to resources, a supportive environment, and institutional commitment to the project and to you as the principal investigator or project director. Although you certainly want to describe the facilities and any equipment that your team will use to do your project, be careful to customize the list to include only those items required for this project to succeed. Access to the necessary equipment and facilities is much more important than ownership or control of these resources. The equipment you need does not have to be in your lab; just explain any arrangements to use equipment in other labs or libraries, and document your access with a letter of commitment. Avoid including irrelevant facilities or equipment that will make this section read like an inventory of everything available at your institution. If multiple institutions are involved in the project, describe the resources available at each site.

It is equally important to describe the environment at your institution and how it will contribute to the success of your project. As you explained in your biographical sketch, the key personnel section of the project narrative, and the personnel section of the budget narrative why you are the person best suited for this project, one of your goals with the resources section is to highlight anything unique about your environment that makes it the ideal place for this work. Place your work within the context of your institution. I once heard a scientist comment to a program officer that "you can't swing a bat around here without hitting a pathologist." Although you may not want to be quite that graphic in your resources section, reviewers do understand the value of your intellectual context and hallway conversations. If your institution is intentionally strengthening its expertise in your area and has added five faculty lines in the last five years in areas related to your work, that increased level of collective expertise is relevant to your project. If the building in which you work was designed specifically to facilitate interdisciplinary conversations and your project cuts across several of those disciplines, then the building design is relevant. The point is that sponsors are thinking more broadly about the resources that can impact the success of projects, so you should think creatively about the elements of your environment that will facilitate the success of your projects.

Particularly if you are in the early stages of your career, it is important to describe the ways in which your institution is committed to your professional success. Some sponsors have very specific definitions of *young* and *early stage* investigators, but regardless of whether your sponsor employs these definitions, detailing your institution's support for your work can be very effective if you are a new investigator. Take the opportunity to emphasize that, though you are new to the field, you have the support system to be successful. Include anything that indicates institutional investment in you and your work. Perhaps you were hired as part of an initiative to increase a certain kind of expertise on campus. You may have been guaranteed "protected" time for research. Your department may have a mentoring program. The campus may offer programmatic support such as grant writing workshops, funding for travel, or training in specialized areas. Think about anything your institution is doing or has done to help you succeed and include those items here.

Budget Justification

Chapter 9 explained how to write a budget justification to explain to reviewers and sponsor personnel how you arrived at your budget numbers and why the budgeted items will be necessary to your project (see Chapter 9, "Budget Justification"). Here we will look at formatting the budget justification for maximum effectiveness.

Each budget category (personnel, supplies, travel, etc.) should have a boldfaced heading. In addition to noting significant changes in the effort of individual personnel from year to year, you may want to summarize personnel effort in a table as well (Table 3).

TABLE 3

Personnel Effort Summary Table

Name	Role	Year 1 Effort	Year 2 Effort	Year 3 Effort
Dr. Phlapyer Wings	Principal Investigator	2 calendar months	2 calendar months	2 calendar months
Dr. Pearl Pureheart	Postdoctoral Fellow	12 calendar months	12 calendar months	12 calendar months
To be hired	Undergraduate Student Researchers (2)	1 calendar month each	1 calendar month each	1 calendar month each

TABLE 4

Budget Justification Summary Table

Supplies

Year 1 Request	Year 1 Cost Match	Year 2 Request	Year 2 Cost Match	Year 3 Request	Year 3 Cost Match
$20,550		$18,695		$19,255	

TABLE 5

Participant Table

Predoctoral Trainees, Including Those Supported by the Institution

Total #: 10 trainees	Year 1	Year 2	Year 3	Year 4	Year 5	Year 6
1	X	X				
2	X	X				
3	X	X Graduate School*				
4		X	X			
5			X	X		
6			X Engineering*	X		
7				X	X	
8				X Medicine*	X	
9					X	X
10					X Arts & Science*	X
Annual #	**3**	**4**	**3**	**4**	**4**	**2**

*Indicates school or college cost sharing.

At the end of each category in the budget justification, summarize the category's total cost for Year 1 and across the entire funding period in a table (Table 4). These tables help to visually frame each section and provide quick overviews of the sections.

In proposals that include participant or trainee costs, the number that will be recruited or served each year can also be effectively summarized in a table (Table 5). It is critical to make this information clear to the reviewer because travel, supplies, and other items will be multiplied by the number of participants in order to arrive at budget numbers.

Formatting for Readability

As a group, academics tend not to think about journal manuscripts and grant proposals as "designed" documents in the same way that brochures and conference programs are designed. By ignoring the design elements of what are arguably some of the most important documents in our careers, we miss opportunities to connect with our readers. We miss opportunities to ensure that what we think are the most important points will be understood by the reader as the most important points. We miss opportunities to pull a rushed reader back into the text rather than continuing to flip through the pages. We miss the implications of the very different perspectives of grant reviewers and journal readers that Shelley Hilton highlights in Chapter 6 (see "Grant Proposals and Other Forms of Academic Writing").

Headers, Footers, and Pagination

Some sponsors require specific headers or footers; some require pagination whereas others do not allow page numbering or headers or footers. Our first advice is to follow the sponsor guidelines, the subtext here being "don't aggravate the reviewer by implying that you are a special case to whom the rules do not apply." We all know how far our students get with such arguments. When the sponsor is not specific, paginate so that reviewers can find text easily in the course of the review panel discussion.

Be sure to use a header or footer that identifies *each page* as part of your proposal. If someone drops a pile of proposals down the steps, you want to be certain that all the pages of your proposal can be identified and placed back in the proper order. This is not as unnecessary as it may seem in this age of electronic grant submissions. When we teach grantsmanship workshops, we routinely ask those in our audiences whether they have ever served as grant reviewers. Then we ask those who have reviewed whether they print out the electronic proposal files. Consistently, across age groups and disciplines, at least 75 percent say that they do. What this tells you as a writer is that your reader is likely reading a hard copy printed on an office laser printer rather than reading a computer screen.

Sentence and Paragraph Length

Proposal reviewers are usually experts in a field related to those of the proposals; for proposals submitted from institutions of higher education, most reviewers are faculty members from other institutions: smart folks, but busy. Think about where there is time in your own schedule to read and evaluate an extra, say, 500 pages. To keep the reader moving, one strategy is to adjust the length of sentences and paragraphs. Sophisticated readers do not decode each letter or even each word in the way that a beginning reader does. Instead, the highly skilled reader takes in chunks of text, often a whole clause at a time. By keeping sentence length to no more than three or four lines, you allow this kind of reader to move through the text very quickly from sentence to sentence. You also minimize the chances that this reader will pick up the first part of the sentence, assume he or she has the concept, and skip the latter part of a long sentence.

Reading at a fast pace is tiring, though, and this type of reading requires frequent small breaks. Think about who reads *USA Today*: certainly not many eighth graders, the reading level to which *USA Today* is purportedly written. Business travelers read it on planes, in airports, at breakfast in the hotel. Again, busy people. To capture and hold these readers, we see short sentences and short paragraphs. Try to keep your grant proposal paragraphs under 10 lines or so as a general rule.

White Space

This is the area of formatting in which we encounter the most resistance from the faculty members with whom we work on grant proposals. The length limits for proposals are getting tighter and tighter. The NIH recently cut space allowed for project descriptions by almost half. It can feel as though there is not enough room to spare for white space between paragraphs and such.

Designers refer to white space on the page as "air," and this is a useful metaphor. White space is what allows the reader to breathe, to come up for air long enough to digest your ideas. The hard truth is that decisions about white space on a page come down to this: do you want the reader to read everything you write, or do you want to write everything you have to say? The crowded page, uniformly grey with text, almost guarantees that the reader will tire and skip over whole passages. These suggestions will help you avoid that fate:

- Do not set line spacing for more than six lines to the inch. The white space between lines of text is visually a white "line" that helps the reader follow the wide single column of text across the page.

- Allow extra space between paragraphs. This helps the reader to grab whole paragraphs as units of thought.

- Left-justified text is easier to read than fully justified text. The ragged right margin helps the reader move from one line to the next more easily whereas with fully justified text, every line looks alike. Spacing between letters and words is uniform with left justification, rather than randomly adjusted to make the margins even.

- Designers refer to margins as "thumb space"—literally the space your thumbs occupy when you hold the page. For most adults, left and right margins need to be at least an inch. This is particularly important for documents such as grant proposals to give the reader room for notes.

Fonts and Typefaces

Many granting agencies specify font and type size requirements for grant proposals. Often, these requirements have arisen in response to reviewer complaints against small type that is difficult to read. Times New Roman is the most readable English font. It is known as a *serif* font, meaning that it has little "feet" at the ends of the strokes of letters. These feet help guide the reader's eye along the line of text, so serif fonts like Times New Roman are best for the main text of a grant proposal.

Sans serif fonts, those "without feet" like Arial and Helvetica, have a cleaner, bolder look. These fonts are best for headings and tables. Use fonts (e.g., Arial, Times) and type styles (e.g., bold, italic) to reinforce meaning, not for decoration. Use one font and typeface size and style for first-level headings and another style for second-level headings. Use a smaller serif font for the main text, and perhaps another small font for figure captions. Consistency with fonts and type styles helps the reader navigate a long document and signals the relationships among the various sections of the document.

Boldface and underscoring are known to slow a reader. Used sparingly, these can be effective strategies for highlighting headings and the most important points on each page. Overused, they have the effect of the many exclamation points junior high students tend to use: eventually, the reader's inner voice is screaming, and the reader tunes it out by ignoring all further emphasis.

Italics are a special case. Some writers consider underlining outdated: historically, underlining was the typesetter's signal to set text in italics. Now that we can italicize text, these writers argue, there is no longer a reason to underline. We disagree for two reasons. First, as mentioned above, underlining is known to slow a reader and can therefore be a useful tool. Second, most italic typefaces print on office laser printers with a finer stroke than the regular typeface of the same font and size. The effect is that italicized text appears to fade rather than creating emphasis. One solution is to bump up the font size one-half point. This will make the italicized text appear a little darker, and the size difference will not be noticeable.

Our habit is generally to use bolding for headings because it takes up more space, and headings tend to be short lines anyway. We use underlining for emphasis within the text, and we try not to underline more than one or two brief passages per page. The goal is that if the reviewer is flipping through the pages of the proposal on the plane on the way to the review panel meeting, the bolding and underlining will communicate the two or three most important points on each page.

Parentheses break up the flow of good writing, making it difficult for the reviewer to maintain the train of thought you are presenting. Studies show that readers believe parenthetical comments are expendable, so reviewers, who are reading long documents with little time, are likely to skip over parenthetical information. Better to state it outright or leave it out.

Use of Color

Color can be a very powerful tool in helping to make your points. The problem with using color in grant proposals is that they are almost always reproduced in black and white. Hard-copy submissions are often placed in the sheet feeder of a copy machine and duplicated for reviewers. Even when you are asked to send an original and 12 copies, the beautiful color copies you send can end up in an administrator's office while the reviewers receive photocopies. Electronic submissions are usually printed by reviewers, and most of us have black-and-white laser printers in our offices. So use color with care. Print the color images on a ratty old copy machine and see if their meaning is still clear. In general, we have found that 12 percent gray usually reproduces as gray rather than disappearing entirely or reproducing as black. Red often reproduces as black. Yellows and golds often disappear. If you need to use color, it is important to experiment to be sure the reviewer will understand the image if it is reproduced in black and white.

Informational Graphics

A picture is worth a thousand words. This inherent emphasis means that graphics must be selected with care. The reader's assumption is that a graphic presents important information. If graphics are used for minor points, then, the reader must work harder to understand the meaning of the text and what the key points actually are. So the first rule of thumb is to use graphics to emphasize important points. Graphics such as flowcharts can preview proposal logic for the reader, setting up important relationships that will be articulated in the text. Graphics can also be used to summarize this logic. Make decisions about the placement of graphics on the page consciously, considering the timing of the graphic with the text and where the graphic will most help the reader grasp meaning.

As with font styles and typefaces, readers will make assumptions about comparisons that are implicit in informational graphics. If there are two similar images on the same page, for example, the reader will expect blue to represent the same thing in both. Used in this way, color can be a great organizer. If there are two graphs side by side that present parallel data sets, the reader will expect the scale to be the same for both graphs. If these expectations are not met, the careful reader can no doubt sort through it. The problem is with the hurried reader, who will just as easily come away with a mistaken impression that can confound the rest of the reading.

Most readers' eyes flow over the page following a Z. We turn a page, and our eyes follow the movement of the turning page to land in the upper left corner of the new page; then they scan across the top of the page (two pages if the document is bound), cut back diagonally across and down to the lower left corner of the left page, across the bottom, and off the right side of the page. Graphics can help manage this eye flow, keeping the reader on the page longer. Placement along the outside margins creates a visual border that helps contain the eyes on the page. Placement of a graphic in the middle of the page, however, can cause the reader to skip text, depending upon how much text falls above or below the graphic. Given that graphics stop the eye and draw attention, a few lines of text stranded above or below a graphic at the top or bottom of the page are likely to be overlooked.

Summary Tips for Formatting a More Readable Proposal

Mary Licklider

Margins and White Space
- Use white space as an active design element.
- Use left and right margins that allow for "thumb space" of about an inch.
- Use left justified text with ragged right margins.

Fonts
- Use only one or two families of type.
- Serif typefaces such as Times New Roman, Courier, and Garamond are more readable.
- Sans serif typefaces such as Arial and Helvetica are good for titles and headings.
- Use bold type sparingly, and all caps even more sparingly.
- Underlining slows a reader down.

Sentence and Paragraph Length
- Limit each sentence to a maximum of two commas.
- Limit sentences to about 15 words.
- Limit paragraphs to 8 to 10 lines.

Titles and Headers

- Limit titles to about 10 words.
- Avoid headers in the lower third of the page.
- Try to use no more than three levels of headings.
- Left justify most headings and captions.
- Use headings and subheadings that are specific to the proposal (not generic).

Lists

- Use numbered lists for items that should be understood in a sequence or priority ranking.
- Use bulleted lists for items of equal importance.

General Formatting Tips

- Check out the funder's materials for font, type size and style, layout, and headers.
- Be consistent: use similar highlighting devices throughout.
- Anticipate skimming, search reading, and critical reading needs.
- Look at the proposal from a distance.
- Use a nonirritating form of binding.

Graphics and Color

- Use color carefully in the graphics, type, and paper choices.
- Avoid complicated graphics.

Design Basics

- Manage eye flow, working with the reader's "Z."
- *Use* the whole page, but do not *fill* the whole page.
- Use graphics to direct the eye to important information and through the piece.
- Use graphics to tell a story, to reinforce the message.
- Be sure that the width of captions fits the graphics.
- Use color as an organizer.
- Use color to portray emotions.
- Setting thin typefaces or small type in color can decrease legibility.
- Double-check the appearance of color:
  - Colors will print differently on colored paper or glossy paper.
  - Color strength will affect intensity—more or less ink on the page.
  - When colors that are opposite each other on the color wheel appear together, they stand out and draw attention—they compete with each other.
  - When colors that are next to each other on the color wheel appear together, they blend together and can reduce readability, depending upon how they are used.
  - Check color to see how it will photocopy in black and white.

Letters of Support and Commitment

Most proposals will benefit by including substantive letters of support from one or more leaders of your institution, discipline, or department—the key word here being *substantive*. Just as you should not include a 10-page inventory of all campus facilities in your resources section, you should not include 10 copies of the same form letter, each signed by a different institutional official. These letters should be customized to your project and to the signer's interest or involvement in it. Letters from individuals who can make meaningful statements about their interest in the project and their investment in its success are useful; anything else is just clutter. Before you ask for letters of support, create a unique draft letter for each individual to use as a starting point. Once the individuals agree to provide letters, send thank-you notes to each person that include the draft letters, emphasizing that the signers can choose to use as much or as little of your draft text as they please. Providing the letters' "authors" with these draft starting points will save them time, help them understand your project and what they are being asked to endorse, and ensure that your project is described accurately. Section Three of the Toolkit includes a template for letters of support and sample letters.

If your project includes a subcontract with another institution, nearly all sponsors will require a letter of commitment from the lead collaborator at the subcontract institution or from someone authorized to commit the institution to the subcontract work, or both. This letter primarily serves as an agreement between your institution and the subcontract institution documenting their intent to enter into a subcontract agreement if the project is funded. At minimum, the letter should include a brief summary of the work to be accomplished at the subcontract institution, the total dollar amount budgeted for the subcontract, and a signature by someone who is authorized to sign for the institution.

You can kill two birds with one letter, so to speak, if you include language expressing support for your project, the value of the project to your collaborators at the subcontract institution, and the skills these collaborators bring to the project. With signatures from both your collaborator and the subcontract institution, this letter can then document the agreement between the two institutions and can also be included in your proposal to document your collaborator's commitment to the project. As you set the deadlines for your collaborators and others to provide letters of commitment, allow a window between receipt of these letters and the point at which you have to finalize the project narrative. Every now and then, something wonderful and unexpected will show up in a letter of commitment that you will want to have time to highlight in the project narrative.

Appendices

As with the page lengths of project narratives, biographical sketches, and sometimes budget justifications, sponsors are increasingly limiting the use of appendices. So the advice we give here should be trumped by any sponsor rules you find in the guidelines for your funding opportunity. Be careful to format these items to match the rest of your proposal as to margins, font and type styles, and headings. You want the appendices to look as though they belong with the rest of the proposal and were prepared with an equal level of care, rather than giving the impression that they were faxed onto a heap the day before the deadline. Keep in mind that appendices are by definition at the end of your proposal and may well be the last thing the reviewer sees, so you will want that final impression to be a good one.

As with all other aspects of the proposal package, include an appendix item only if it is required or adds to the proposal in a meaningful way. Reviewers are very sensitive to appendices that appear to be vehicles for circumventing page limits for other sections of the proposal. That said, when items in appendices are allowed or requested, articles, media, lists of board members, samples, and financial documents are among the most common.

Articles

Generally speaking, journal articles may be included in the appendix if they are not readily available. An example is an article that has been accepted for publication but is not yet in print. Sponsors that allow you to append copies of journal articles often limit the number you can include.

Media

Some sponsors, particularly for projects in the arts and humanities, allow a CD or DVD with images, video, or sound recordings to be included with your proposal. CDs typically include images from the proposal that are not easily viewed within the proposal format or do not reproduce well when scanned or photocopied. Any media files should be labeled and paginated so that they can be matched easily with references to them in the proposal text. With proposals for scientific projects, very few sponsors accept multimedia information that is not already in the proposal package in another form.

Board Members

Lists of governing boards or stakeholder councils may be allowed or required.

Samples

If your project will result in the development of some sort of "product"— new curriculum, a scholarly book, an original opera, a piece of equipment, a software application—you may want to include a sample or draft of some sort in the appendix of your proposal. The existence of such items tends to be more important to the proposal than the details of their content. Although many reviewers will not read every word of a sample survey instrument, for example, the inclusion of the sample in your proposal proves that it exists, that the work is already started, and that you have a process in place. These do not necessarily have to be in final form but should be clearly marked as drafts if that is the case.

Other samples that can help communicate the work already completed on your project include screen shots of software under development, images of pilot versions of instruments you propose to refine, or an outline for the book you propose to write. If your project involves developing a certificate or degree program, a course list or draft syllabi could also be included in the appendix to document your planning to date.

Financial Documents

Sponsors sometimes ask for your institution's IRS determination letter (this documents the institution's tax-exempt status), the most recent audited financial statements, or the facilities and administration rate agreement. Some of these documents can take time to round up, so you may want to begin early by asking your grant writing consultant, fiscal manager, or sponsored programs contact person where to get the documents you need.

For large, state-sponsored institutions, the financial statements can be very long documents. Most audited financial statements include an executive summary at the beginning of each year's document. If this is the case for your institution, our recommendation is to send only the executive summary pages so as not to load your proposal with pages and pages the reviewers will not read. Be sure, though, to offer to send the full document if the sponsor requests it. The requirement for financial statements often comes from sponsors that sometimes fund small community nonprofits, and the purpose of the requirement may be to establish the financial stability of the grantee institution. For many of us in higher education, this thankfully is not an issue, and the executive summary of the annual financial statement will satisfy the sponsor's requirement.

Submission Processes

The sponsor's submission process will have a significant effect on your decisions about how best to present your proposal package. Proposals are increasingly submitted in some type of electronic format. This can range from simply e-mailing the proposal documents as an attachment to uploading all documents to your individual account on the sponsor's website. Despite the ubiquity of e-mail and the Internet, some proposals are still submitted as paper copies by mail or parcel service.

Paper Submissions

Many sponsors require paper proposals to be sent without any binding other than large clips or rubber bands. Occasionally, proposal guidelines require a binder with dividers for the sections or other types of organizing devices. If binding is allowed or required, be sure to choose a method that allows page to lay flat so the binding doesn't become a source of annoyance for the reviewer. Whether bound or not, paper submission opens two potential issues that will influence the way you format your proposal. First, there is the chance that someone could drop the proposal or that the envelope or box in which you ship it comes open. If you have identified the proposal by placing the title or the name of your institution in a footer or header or both, the sponsor will be able to tell which papers go with your proposal. If you have also included page numbers in the header or footer, the sponsor will know the order of the pages and whether all the pages are there.

The other scenario that paper submission opens is that sponsor personnel may place the proposal in the document feeder of a photocopier and run additional copies. Planning for black-and-white duplication of color images is covered in the "Use of Color" section above. Some copiers handle color images better than others. Some copiers jam more consistently than others. Page numbers and a proposal identifier in a header or footer will help sponsor personnel sort pages if the copier jams. (Have we said yet that Murphy rules the grant process?)

Electronic Submissions

Although the variety of electronic submission methods is considerable, there are a few major proposal processing services, such as Grants.gov and Fastlane, that handle a large number of online submissions. Each has specific requirements, but the following list represents rules and restrictions that are common to many proposal processing services and will influence how you package your proposal:

- **File Name**. Some electronic systems cannot process files with special characters (such as @ # $ % ^ & *—+ " ?). Other systems may require a particular naming convention that streamlines identification, retrieval, and assembly of the documents. Failure to follow these rules can cause an online system to reject or misplace the files.

- **File Type**. Many sponsors require documents to be in PDF format. Others may require a specific word processing format or may require the budget to be submitted as an Excel file. The sponsor's system may not be compatible with specific versions of particular programs. Knowing which file types are allowable before you start writing your proposal can save time as you prepare to upload files to the sponsor's online system.

- **File Size**. Some systems are limited as to the maximum file size they can accept. This can especially be an issue if your proposal includes high-resolution images. File compression is an option, but this process often affects the sharpness of the images. If you run into problems with file or image sizes, try contacting your institution's printing services, publications, or information technology personnel for help in reducing the file size without losing the details of your images.

- **Headers, Footers, and Page Numbers**. Electronic submission systems often require many separate documents to be uploaded. The system then compiles them into one master document. In these cases, the compilation process sometimes adds the headers, footers, and page numbers, but not always. If the sponsor's system adds these elements, including them in your document can result in confusing duplication or even rejection of the submission package. Although you will probably want at least page numbers on your draft documents as you develop your proposal, you may need to make a note to yourself in some prominent place in order to remember to delete these from the final documents if your sponsor's system does not allow them.

Electronic submissions sometimes involve uploading your proposal to a large proposal processing service, which in turn sends the proposal on to your sponsor. If this is true for your proposal, you will have two sets of formatting guidelines to deal with: the sponsor's and those of the processing service. We have not run into any situations in which the two sets of guidelines were in conflict, but we have seen variances. Sometimes the sponsor's guidelines are more stringent as to the acceptable fonts or page lengths. These differences may allow your proposal to be submitted to the proposal processing service, only to be rejected when it reaches the sponsor. Sometimes the sponsor uses an electronic "slot" in the processing service's system in a manner that is less than intuitive. NIH, for example, uses the "project narrative" slot in the Grants.gov submission system for a statement of the proposal's public health significance. What most of us call the project narrative goes in the "research strategy" slot.

Summary

Although careful formatting and presentation will not cause an otherwise weak proposal to be funded, carelessness in these areas can prevent your proposal from even being reviewed, and careful attention to these elements can help to push a strong proposal over the line into the "funded" category.

Some of these issues must necessarily be dealt with at the end of the proposal process. Many of them, however, can be incorporated into your proposal outline and file naming conventions as you work on the proposal, and doing so will help avoid last-minute drama as you submit your proposal to the sponsor.

Section Three

Next Steps

Chapter 11

Review, Rejection, and Reshaping

Susan Hazelwood and Diane Oerly

THE SENSE OF relief when your proposal leaves your hands and moves to your sponsored programs office is amazing. But don't feel too relieved until you know the sponsor has actually received your submission. Until the proposal has been received and accepted by the sponsor, you will be on call to make corrections or fix problems. Once the submission deadline has passed and you realize that your proposal really is gone, allow yourself some time to get reacquainted with your graduate students, your family, your pets, and your friends. Relax, catch a few extra hours of sleep, and try to catch up on everything that fell by the wayside under the pressure of meeting the submission deadline. This is not the time, however, to forget about the proposal and its proposed work scope.

While the sponsor is finding peer reviewers (see the boxed text "Becoming a Reviewer" later in this chapter), conducting the review, and determining which proposals will be funded, you need to continue thinking about the proposed project. Begin by thanking those who helped with proposal preparation. We all like to feel appreciated, and these small acts of recognition will strengthen your team.

Consider submitting compliance forms, such as human subjects or animal care protocols, while the details of the project are fresh in your mind. Think about any additional pilot data you could collect to further your project, even before the funding arrives. There were probably questions, problems, and activities which could not be included in this particular proposal but which could logically follow on the heels of or in parallel with this project. Now is a good time to think through the priority that these issues should hold in your research agenda.

While the proposal is still fresh in your mind, jot down some notes about how it might have been made stronger and more likely to receive full funding. If there are bits of preliminary data, additional letters of commitment, or other elements that you wish you could have included, put those on your list. Consider as well how the proposal development process might have been improved. At MU, the Department of Family and Community Medicine has a tradition of conducting a "well grant checkup." After a proposal is submitted, everyone involved meets to discuss the process, what went well, and what could be improved next time.

It is much easier to view your proposal with objectivity a week or two following submission, when the ideas are still reasonably fresh but you have had time to gain a little distance from the proposal. NSF regional seminars often include this description of a good proposal: "a good idea, well expressed, with a clear indication of methods for pursuing the idea, evaluating the findings, and making them known to all who need to know." If, upon reflection, you think any of these items were weak in the proposal you submitted, now is the time to begin reworking your proposal for resubmission.

Our purpose here is not to be the bearer of bad news or to discourage you. You should prepare for your proposal to be declined simply because the odds are that it will be. It is very challenging to get a grant proposal funded, and we view getting funded as a process rather than as an event. The success rates posted on the National Institutes of Health (NIH), National Science Foundation (NSF), and other federal agency websites show just how high the odds against funding are at those agencies, and the competition for funding is increasing. At the NSF, the number of proposals submitted rose by 74 percent between 2001 and 2010.

Research proposal success rates at NSF have dropped from 33 percent in 2000 to 23 percent in 2010. In 2010, the success rate for new principal investigators was only 17 percent, and the average number of proposals submitted by an individual to the NSF before receiving an award was 2.3. The data from the NIH shows similar trends except that the 2010 funding rates for the NIH are even lower: R01s, the bread-and-butter NIH research proposals, were funded at 18 percent; R03s, small research grants, at 19 percent; and R21s, exploratory/developmental grants, at 15 percent.

Applying for a grant award is almost always a repeat process. It is not worth investing your time and energy to prepare the initial application if you are not willing to rework your project into another application to a different sponsor, or to use what you learn from the review process to resubmit the proposal. Grant proposal development is far less stressful when you understand that resubmissions are the norm.

A rejection notice does not necessarily mean that you should give up. As you will find from conversing with someone who has served on a review panel—or better yet, learn for yourself by serving on a review panel—there are many more excellent proposals than there is money to fund them. The number-one reason that grant proposals fail is that the sponsor does not have enough money to fund all the good ideas. Of course, there are some situations in which you should not resubmit—more on those later.

Review Processes

What happens to your proposal after it is submitted depends on the sponsoring organization to which you submit and the type of grant award you request. Sponsors use several different approaches to determine which individuals or organizations will receive their money. If you can learn who will review your proposals and make the funding decisions, you will be able to write to that audience and respond to the review criteria with that audience in mind.

The first hurdle your proposal must clear is compliance with the guidelines. Most sponsors have personnel whose job is to triage any applications that violate format guidelines or content requirements. Because of the large volume of proposals and the significant amount of time and effort a review panel invests, applications in violation of the guidelines are often rejected without review. When this happens as a result of screening via an electronic submission system, you may or may not receive detailed information as to where the problem is in your proposal. This can make it difficult to find the problem, fix it, and resubmit the proposal before the agency deadline. Even if such errors are overlooked at this screening stage, sometimes peer reviewers, who tend to be overworked and also fully aware that the sponsor cannot fund every good proposal, are looking for a reason to decline a proposal. Violations of the sponsor's guidelines can provide such a reason.

Beyond this compliance screening, the review process depends largely on the size of the sponsoring agency and whether the funder is a private entity or a governmental agency. Although we provide general information about typical review processes below, be sure to study your sponsor's website or other information carefully to learn what you can about the specific review process for your proposal.

Private Sponsors

A family foundation often has family members on its board who decide which proposals to fund based on their own viewpoints without any outside involvement. A community foundation typically has a board composed of leaders from the community who review applications and decide which projects to fund. Some of these leaders may offer expert input; many will not be experts but simply engaged members of the community. Corporate foundations vary. In some cases, the corporate board makes funding decisions. In other cases, this responsibility is delegated to hired experts or knowledgeable employees. Funding from these types of foundations is typically for projects or interventions in education, community services, and similar areas.

Professional associations such as the American Council of Learned Societies and "disease" associations such as the American Cancer Society are more likely to use formal review panels to rank the grant proposals they receive. These panels will certainly include experts in fields related to those involved in the proposed projects they review, but the panel may also include stakeholders such as family members of individuals suffering from a particular disease. It can be tricky to strike the right balance between lay and technical language in writing for review panels with this kind of mixed level of expertise. This makes it especially important to ask about the review process and the composition of the review panel early in the proposal development process.

Government Agencies

Government entities are generally much more transparent and typically have a specific set of review criteria and a specific review procedure. An agency may have its own internal review processes using agency personnel, or it may bring in a panel of external experts to independently evaluate grant applications. Most government agencies use a process known as peer review in which all the reviewers are knowledgeable in the area of work to be reviewed and at least one or two are experts in the specific area of your proposal.

The program officer or the peer reviewers, or both, make sure that the information presented is reasonable and understandable and that the activities proposed in the application are achievable and consistent with programmatic or legislative requirements as they were presented in the funding opportunity announcement. In some cases, proposals are ranked against each other. In other cases, proposals are scored against the review criteria independent of the other proposals in the queue. Sometimes the reviewers meet in person, sometimes they review and respond independently, and sometimes a panel meeting occurs by conference call. Sometimes reviewers post their preliminary scores for each proposal online before the review committee meets; other times they do not communicate at all until they meet in person or by phone.

The agency will also conduct a financial review to evaluate the fiscal integrity and capacity of your institution and to examine your budget and budget narrative to determine whether costs are reasonable, necessary, allocable, and allowable under the applicable federal cost principles and agency regulations. Some sponsors have a second layer of review by the board or advisory council that created the agency's strategic plan and oversees all of the agency's funding decisions. To illustrate how the review process plays out at particular agencies, the following paragraphs provide examples from the National Institutes of Health (NIH) and the National Science Foundation (NSF).

The NIH (the largest research sponsor in the US government) uses standing committees of experts who typically serve three-year terms, with one-third of each committee rotating off and on each year. NIH's first level of review is carried out by a scientific review panel, called a *study section*, composed primarily of nonfederal scientists with current expertise in relevant scientific areas. The second level of review is performed by the national advisory council or board for each institute and center. These councils are composed of both scientific and lay members chosen for their expertise, interest, or activity in matters related to health and disease. Only applications that are favorably reviewed at both of these levels will be funded. At the NIH, program officers have relatively little influence on the selection process.

At the NSF, ad hoc peer review committees typically review proposals. After the peer review by these external committees, the program officers make the final funding decisions, taking into account the balance of their portfolios of funded projects among senior and junior investigators and across the fields of science for which they are responsible, as well as similar issues that affect the balance of science funded by a given directorate.

Rejection

When your proposal is declined, it is common to feel insulted, dejected, and rejected and to think the peer reviewers were stupid, careless, or politically motivated. So the first step is to let some time pass while you overcome anger or any other negative emotions generated by the notice of declination and summary of the review panel's comments. Share the review summary with the rest of your team. Your initial proposal benefitted from the insights and expertise of the other members of your team, and decisions about whether to resubmit and, if so, how to revise the proposal will benefit from the shared vision of the group as well.

When you can objectively review the feedback you received, it will be time to develop and implement a plan of action. Using reviewer comments to guide the changes you make will increase the likelihood of being funded with your resubmission. The reviewer comments will help you understand where you failed to effectively make your case for funding. If you did not receive comments by the peer reviewers, check with the sponsor's program officer to see if reviewer comments are available or if the program officer can give you feedback on your proposal. If so, schedule a time to discuss the reviews with the program officer.

Program officers are typically scholars who have had considerable success in their own careers. They can often help you adjust your proposal's methods or otherwise lead you to more productive approaches. Program officers usually sit in on the review panel discussions. Consequently, they can help you to better understand the peer reviewers' comments and will often share discussion points that may not be recorded in the summary you receive. The program officer can offer valuable insights that may help you to decide whether to resubmit your proposal. In addition, the program officer may be able to inform you of upcoming initiatives or programs in other parts of the agency for which your project may be better suited. Do call!

Becoming a Reviewer: Selected Funding Agencies

Sara Vassmer

There is no better grantsmanship training than serving as a reviewer. Although it does take time and typically pays little, if anything, the investment of your time is well worth it because of the knowledge you will gain of your sponsor's culture and the relationships you build with program officers.

Administration for Children and Families

A step-by-step process to becoming a grant reviewer is available at http://www.acf.hhs.gov/programs/grantreview/. This page also includes a list of frequently asked questions.

The Administration on Children, Youth, and Families encourages participation in the review of grant proposals as a means to better understanding its processes. A reviewer registration form is available at https://www.acfgrantreviewer.com/public/regRef.aspx.

Department of Agriculture, National Institute for Food and Agriculture

To be considered as a reviewer, send an e-mail message noting your institution's name and your areas of expertise (limit to four or five keywords) to newreviewer@nifa.usda.gov.

Department of Education

Contact the program office that handles grant programs in your area of expertise and inform them of your interest in being a reviewer. Phone numbers for program offices can be found in the *Guide to US Department of Education Programs* (http://www2.ed.gov/programs/gtep/index.html). You will usually be asked to send a résumé or curriculum vitae to the department to enable the team to evaluate your credentials as a potential reviewer.

Health Resources and Services Administration

Register and learn more about the reviewer recruitment process for the US Department of Health and Human Services' Health Resources and Services Administration at http://www.hrsa.gov/grants/reviewers/index.html.

Institute of Museum and Library Services

Download reviewer handbooks and become familiar with the IMLS review process before applying at http://www.imls.gov/reviewers/default.aspx.

National Endowment for the Humanities

Log in and register for the NEH Panelist and Reviewer Information System (PRISM) at https://securegrants.neh.gov/prism/.

National Institutes of Health

The NIH primarily calls upon NIH-funded investigators for voluntary peer review services. The process is explained at this site: http://grants.nih.gov/grants/peer/becoming_peer_reviewer.htm. To volunteer, send an e-mail to the Enhancing Peer Review mailbox at ReviewerVolunteer@mail.nih.gov. Include a brief description (one or two sentences) of your areas of expertise in the body of the e-mail and a copy of your biographical sketch as an attachment.

National Science Foundation

Send an e-mail message to the NSF program officers of the programs that fit your expertise. To find the appropriate NSF program officers, go to the NSF website (www.nsf.gov). Select one of the program areas listed in the pull-down menu on the left side of the home page. This will take you to the home page of the selected NSF directorate or office. Select the Staff Directory, and you will find names of program officers listed by divisions or programs they manage. You can then send the program officer an e-mail with the information indicated on the NSF web page: Introduce yourself, identify your areas of expertise, and express your interest in becoming a peer reviewer. Attach a two-page biographical sketch with current contact information.

Substance Abuse and Mental Health Services Administration

Applicants who wish to serve as new SAMHSA grant reviewers are asked to attach the completed reviewer contact form and a résumé to an e-mail to reviewer@samhsa.hhs.gov. The reviewer contact form is available at http://www.samhsa.gov/Grants/emailform/index.aspx.

Reshaping Your Proposal

There are many valid reasons that a proposal is not funded. NIH regional workshops typically include a slide or two that detail the most common problems in proposals that lead to a failure to receive funding:

- Lack of new or original ideas

- Absence of an acceptable scientific rationale

- Lack of experience in the essential methodology

- Questionable reasoning in the experimental approach

- Diffuse, superficial, or unfocused research plan

- Lack of sufficient experimental detail

- Lack of knowledge of published relevant work

- Uncertainty concerning future directions

Reading the reviewer comments, discussing the proposal with the program officer, and talking about this information with the rest of your team will probably lead you to strategies for telling your story better or overcoming weaknesses with your original submission. The strategies below address several of the most common problems we have seen.

Sponsor Match

If the program officer says your work is not a good match for the sponsor, this may mean that you did not learn enough about the agency or funding opportunity. But it may also mean that you failed to convey the connection between your project and the agency's goals and objectives.

To avoid the first possibility, try to call the sponsor to discuss your project before you submit your proposal. If the sponsor does not have staff that you can reach, check its recent IRS 990s (for foundations) or website to see what they have funded in the past.

To avoid the second possibility, be sure to find someone who has not been involved in your proposal's preparation to read it against the sponsor's guidelines before you submit it. Any gaps in the logic of the proposal will be more obvious to an "outsider" than to members of the team, who are immersed in planning the project.

If you find that your proposal is truly a mismatch with the priorities of the sponsor, the solution is usually to identify a sponsor that is a better match with your project, but you may also be able to resubmit a proposal that presents only the portion of your project that is a good match with the original sponsor's priorities.

Too Ambitious

If you are told your proposal is too ambitious, your proposal failed to convey that you fully understand the scope of the work and what the project entails. This kind of comment usually means that the reviewers did not believe you had clearly thought through the details of the project. This is a common problem among inexperienced grant writers. The tendency is to want to be sure the sponsor is getting a good deal for its money, and these good intentions lead to a proposal that includes more work than the budget and time frame can support. Start by discussing the project with an experienced colleague to see whether the problem really lies with your timeline for the work or with the way you presented the work in your proposal.

If the problem is a too-ambitious timeline, consider subdividing your proposal into several smaller projects. Once you have parsed the work, you may find that you need to seek multiple funding sources. Alternatively, if the problem is with your presentation, providing pilot data and explaining your process and timeline for securing that data can demonstrate to reviewers that you know how long the early phases of the work will take. The addition of a timeline that indicates major project milestones and when they will be accomplished can also demonstrate that you have thought through the details of the work.

Relevant Expertise

If your proposal failed to convey that your team has the expertise and experience to successfully complete the project, you may need to add collaborators or consultants to strengthen the expertise of your team. This can be particularly true if you are a junior faculty member and lack experience as a principal investigator. To address this reviewer concern, identify an externally funded senior faculty member who will agree to mentor you. Arrange to have lunch each month to discuss the progress of your project, and write these plans into your revised proposal, including a letter of commitment and a biographical sketch of your mentor.

If the concern is instead about the team's expertise to do the project, expand your team to include an individual or individuals who can provide the missing credibility. Look at your descriptions of the key personnel to be sure they include very specific statements as to individuals' qualifications to fulfill their roles on the project. Instead of relying upon the reviewers to glean the relevant information, point out in the project narrative or the budget justification, or both, each person's experience, skills, and strengths pertaining to the proposed work.

Adequate Resources

If your proposal failed to convey that you have the necessary resources to do the work, the reviewers may have a perception that your institution does not have, or is not willing to provide, adequate institutional support for your work. Letters of support or, better yet, letters of commitment from consultants, mentors, department chairs, or more senior institutional officials can help persuade reviewers that your work will not be done in isolation and that the resources you need will be available. Commitments of institutional resources such as cash, space, equipment, and personnel time go beyond simple acknowledgment of the project. These kinds of commitments demonstrate clear institutional support for your work.

Obstacles and Alternatives

If reviewer comments include phrases like "insufficient discussion of obstacles and alternative approaches," the reviewers believe there is a high probability that some phase of the work will not pan out as you have proposed. If other objectives and phases of your project depend on that phase, this could bring the whole project to a halt. Sponsors will not give you money for work they are not confident you will be able to complete.

The best proposals usually include a potential-pitfalls-and-solutions section for each major activity. If you acknowledge what could go wrong with the project and what you will do if it does, you take control of this issue. The reviewer is then more likely to believe that you understand the work and have fully considered and planned for what might go wrong. For a particularly risky or complex project, the addition of a graphic clearly displaying your decision tree will demonstrate that you have given thought to what might go wrong and the alternatives you will follow in each case.

Budget

If reviewer comments suggest that your project is not an appropriate or best use of the sponsor's funds, this can mean that you did not adequately justify your budget request, the reviewer did not see the connection between the budget items and the proposed activities, or the reviewers were not able to understand how you determined "the ask" that you were making. Check back through your budget to be sure there are no costs associated with an activity that was dropped as the proposal was revised. Part of planning the budget is to see what pilot data collection or a pilot of the activity costs. Ask a colleague to look at your budget to see if the costs for travel, equipment, and supplies appear to be reasonable. Think carefully about the tasks each person will be assigned and whether all the personnel time is really needed. Vendor quotes for equipment are helpful and are sometimes required. Be sure your budget justification explains, in detail, how you arrived at the numbers in the budget.

Outcomes

If reviewer comments cite a failure to include measurable outcomes, consider including a timeline that contains milestones and outcomes. Sponsors want to know how you and they will know when your project is completed and whether it was successful. A table of objectives, milestones, and outcomes can accomplish this in a minimal amount of space. Logic models are increasingly popular with sponsors and can help you and the reviewers understand your project's outcomes and how they will be measured.

Planning in Isolation

If reviewers comment that your proposal appears to have been built in isolation, this can mean any of several things. Sometimes this comment means you did not cite the literature, giving credit to others and incorporating their work as a basis for your proposed work. Sometimes it means that you are too close to your own work to see what others may not readily understand and that your text is not clear. Or it may mean that you failed to involve stakeholders in the planning process.

To address this comment, start by going back through your background or need section to be sure you have acknowledged important contributions by those who may be serving as the peer reviewers of your proposal. Doing so recognizes the contributions that have already been made and gives your work intellectual context.

To identify a lack of clarity for a reader who is not an expert or who is reading quickly, arrange for a friendly review before you resubmit the proposal. Build time into your proposal preparation timeline for this review and also for the time to improve your proposal in response to the reviewer comments. We guarantee this will improve the quality of your proposal. Be careful not to call upon individuals as friendly external reviewers who the sponsor may ask to serve as reviewers. If they give you a presubmission review, they will have to recuse themselves from reading and voting on your proposal.

When Not to Resubmit

As we mentioned early on, there are situations in which you would not resubmit a proposal. You may have reached the agency's maximum number of submissions for this project. For example, the NIH allows only one resubmission, so if your resubmission is not funded, you cannot submit that particular proposal a third time.

Other situations in which you would not resubmit your proposal would be driven by "fatal" reviewer feedback. If the reviewers clearly do not think the work is important, the project will not be funded regardless of how perfectly the methods and other parts of the proposal argument are presented. If reviewers comment that your hypothesis is not supported by your preliminary data or data from the work of others, this is a criticism that cannot be overcome. If reviewers comment that the work has already been done by someone else, there is no point in funding your project as original work. Finally, if reviewers comment that your proposed methods are not suitable for testing your hypothesis, correcting this problem would result in such a complete rethinking of your approach to the project that it would result in a new project rather than a resubmission.

Summary

In grant work, rejection is the norm. Knowing that, you have every right to be thrilled with a notice of award. After you submit a proposal, begin right away to consider how you might improve your proposal in anticipation of receiving a declination from the sponsor. The time devoted to considering how to improve the proposal can help to position you for your next submission, even if this first one is funded. The most successful investigators are always planning their next proposals rather than waiting until the currently funded work is completed.

Chapter 12

Your Project Is Funded—Now What?

Elizabeth D. Miller

IT OFTEN TAKES a year or more from the time you first submit the proposal until you are notified of funding. Most often, however, faculty members know they will be funded long before the award notice officially arrives. This award limbo can be agonizing, but there are things to do if you are to receive the official award notice. With federal grants, there are just-in-time items that must be submitted to the agency before an award can be issued, and you will likely get a request for this information. Not-for-profits, foundations, and associations are increasingly requesting similar information. Many sponsors ask for a list of your current and pending research support and about your ongoing, upcoming, and potential time commitments at this time.

Your institution likely has resources available to help you gather and submit this information to the sponsor. Getting from the award notice to project implementation is usually a routine institutional process supported by grant personnel. In fact, the institution's sponsored programs office is often the only campus entity authorized to submit this information on your behalf. These processes can be as varied as the many institutions of higher education. Just as Bob Glidewell and Diane Oerly recommended in Chapter 3 for the proposal development stage of your project, you will want to seek out any support available to you at this stage as well. So, when you get the notice that you are likely to be funded, perform the happy dance of your choice. Then contact your sponsored programs office.

Many compliance requirements are referred to as just-in-time information. In the past, these approvals were all required at the time of proposal submission. In an effort to eliminate unnecessary work on proposals that are not funded, these requirements were moved to the point of award. Now, required approvals must be in place before your grant account can be set up in your institution's accounting system and you actually begin to spend money. These approvals include any animal care and use proto-col, human subjects protocol, and biohazards considerations. If you did not do so after the proposal was submitted, finalizing research compliance approvals is a good use of this limbo time so that, once the award is made, you will be ready to begin the work of the project.

Research Compliance Issues

This is a book about grantsmanship rather than research compliance. Con-sequently, the following sections are not intended to offer in-depth compliance information but rather to alert you to the issues in this area that may apply to your project. Although technically the federal research compliance policies only apply to federally funded research, many research institutions apply them to all research conducted by the institution. The following list is intended to provide a broad-brush awareness of compli-ance issues that may apply to your project.

Responsible Conduct of Research

Responsible conduct of research is a term of art that refers to training in safe, ethical research practice. The current rules and guidance for this training are not well organized. Some practices are defined by laws and institu-tional policies; others are set in nonbinding codes and guidelines; some are tied to granting agencies; still others are just practices commonly accepted by most researchers and learned from mentors in a given field. Monitoring this mishmash of regulations can be difficult, but you should be aware that some agencies require this training of anyone involved in research activities.

Conflict of Interest

There will inevitably be conflicts of interest and conflicts of commitment as researchers fulfill their obligations in today's world. Faculty members are expected to serve on committees, train the next generation, review grants and manuscripts, and move their own research agendas forward. These many roles practically guarantee some conflicts of interest and com-mitment. These are not necessarily bad as long as they are managed. Institutions are required to manage potential conflicts in three critical areas: finances, work commitments, and intellectual and personal matters. If you have a potential conflict in one of these areas and do not know who handles these issues for your institution, contact your institution's research or sponsored programs office for advice.

Human Subjects

If your project qualifies under the federal definition of *research* and involves living human beings, you will need institutional review board (IRB) approval to proceed with the work. For these purposes, *research* is defined in the *Code of Federal Regulations* as "a systematic investigation designed to develop or contribute to generalizable knowledge" (Protection of Human Subjects, 2009). A *systematic investigation* is any activity that involves a prospective plan that incorporates data collection, either quantitative or qualitative, and data analysis to answer a question. *Generalizable knowledge* comes from projects designed to draw general conclusions, inform policy, or generalize findings beyond a single individual or an internal program.

Most institutions have a standing IRB, along with a dedicated office and personnel to support this work. Any IRB will be comprised of at least five members with varying backgrounds, including members from different fields and diverse race, gender, and cultural backgrounds and sensitivities. If an IRB regularly reviews research that involves a vulnerable category of subjects (for example, children, prisoners, pregnant women, or people with intellectual disabilities), it should also include people who are knowledgeable about and experienced in working with these subjects. The goal is to have sufficient expertise on the committee to provide a meaningful review and to have counsel in safeguarding the rights and welfare of human subjects.

If you are at a small institution that does not do much research and does not have an IRB, there are other options available. For example, your institution can enter into an agreement with another institution to use its IRB. The federal Office of Human Research Protections maintains a listing of established IRBs that can help you find one in your area (http://ohrp .cit.nih.gov/search/search.aspx?styp=bsc). Where there is a will, there is a way!

Besides securing IRB approval, anyone engaged in research with human subjects must complete training to understand the historical foundations and basic ethical principles that underlie the conduct of biomedical and behavioral research involving human subjects. Personnel with your local IRB can point you to local sources of training. The *Belmont Report* (U.S. DHHS, Office of Human Research Protections, 1979) identified three fundamental ethical principles: respect for persons, beneficence, and justice. The uniform set of regulations is the Federal Policy for the Protection of Human Subjects and is informally known as the *Common Rule* (Korenman, 2006).

IRB review and approval of your project may take from a day up to several months to finalize depending upon the risks entailed for the subjects in your project and your responsiveness to requests for further information. This is why we recommend that you start the process soon after your proposal is submitted. When the IRB approval process is taking longer than expected, it is usually because the IRB personnel are waiting for the principal investigator to provide information they requested. You will want to stay in touch with IRB personnel to be sure they have what they need from you.

One final note: Research with the lowest levels of risk to human subjects is labeled *exempt*, and this is a bit of an unfortunate label. It does not mean that the work is exempt from IRB regulations, as the label might imply. This level of work must be submitted for IRB approval just as work with higher levels of risk.

Even with all of this review by the IRB, you know the intricacies of your project the best. As the principal investigator or project director, you are responsible for carrying out sound ethical research consistent with the research plan as approved by an IRB. Use the IRB personnel to be sure that you are clear about your responsibilities for each project you do.

Vertebrate Animals

Although there is no Common Rule as there is for research with human subjects, the Animal Welfare Act regulates how animals are cared for and used in research (U.S. Department of Agriculture, 2012). The federal government requires that if you involve "any live, vertebrate animal used or intended for use in research, research training, experimentation, or biological testing or for related purposes," then you must obtain clearances from a local animal care and use committee (ACUC). This committee is composed of local scientists, nonscientists, community members, and veterinarians. Its roles are to closely monitor the research and ensure that it is conducted within the laws and regulations, to monitor the care and use of research animals at the institution, and to suspend any activities involving animals if the research is not in compliance with federal requirements.

As with IRB approval for human subjects, ACUC approval is required before an associated grant award can be finalized. You will submit a protocol that includes such information as your rationale for animal use and consideration of alternatives, justification for the choice of species and the number of animals, research procedures involving animals, procedures to minimize pain and distress, animal living conditions and veterinary care, the method of euthanasia, and endpoint criteria.

Biohazards

Biohazardous materials are defined as any microorganism; infectious substance; or naturally occurring, bioengineered, or synthesized component of any such microorganism or infectious substance capable of causing death, disease, or other biological malfunction in a human, animal, plant, or other living organism; deterioration of food, water, equipment, supplies, or material of any kind; or harmful alteration of the environment (University of Missouri Environmental Health and Safety, 2004, p. 1). These include but are not limited to certain bacteria, fungi, viruses, rickettsiae, protozoa, and parasites; recombinant products; listed select agents and toxins; allergens, cultured human or animal cells, and the potentially infectious agents these cells may contain; or other infectious agents as outlined in laws, regulations, or guidelines. If your project includes work with biohazards, contact your institution's research office to learn about your institution's policies and procedures in this area.

Export Controls

The US government regulates the distribution of strategically important products, services, and information to foreign nationals and foreign countries for reasons of foreign policy and national security under rules collectively known as *export controls*. An *export* for these purposes is defined much more broadly than just a package heading out in the mail: it is "the transfer of controlled technology, information, equipment, software, or services to a foreign person in the US or abroad by any means" (May, 2005, p. 3). For example, an export could be simply a visual inspection of controlled equipment, an oral disclosure of controlled information, or review and comment on a research protocol. This kind of information sharing, even if it happens within the United States, is considered a *deemed export*. Export control regulations apply to all activities, not just sponsored research, and the penalties, including heavy fines, reach through to the individual rather than stopping at the institution.

That's the bad news. The good news is that these regulations have relatively little effect on the majority of the research and other activities at institutions of higher education. This is because the *fundamental research exclusion* applies to most research conducted by institutions of higher education. This exclusion applies to work where "the resulting information is ordinarily published and shared broadly in the scientific community" (May, 2005, p. 11). To invoke this exclusion, your institution cannot accept any contract clause that forbids the participation of foreign nationals, gives the sponsor a right to approve publications resulting from the research, or otherwise operates to restrict participation in research or access to and disclosure of research results. Note, though, that the provision of things (that is, tangible items) and services (such as training) are not included under this exclusion and may require a license when controlled items or information are involved.

Budget Negotiations

As the individual ultimately accountable for implementing your project, you hold much of the responsibility for its successful and compliant completion. You know the intricacies of the project and understand the resources it requires, so it is up to you to avail yourself of institutional resources to be sure that you understand the export control, human subjects, animal care and use, biohazard, intellectual property, and other compliance issues and requirements that are relevant to your project. Similarly, it will be your responsibility to manage the budget, spending only on allowable costs and in keeping with the budget you negotiated.

It is very important that you never complete and deliver the work for a grant project before the award documents have been signed by both parties. Doing the work before there is an award agreement in place puts you and your institution at risk of not getting paid. In fact, we know of cases in which this happened. This is not to say, however, that you should do nothing at all until you have the last t crossed on the award documents. As discussed below in the "Period of Performance" section, pre-award expenditures always entail the risk that the award may not materialize, but there are cases in which the nature of the project's activities requires you to begin or risk missing a window of opportunity.

In today's financial climate, it is reasonable to expect that the sponsor will fund only part of your budget request. There just is not enough money to fully fund all the excellent proposals. If the sponsor does offer less money than you requested, carefully consider which elements to drop from the project. As Sheryl Koenig and Susan Hazelwood explain in Chapter 9, we do not recommend that you attempt to do the whole project as proposed without an adequate budget. To accept a lesser budget for the full scope of work tells the sponsor that you really asked for more money than you needed and your original budget was therefore dishonest, or that you did not know what the project would cost and therefore may not really know what you are doing. Neither is a good start with the sponsor.

Award Terms

Who negotiates? This responsibility is often split between you and your institution. As the designer of the project and the expert regarding the work of the project, you are probably the only person qualified to negotiate the programmatic and technical aspects of the project. You are probably the only person qualified to decide how to restructure the project in response to a reduction in the budget, for example. However, most institutions' bylaws or state laws in the case of public institutions restrict the terms and conditions to which the institution can legally agree. You as a faculty member are probably not authorized to negotiate such terms and conditions. This means you probably will work with someone in the sponsored programs office or other entity to negotiate your grant award on behalf of your institution.

What are these terms, you ask? Well, they are mostly issues that will not affect your science or scholarship, such as indemnification, arbitration, and governing law (most state institutions do not have the right to agree to be governed by another state's laws). You may not care much about these issues, but award terms include other issues that you will care about, such as publishing rights for the work, patents arising from the work, and your ability to retain your intellectual property. We have seen terms from one organization, for example, that would have limited the principal investigator's ability to continue working in the field if the award had been accepted. The lesson is to make time to read the award documents and be sure you understand them before accepting the sponsor's money.

There are reasons that investigators conduct their research at universities and not in the basements of their homes. The days of Dr. Frankenstein and Dr. Jekyll are long gone. Institutions provide researchers with a plethora of resources to conduct research and scholarship safely and in compliance with the myriad requirements of federal agencies. If an award were made to you personally, you would personally be liable for taxes on the whole of the award. You would carry legal liability for the work. You would be expected to provide an external audit each year and to comply with all manner of other requirements. By making awards to your institution rather than to you personally, sponsors deal with the institution on these issues of legal and fiscal compliance, leaving you to focus your time and attention on conducting the work. You do, however, share with your institution the responsibility for the manner in which you conduct your project.

Statement of Work

Most often, award documents simply reference your proposal as the scope of work for the project. However, cutting-edge science changes rapidly, and there can be a time lag of more than a year between proposal submission and award. If there have been significant changes since you submitted your proposal and these will affect the work you do, be sure to discuss them with the sponsor's program officer during the award negotiations.

Period of Performance

An award has definite start and end dates. This is known as the period of performance, and all expenses for the grant should happen during this time. Sponsors sometimes allow for *pre-award costs*, or costs incurred before the period of performance. Examples of generally allowable pre-award costs include hiring efforts, training costs, and survey development. There are also often pre-award cost limitations. Some awards allow for no pre-award costs at all, whereas others allow for acceptable costs for as many as 90 days prior to the beginning of the period of performance.

For many awards the start date can be almost any time, but if your project must be timed with other events, you may need to negotiate an appropriate start date. Examples include a curriculum project that must be timed with the beginning of a semester or academic year or with agricultural research that must be timed with the growing season in your area.

Project Costs/Award

This section of the award notice is generally either your proposal budget or a revised budget that will be funded. Remember, if the sponsor has cut your budget, you should adjust your scope of work accordingly.

Invoice Submission and Payments

Most grants are set up to reimburse your institution after the expenses have been incurred rather than simply transferring the funds and leaving you to spend them. Each sponsor has its own preference for how often invoices can be submitted to request payment, and you can probably rely upon your sponsored programs office to handle this for you.

Title to Equipment

If you plan to purchase equipment as part of your project, ownership of that equipment does not necessarily rest with your institution. The sponsor can usually retain that title if it chooses. In general though, if you purchase equipment on a grant, the title most often will stay with your institution. This means that if you take a position at another institution, the equipment will probably stay behind at your current institution.

Deliverables/Reports

Sponsors generally want to know how your project is going, not just what you are spending. Most often, project reports are submitted annually, but some sponsors have other preferences. When you finish your project, the final report is usually due 90 days after the end date.

Records

Sponsors generally require you to retain both financial and scientific records for three to seven years. If your project is audited, you will need to keep all your records until any findings are resolved.

Publication

Institutions of higher education are always interested in protecting your right to publish because that is the means of expanding scholarship. It is common practice, however, to give the sponsor notice that you intend to publish and to give the program officer the manuscript for review and comment within a set time, such as 30 days.

If a sponsor's award terms seek to limit your right to publish, your institution will negotiate this on your behalf. Be especially careful about accepting any publication restrictions if your project includes graduate students whose work is part of the project and whose theses or dissertations (and hence, graduation) could be affected by publication restrictions.

Many sponsors want you to publish and request that you note the sponsor's funding in your publications.

Confidentiality

If your project involves information that is proprietary to the sponsor or to you, confidentiality terms can be included in your award agreement unless disclosure of information is required by law.

Publicity/Use of Sponsor Name

Sponsors typically want you to cite their support when you publish the results of your project in professional journals but not when you promote products or engage in commercial publicity or advertising.

Indemnification and Arbitration

The indemnification and arbitration legalese in award documents can be very sticky because it assigns liability and determines the laws that will govern any disputes between your institution and the sponsor. State institutions cannot agree to arbitration under the laws of another state, for example. Sponsored program and university legal personnel are aware of the issues in these areas and can work through them on behalf of you and your institution.

Subcontracts

If your project includes a subcontract with another institution, it is important that the subcontracting institution invoice your institution regularly. Be sure to ask your subcontract collaborator and his or her institution to provide you with the same information for its work scope as you will provide to the sponsor for the work at your institution so that your reports to the sponsor reflect the whole project. Your sponsored programs office will work with its counterpart at the subcontract institution to create a subcontract agreement. Your collaborator will not be able to begin work on the project until this agreement is in place.

Award Setup

Once you have reviewed and approved the terms of your award, most institutions require certain approvals and assurances before you can start spending money, as discussed earlier. After all the compliance issues are settled, the next step is to notify your sponsored programs personnel so that they can set up a fiscal account for your project.

Your Project, Your Business

It is helpful to think of your work in academia as a small business within a larger one. Your "business" will have a mission (see the "draw a box" exercise in "Planning Your Research Agenda" in Chapter 1), clients (the grant sponsors), a budget, and employees. Yes, your institution makes a plethora of resources available to you (for example, human resources, sponsored programs, compliance, accounting, and legal services), but you are still responsible for tapping and managing these resources as they apply to your work. The sections that follow will look at your role as a leader and supervisor as you manage the people, the money, the data, and the sponsor relationships associated with your project. We also include "A

Model for Success," a profile of a professor who brought her skills from a previous corporate career to academia.

Numerous interruptions and issues compete for your time and attention. Set priorities. Break large tasks into smaller ones that can be more easily accomplished. Create and protect blocks of time on your calendar for both writing manuscripts and completing the project tasks. Note when in the day you tend to be most productive, and use that time. Use your proposal, particularly the project narrative, project timeline, budget, and budget justification, to guide your work.

Managing People

Hiring people to work on your project will be among the most important decisions you make. Your goal is to hire and retain folks with the skills, personalities, and work ethics that best fit your project and your leadership style. Tips for sound personnel practices include the following:

- Create a written job description that defines specific duties and objectives for each position.

- Ask applicants to complete some of the tasks that you are hiring them to do on the job—if you are hiring them to write, for example, ask for an impromptu writing sample as part of the interview process.

- If the job involves working with others, ask a committee of other project personnel to conduct the first-level interviews and provide feedback to you as to their top choices for second-level interviews.

- Ask each applicant the same questions so that you can compare apples to apples.

- Be careful to not do all the talking during the interviews; ask open-ended questions during the interviews and also when checking references.

- Check references. Always.

- Communicate the objectives of the position to the employee, and provide regular performance reviews to keep everyone on track.

- Above all, use your institution's human resource professionals to help guide your processes.

If you are conducting research at an institution of higher education, there is a good chance you will be able to hire student workers for some tasks. Your institution or department may have guidelines regarding appropriate responsibilities and pay scales for students. Student workers differ by definition from other employees simply because they are primarily students, and this in turn affects your role as the supervisor. Your role with students is to mentor and nurture them. In contrast, other employees are hired solely for the skills and expertise they bring to a defined job.

Hiring internationally has always entailed jumping through some extra hoops, and attention to export control laws means that these days, there are even more hoops. Be sure to contact your institution's human resources or international programs office for help with these requirements.

You no longer have to do everything yourself. In fact, you should be supervising and training others to do tasks that do not represent the best use of your time. You will likely assemble a team to complete each project. Regular team meetings are essential to keeping any team focused and on track. As the team's leader, you have set priorities and developed measures for success. Communicate with the team about your goals and how you will manage the project's resources. Allow for input from team members. Discuss contingency plans and, if necessary, clear obstacles to success by shifting responsibilities or rotating duties among the members of your team. Be sure to follow any team meeting with a note that highlights decisions made, action items, and any changes of duties.

A Model for Success

Elizabeth D. Miller

Jung Ha-Brookshire has been an assistant professor in the MU Department of Textile and Apparel Management since 2007. Ha-Brookshire worked in the corporate world for nine years prior to coming to academia and managed an international apparel business of $300 million annually. As I have observed her on her path to tenure, I can see that sound business practices have given her the tools to succeed in academia. Upon arriving, she was disappointed to learn that her corporate experience would not directly help her in her quest for tenure, but she has since realized that the skills and habits she developed in the corporate world have made the tenure process easier. In the past four years, she has had 19 publications, four in review, and three more in process. In a field with relatively little access to extramural funding, she has garnered nearly $250,000 in research and education funding. Ha-Brookshire sailed through her third-year review. In fact, her professional organization, the International Textile and Apparel Association, gave her its Rising Star Award. So what habits and skills has she tapped to make such a smooth transition to academia?

A lot of business success derives from knowing the right people, and Ha-Brookshire positions herself well. When she attends a conference, she networks. This leads to new ideas and new collaborations. She listens to others and takes constructive criticism to heart.

She tracks funding opportunities and targets her efforts to meet the goals of the sponsor. There are times when I actually think this woman could find money under a rock! She does not allow herself to fixate on seeking funding for a single idea. Rather, she applies her skills to numerous topics. She does not wait for the latest funding opportunity announcement to be released but works her concepts around the last one available and then follows the news of the funding agency. Most often, she needs to make only minor tweaks once the new funding opportunity announcement is released.

In business, if you miss a deadline, you fail. Ha-Brookshire works well ahead of deadlines—often a year before the due date. If it is due in March, she has her proposal ready for submission in February. This allows time for others to review her work and for her to focus without the deadline pressure that can trigger mistakes.

Managing the Money

At most institutions, the PI or PD is responsible for ensuring that all expenses are both allowable under the general cost principles and allocable to the specific project. Keep track of your project's budget on a regular basis. Verify all the expenses charged to your award each month. Even though you may have departmental fiscal or grant personnel who help with this, you are ultimately responsible.

You usually have some latitude to move money between budget lines, and your contact person in the sponsored programs office will be able to tell you how much you can do this. Be aware that there are limits; for example, you probably will not be able to buy office furniture with your grant funds. At most institutions, office furniture is part of facilities and administration costs and thus not allowable as a direct cost on a grant budget.

The Office of Management and Budget (OMB) issues circulars that define the federal budget and how those funds are spent and monitored. Three of these OMB circulars directly pertain to higher education and grants: A-21, A-110, and A-133. OMB's *Circular A-21*, "Cost Principles for Educational Institutions," addresses how to determine direct costs associated with the work on specific grants, contracts, or other agreements; it also defines facilities and administration (F&A) costs (OMB, 2004). OMB's *Circular A-110*, "Uniform Administrative Requirements for Grants and Agreements with Institutions of Higher Education, Hospitals, and Other Non-Profit Organizations," covers such issues as the terms of agreement, forms to use when applying for funding, standards of financial management, payment methods, cost matching, program income, equipment, record keeping, and award closeout procedures (OMB, 1999). OMB's *Circular A-133*, "Audits of States, Local Governments, and Non-Profit

Organizations," is about consistency and uniformity among federal agencies for annual audits (OMB, 2007). If your project is selected for an audit, check with your sponsored programs office to see who can assist you with this process.

Managing Data

Research produces data, and as the researcher, you may or may not own that data. Funders, research institutions, and data sources may impose their own conditions. In general, the government gives institutions the right to use data collected with grant funding as an incentive to put research to use for the public good. Data gathered as a result of government contracts is generally owned or controlled by the government. Similarly, private companies generally seek to retain the rights to the commercial use of data produced by projects they fund. Foundations and other philanthropic organizations are less consistent—some give away and others seek to retain ownership of intellectual property resulting from their grant awards.

Because awards are generally made to institutions and not to individual researchers, institutions have obligations for data management and may have rights and duties to retain control over research data produced by their employees. This means that your institution may have standards and resources available to assist you with managing your research data. It also means that you may not necessarily be able to take data with you if you relocate.

Data Sharing

Data sharing fulfills many goals. It encourages scientific and scholarly inquiry, diversifies opinions and analysis, promotes research, facilitates training of new researchers, and saves money by helping to reduce duplicative work. There is an expectation that data from grants funded with public dollars will be shared when this is appropriate. Keeping data confidential prior to publication is a commonly accepted practice, but once you publish your results, it is generally expected that your final data will be made available for others to use.

Data Management Plan

If your project is to be successful, you need a plan for collecting, managing, and archiving your data. Thinking through all the ways in which you might want to retrieve the data later will help to identify the sortable fields you need. Establish consistent standards for file names, samples, and specimens. Numerous resources offer guidance on preparing, sharing, and archiving data. The NIH, for example, recommends a resource developed by the Inter-University Consortium for Political and Social Research at the University of Michigan (2009).

Managing the Sponsor Relationship

Sponsors generally want to know the outcomes of the research projects they fund. As a result, you will be asked to report both during the project period and at the end of the project. Keep in mind that this award will, with any luck, be just one step in a long relationship with the sponsor. The following tips can help ensure an ongoing and positive relationship:

- File reports on time, and be sure they include all required information.

- Know the level of effort you have committed to each project, and verify accordingly.

- Know when to request a no-cost time extension.

- Provide the sponsor with information about your project that serves the sponsor's needs and audience.

- Anticipate your next project, planning for the next award before the current project runs out.

Reporting in a timely and accurate manner is important. If you have similar projects funded by the same sponsor, never cut and paste identical sections into multiple reports. Doing so will lead the program officer to believe that there is substantial programmatic overlap between projects and that you have accepted funding more than once for the same work.

OMB's *Circular A-21* requires institutions to document 100 percent effort for personnel whose salaries and wages have been charged to grants and contracts, paid from other funds identified as cost sharing, or paid from other federally sponsored sources (OMB, 2004). Effort verification reports must be filed on a regular schedule (often semiannually) and should document each person's actual effort on the project.

Many grant awards allow for what is known as a no-cost time extension. These allow grantees to extend the final budget period, usually for up to an additional 12 months. This gets you extra time but not extra money to finish your project. Having money left over is not an appropriate reason to request an extension. On the other hand, if you need more time to adequately complete the original work scope, to provide continuity while a renewal application is under review, or to phase out a project that will not receive continued support, a no-cost extension is a reasonable request. Some administrators will tell you that a no-cost extension reflects poor planning or poor time management, but the reality is that many projects do not get under way on time or are delayed due to recruitment, hiring, or any number of other issues.

Knowing how your sponsor's culture works and makes decisions will enable you to target your work to meet its needs. Each sponsor has its own agenda and constituents. Keep the sponsor's audience in mind as you complete your project and share information with the program officer that might be of interest to the sponsor's audience. If you can help meet these needs, you will have better odds of receiving funding. Visit your program officer every chance you get. Build a trusting and professional relationship. Often, at the end of the fiscal year, agencies sweep up tidbits of money and award these dollars administratively; this is just one way in which knowing your agency and its program personnel can pay off.

Summary

From the individual perspective, a grant award can seem deceptively simple: you get the money, you do the work. From a broader perspective, however, a grant award is a fairly complex affair that brings together the missions, policies, and procedures of at least two organizations (your institution and your sponsor). Although there are many human, compliance, fiscal, and reporting issues for which the principal investigator or project director is ultimately responsible, most institutions of higher education have systems in place to help you manage this complexity.

Part Two

Grant-Seeking Toolkit

Assembled by Larry Nossaman

Section 1

Diving into Grants Culture

Grant Glossary

We begin with a glossary of grant-related terms (Table 6) to help orient the novice. The list of terms included in this glossary was not assembled in any scientific manner. Rather, these are simply the resources and terminology we have found useful and about which we get questions in our work as grant writing consultants.

Note: Items that are <u>underlined</u> are defined elsewhere in the glossary.

TABLE 6

Grant Glossary

A	
A-21	Office of Management and Budget *Circular A-21:* "Cost Principles for Educational Institutions." Available at http://www.whitehouse.gov/omb/circulars_default
A-110	Office of Management and Budget *Circular A-110:* "Uniform Administrative Requirements for Grants and Other Agreements with Institutions of Higher Education, Hospitals and Other Non-Profit Organizations." Available at http://www.whitehouse.gov/omb/circulars_default
A-133	Office of Management and Budget *Circular A-133:* "Audits of States, Local Governments, and Non-Profit Organizations." Available at http://www.whitehouse.gov/omb/circulars_default
abstract	A brief summary (usually one page or less) of the <u>grant</u> proposal. It is often the first part of the proposal reviewers read and may be the only part some reviewers read. After the grant is <u>awarded</u>, the <u>sponsor</u> often publishes the abstract.
activity	A specific step taken within each <u>objective</u> to achieve your <u>goal</u>.
ADVANCE	<u>NSF</u> funding program, Increasing the Participation and Advancement of Women in Academic Science and Engineering Careers (ADVANCE). Details are available at http://www.nsf.gov/funding/pgm_summ.jsp?pims_id=5383

(Continued)

TABLE 6
(Continued)

AGRICOLA (AGRICultural OnLine Access)	The catalog for the collections of the U.S. Department of Agriculture's National Agricultural Library, as well as a primary public source for worldwide access to agricultural information. The database covers materials in all formats and periods, including printed works from as far back as the 15th century. Available at http://agricola.nal.usda.gov/.
allowable costs	Expenses that can be charged to a grant project in keeping with the sponsor's guidelines and the relevant OMB circulars.
animal care and use committee (ACUC)	The campus committee which reviews animal research protocols and ensures that the institution's animal care and use policies and practices are in compliance with federal animal care and use policies and regulations.
authorized signer	An individual authorized to commit the institution to follow a certain course of action, such as submit a proposal to a grant sponsor. Individuals within sponsored programs offices typically perform this function at institutions of higher education.
award	Funds provided by a sponsor to pay expenses for a specific project.

B

biosketch or biographical sketch	A short description (usually 2–4 pages) of an individual's qualifications, usually including education, other professional preparation, work experience and appointments, publications, and honors/awards. NIH biosketches also require a personal statement and a list of current and recently completed research support. NSF biosketches require lists of synergistic activities. Both NSF and USDA require information about collaborators.
broad agency announcement (BAA)	An announcement of a federal agency's general research interests that invites proposals and specifies the general terms and conditions under which an award may be made.
budget justification	A narrative description of all budgeted expenditures in a project.

C

CA (confidentiality agreement)	A legal agreement that defines the rights and obligations of all participants involved in exchanging confidential information between or among the signing parties.
CAREER	NSF funding program, Faculty Early Career Development (CAREER) Program. Details are available at http://www.nsf.gov/funding/pgm_summ.jsp?pims _id=503214. See K awards for the NIH's career funding mechanisms.
CFDA (Catalog of Federal Domestic Assistance)	A database of all federal programs, projects, services, and activities for which spending is authorized. Every authorized program does not necessarily receive funding, however. Every federally sponsored funding opportunity announcement will be associated with a CFDA number. Access is available at https://www.cfda.gov/.

TABLE 6

compliance	Adherence to all applicable federal, state, and institutional research-related rules and regulations. Research compliance includes research integrity, human subjects protection (see institutional review board [IRB]), research animal care and welfare (see animal care and use committee [ACUC]), export controls, classified and sensitive research, lobbying activities, and conflict of interest. Additional areas include radiation safety and biological safety. Fiscal and sponsored programs aspects of research compliance (such as effort verification reports and grants management) are typically handled by the institution's sponsored programs office.
conflict of interest	Any circumstance in which an individual could potentially benefit personally from performing a sponsored project or other institutional responsibility. Any potential conflict of interest should be called to the attention of the institution's conflict of interest contact person as soon as possible.
consortium agreement	Terms and conditions for personnel from two or more organizations to work together on a project.
consulting	Professional activity related to an individual's field or discipline where a fee-for-service or equivalent relationship with a third party exists. For grant proposal budgeting purposes, the consulting line is used when the work to be performed is a small part of the project, is work routinely provided for the general public and not unique to the project, and involves little discretionary judgment.
cooperative agreement	A type of award requiring a written agreement in which substantial involvement is anticipated between the sponsor and the awardee institution during the performance of the project.
co-principal investigator (co-PI)	A member of the research team with status equal to the PI (principal investigator).
COS (Community of Science)	A set of subscription information resources accumulated for the global research and development community. Includes funding opportunities, an expertise database, and customized access to a range of professional reference databases including US Patents, MEDLINE, AGRICOLA, and GeoRef, among others. Recently replaced by PIVOT. PIVOT access is available at http://pivot.cos.com.
cost sharing	That portion of the total project costs which is not paid by the sponsor and is the responsibility of the grantee institution.

D

Data Universal Numbering System (D-U-N-S®) Number	A unique nine-digit number which identifies a particular entity or organization. This free number is assigned by Dun & Bradstreet and is required for all businesses and institutions that register with the federal government for contracts or grants. Further details and an application form are available at http://fedgov.dnb.com/webform.

(Continued)

TABLE 6
(Continued)

DHHS	U.S. Department of Health and Human Services. The National Institutes of Health (NIH) are part of DHHS. See http://dhhs.gov/ for further information.
direct costs	Costs that are easily identified with a particular project, in contrast to costs which are part of the institutional infrastructure and not readily assigned to one specific project.
dissemination	Activities to inform other individuals and institutions about the results of a project. These activities can include publishing, presenting results at professional conferences, creating websites, sharing data, conducting webinars, hosting classes or seminars, and submitting progress reports to sponsors.
DOE	U.S. Department of Energy. See http://www.energy.gov/ for further information.

E

ED	U.S. Department of Education. See http://www.ed.gov/ for further information.
effort	The portion of time an individual spends on a project or activity, typically expressed as a percentage of full-time effort (FTE) or as person months per year.
effort verification	Reporting in response to the mandate that applies to all federally sponsored contracts or grants requiring that the distribution of pay must accurately reflect the effort devoted to a project.
endowment grant	A grant to be invested in perpetuity for the ongoing operations of an organization.
export controls	Federal rules about the distribution of strategically important products, services, and information to foreign nationals and countries for reasons of foreign policy and national security.
extension	Additional time to complete a project beyond the agreed-upon end date.
evaluation	The systematic monitoring and assessment of resource allocation; programs, interventions, and activities; management actions; program performance; and resulting outcomes.

F

F&A (facilities & administrative costs)	Infrastructure costs associated with sponsored projects; the percentage is periodically negotiated with the institution's federal cognizant agency to allow the institution to recover some of the infrastructure costs associated with sponsored projects. Also known as *indirect costs* or *overhead costs*.
funding opportunity announcement (FOA)	Grants.gov term for any agency announcement of the availability of funding.

TABLE 6

G	
GeoRef	Database established by the American Geological Institute in 1966 to provide access to the geoscience literature of the world. Available at http://www.agiweb.org/georef/index.html.
gift	In contrast to grant, funds that are awarded with few or no restrictions.
GK–12	NSF funding program, Graduate STEM Fellows in K–12 Education (GK–12). Details are available at http://www.nsf.gov/funding/pgm_summ.jsp?pims_id=503369 &org=DGE&sel_org=DGE&from=fund.
goal	The overall, broad purpose of a project or organization.
GOALI	NSF funding program, Grant Opportunities for Academic Liaison with Industry (GOALI). Details are available at http://www.nsf.gov/funding/pgm_summ .jsp?pims_id=13706&org=DGE&sel_org=DGE&from=fund
grant	In contrast to gift, funds pledged by a sponsor to support research or another specific project.
Grant Proposal Guide (GPG)	Guidelines published by NSF for grant proposal development and submission. Available at http://www.nsf.gov/publications/pub_summ.jsp?ods_key=gpg
H	
human subject	Living human being involved in a research project as a subject. The protective oversight for research activities involving living humans is delegated to the institutional review board (IRB).
human subjects narrative	Narrative section of a grant proposal describing the project's human subjects research activities and the protections planned for those human subjects.
I	
IGERT	NSF funding program, Integrative Graduate Education and Research Traineeship (IGERT) Program. Details are available at http://www.nsf.gov/funding/pgm _summ.jsp?pims_id=12759
indirect costs	See F&A.
institutional review board (IRB)	Committee that oversees research involving human subjects to ensure protection of those subjects in keeping with federal and institutional compliance regulations. IRB approval must be obtained before a project involving human subjects can begin and before grant funding can be awarded.
intellectual property	Works created by human beings, such as discoveries, inventions, and musical, literary, and artistic works. Common types of intellectual property protections include copyrights, trademarks, patents, industrial design rights, and trade secrets.

(Continued)

TABLE 6
(Continued)

K	
K awards	A range of <u>NIH</u> funding mechanisms for supporting career development of biomedical scientists. Details are available at http://grants.nih.gov/training /careerdevelopmentawards.htm
key personnel	Any person whose intellectual involvement is essential to the success of a project; also known as *senior personnel*.
L	
letter of commitment	A notice describing commitments of resources (such as personnel time, space, equipment, or funding) made by an organization or individual to a given project. A letter of commitment may also contain elements of a <u>letter of support</u>.
letter of intent (LOI)	A notice of intent to apply to a specific funding opportunity. LOIs usually contain contact information and a brief description of the proposed project that enables the <u>sponsor</u> to plan for the proposal review process.
letter of support	A notice of support for a particular area of scholarship or project without making any commitments of resources for the project.
limited submission	Programs for which the <u>sponsor</u> limits the number of applications or nominations that a given institution or individual may submit.
logic model	A graphic or table representing how the project team will manage the project's inputs, <u>activities</u>, outputs, and <u>outcomes</u> to solve identified problems.
M	
matching grant	A <u>grant</u> that requires a portion of the project's cost be supplied from sources other than the <u>sponsor</u>.
material transfer agreement (MTA)	A document used for the transfer of materials between institutions.
MEDLINE®	A database containing journal citations and abstracts for biomedical literature from around the world. The National Library of Medicine's PubMed® provides free access to MEDLINE and links to full-text articles when possible. Access is available at http://www.ncbi.nlm.nih.gov/pubmed
memorandum of understanding (MOU)	An agreement describing the roles and responsibilities of the individuals or organizations involved in a specific project or activity. An MOU is usually signed by an <u>authorized signer</u> from each party.
modified total direct costs (MTDC)	That portion of <u>total direct costs</u> against which the <u>F&A</u> rate can be applied; for example, total direct costs modified by removing those budget items to which F&A charges cannot be applied.

TABLE 6

modular budget	The <u>NIH</u> allows many projects with <u>total direct costs</u> of up to $250,000 per year to submit only limited budget information to reduce the administrative burden to applicants, reviewers, and NIH staff. Modular <u>grant</u> applications request <u>direct costs</u> in $25,000 modules and may request up to 10 modules per year. The <u>NIH</u> Modular Research Grant Application web page at http://grants.nih.gov/grants/funding/modular/modular.htm provides detailed information about the application process, including samples of relevant pages from a grant application.
MRI	<u>NSF</u> funding program, Major Research Instrumentation Program. Details are available at http://www.nsf.gov/funding/pgm_summ.jsp?pims_id=5260

N

NSF	National Science Foundation. Details are available at http://www.nsf.gov/
NIH	National Institutes of Health. Details are available at http://www.nih.gov/

O

objective	The interim benchmarks to be achieved during the project toward the long-term <u>goal</u> or goals that the project addresses.
OMB circulars	Government-wide policy directives issued by the Office of Management and Budget that apply to <u>grants</u>. Circulars that apply to institutions of higher education include <u>A-21</u>, <u>A-110</u>, and <u>A-133</u>.
outcomes	The results of a project. Outcomes are often designated as short-term (for example, increasing awareness), intermediate, and long-term (for example, larger-scale, longer-term social, economic, civic, or environmental conditions).
overhead	See <u>F&A</u>.

P

peer review	Objective assessment of the merit of applications by peers, or individuals with expertise equivalent to that of the individuals whose applications they are reviewing.
person months	The portion of time an individual spends on a project or activity, expressed as the number of months per year.
PHS 398	Public Health Service (PHS) <u>grant</u> application forms used by the NIH and other PHS entities. Available at http://grants.nih.gov/grants/funding/phs398/phs398.html
preproposal	Comparatively brief documents containing technical information submitted to a <u>sponsor</u> which can lead to an invitation to submit a full proposal.
principal investigator (PI) or project director (PD)	Team member who is responsible for all aspects of the work described in the <u>grant</u> proposal and serves as the <u>sponsor</u>'s primary programmatic contact for the project.

(Continued)

TABLE 6
(Continued)

program announcement	Request for <u>grant</u> applications in stated scientific areas. The sponsor may or may not set aside funding specifically for these programs.
program income	Gross income that is directly generated by a supported activity or as a result of a <u>grant award</u>. The income may derive from such sources as fees for services performed as part of the project, the use or rental of real or personal property acquired under a funded project, the sale of commodities or items fabricated under a funded project, or interest on loans made with award funds.
program officer	An employee of the <u>sponsor</u> who provides information about sponsor activities and funding opportunities. Some program officers review drafts and discuss reviews of previously submitted proposals.
program project grant (PPG or P01)	<u>NIH</u> funding mechanism that usually includes several closely related research projects and several core facilities to support those projects.
progress report	Report summarizing the work to date on a funded project. Multiyear <u>award</u>s frequently require a progress report before the next year's funding is released.
project director	See <u>principal investigator</u>.

R

request for applications (RFA)	Announcement detailing availability of <u>grant</u> funds for well-defined scientific areas, generally with a single receipt date and funds set aside specifically for the announced program.
request for proposals (RFP)	Announcement with a single receipt date requesting proposals for a contract to meet a specific need.
resubmission	Submitting a revised proposal to the same <u>sponsor</u> after it failed to receive funding when it was submitted earlier. Some sponsors limit the number of resubmissions.
RET	<u>NSF</u> funding program, Research Experiences for Teachers (RET) in Engineering and Computer Science. Details are available at http://www.nsf.gov/funding/pgm _summ.jsp?pims_id=5736
REU	<u>NSF</u> funding program, Research Experiences for Undergraduates (REU). Details are available at http://www.nsf.gov/funding/pgm_summ.jsp?pims_id=5517&from =fund

S

scope of work (SOW)	A written description of work to be performed on a project.
senior personnel	See <u>key personnel</u>.
SF (standard form) 424	Standard cover sheet used by most federal agencies for <u>grant</u> applications. Available at http://grants.nih.gov/grants/funding/424/index.htm

TABLE 6

solicitation	Formal document that elicits <u>proposals</u> for acquisition or financial assistance awards. Includes <u>requests for proposals (RFPs)</u>, <u>requests for applications (RFAs)</u>, and <u>broad agency announcements (BAAs)</u>.
sponsor	An organization that provides funds to other entities to carry out programs or projects.
sponsored programs office	Administrative office that helps personnel acquire and manage external funding for research, training, and public service projects. Sometimes called *sponsored research office*.
start-up grant	A <u>grant</u> to cover the costs of starting a new program or organization.
stipend	A fixed sum of money paid for services or to help cover expenses.
subcontract or subaward	Agreement for personnel from another organization to carry out a specific portion of the <u>scope of work</u> described in a proposal.

T

technical assistance grant	A <u>grant</u> to support organizational development.
total direct costs (TDC)	The sum of all <u>direct costs</u> for a project.

U

unallowable costs	Costs that cannot be included in a project budget because of specific laws, regulations, or <u>sponsor</u> limitations.
unitized cost	Costs that are calculated on a per-unit basis to include all personnel, supplies, and other expenses involved in producing each unit.
USDA	U.S. Department of Agriculture. Details are available at http://www.usda.gov/

Tools for Finding Funding

The "Deal or No Deal?" worksheet (Table 7) that follows can be helpful as you seek to contextualize the project you have in mind in terms of the other work on your plate and those of the other members of your team, the experience and priorities of your team and institution, and the competitive climate in which your proposal would need to succeed. The worksheet is designed to allow you to quantify each issue, though we are not very often

TABLE 7

Deal or No Deal?

	Factors	Decision criteria
		Negative
		1 **2** **3**
The Project	**Will project activities fit with our mission, values, goals, and objectives?**	Activities fall outside our mission and plan.
	Is there credible in-house expertise to do the work?	Expertise is weak, or this is a totally new area for our organization.
	Will partnering consultants or organizations be involved in the project?	Partners have not been contacted yet, or working relationships have not yet been formed.
	What organizational resources will the project require?	A significant investment of organizational resources will be required.
	What will be the return for clients on the organization's investment in this proposal and project?	Poor long- and short-term return on investment in benefits to clients.
The Odds	**How will stakeholders respond to this project?**	Key stakeholders are likely to oppose the project or an association with this funder.
	How well prepared is the organization to respond to this particular funding opportunity?	The staff did not expect the opportunity, and the guidelines are not clear.
	How much work will be involved in preparing the proposal?	Our organization does not have the staff time to respond adequately or the funds to hire a grant writer.
	How stiff is the competition expected to be?	Competition will be very strong and/or there will be very few awards; odds of receiving funding are probably less than 10 percent.
	How familiar is our organization with this funding agency?	Our organization is unknown to this agency and its staff.
	Total Score	10–30: This proposal and/or project is likely to siphon staff time with little return.

this precise in our use of this tool. We have found this to be especially useful for our graduate students and for faculty members who are new to grant work as they consider whether the time invested in a given proposal is likely to be worthwhile.

The "Funding Search Cheat Sheet" summarizes the funder research process described in Chapter 2. We have found this to be a useful handout for workshops and classes that meet in a computer lab to learn how to conduct funder research.

							Score
Neutral				**Positive**			
4	**5**	**6**	**7**	**8**	**9**	**10**	

Neutral	Positive
Activities match minor elements of our mission and plan.	Activities will help fulfill important priorities of our mission and plan.
Organization has average expertise in this area.	Organization has strong expertise and on-the-ground experience in this area.
Partners are on board but will not have an effect on the quality of the project.	Partners are on board and will enhance the quality of the project.
A marginal investment of organizational resources will be required; they will be balanced by funder resources to be received.	Only minimal organizational resources will be required; they will be outweighed by funder resources to be received.
Some short- and/or long-term benefits for clients, but benefits are not key to our organization's mission or plan.	Excellent short- and long-term benefits for clients, and benefits align well with our organization's mission and plan.
Key stakeholders are likely to be neutral about the project and the funder.	Key stakeholders are enthusiastic about the project and association with this funder.
The staff anticipated the opportunity but not in enough detail to begin to position our organization to respond.	The staff anticipated the opportunity, and our organization is well positioned to respond.
Proposal preparation will place stress on personnel, but our organization can prepare an adequate response.	Our organization has the staff time to prepare a highly competitive proposal and/or the funds to hire a grant writer.
The competition is relatively open and there will be a reasonable number of awards; odds of receiving funding are probably between 10 and 50 percent.	The competition is weak relative to our project and many awards will be made; odds of receiving funding exceed 50 percent.
Our organization is known to this agency and its staff.	Our organization has well-developed working relationships with this agency.
31–70: This project should be pursued if there is extra time and staff expertise available for the proposal and the project work.	71–100: Go for it!

Funding Search Cheat Sheet

How to Turn Over Every (or Almost Every) Rock
Guiding Principles

- Be persistent and thorough—look at dozens of funding opportunities to find one.

- Identifying a funding agency and program is square one. More than half the work is in assessing the match. The general process is (1) generating a prospect list and (2) narrowing the prospect list to one or two likely candidates.

- It will get easier as you learn the funding field in your area.

- We rarely suggest to faculty members that we pursue a foundation; good matches are less likely compared to state or federal sources.

PIVOT (Previously COS)

Link: http://pivot.cos.com

How we use them: We find the weekly alerts very useful. We set up multiple searches by topic area and read the alerts for new announcements. PIVOT offers a comprehensive and fast way to generate a prospect list.

Foundation Center

Link: http://foundationcenter.org/

How we use it: This site has a free portion and a subscription-only portion. The free portion will allow you to look up a specific foundation and view the 990 tax returns. Toward the end of the 990 is a list of grant awards. We usually print this section (or a portion of it) and see what we can learn. Of interest is information like the following:

- What size of award is typical?

- Do they give to any universities?

- Do they give to only big-name places like the United Way and Boys & Girls Clubs?

- Do they give in our state?

Note that these questions can be answered quickly using the subscription-only portion of the Foundation Center database or Foundation Search America (see its URL below). The graphs are generated from 990 data, so they have done the looking already and turned it into a useful interface.

The subscription portion will also allow you to search foundation awards using keywords, geographical limitations, and the like. This is useful for generating a prospect list and offers some utility for narrowing a prospect list.

Foundation Search America

Link: http://www.foundationsearch.com/

How we use it: Once we have a list of prospects (generated through either COS/PIVOT or the Foundation Center), we use this site to narrow those prospects. Specifically, we look up individual foundations and use the graphing options to investigate giving history. Things we look for here include questions such as the following:

- Do they give in our state, and if so where did those awards go?
- Are they giving out new awards, or do they fund only existing grantees?
- Has there been a big drop-off or increase in giving over the past few years?

A second use of this site is to generate a list of prospects by looking at the foundations that have given money to our state in broad categories. The categories here are quite broad, though—we generally find the Foundation Center search more useful for this purpose.

Grants.gov

Link: http://www.grants.gov

How we use it: We use Grants.gov to download the required electronic application packages for specific grant programs to which we have decided to apply. We find the search functions here almost, but not quite totally, useless. The ability to track a particular funding opportunity is useful since Grants.gov often receives revisions to funding opportunities before any of the other subscription services.

Prewriting Questions

Developing a successful grant proposal requires coordination and tenacity. The first step in this process is to think through the project carefully and at some level of detail. The prewriting questions below will help with that process.

Problem Statement/Need for Funds

- What is the problem that will be addressed by your program/research/ technology? What is the need for this project?

- What are the target audiences/populations that will benefit from your project? (Include information about geographic locations of target populations, numbers of employers and employees, and so on.)

- What are the existing or potential barriers that have prevented current programs/technology from addressing the need that your project will address?

- If this is a technology transfer or development proposal, what is the current technology and why would yours be better? What competitors exist? How and why is your technology better than what is currently being used?

- If this is a training grant, list the types of training and methods this project will use and the topics to be covered. Explain why or how these methods and topics were chosen.

- How many months or years will be needed to fully develop this project? How much funding will be needed to fully implement this project?

- What, if any, additional funding will be needed (and from where) once the requested grant funding ends?

Administrative, Department, and Program Capability

- Describe your group's functions and activities. (Include an organizational chart of your organization.) Do you have a mission statement? If so, what is the mission statement?

- Within the last five years, has your group conducted any program, research, or project funded by federal, state, or city grant monies?

- If so, answer the following questions:

  - What entity sponsored each project?

  - What was the dollar amount of each grant?

Program Experience

- What is your group's experience with the type of work proposed? (If you were funded by a training grant, who and how many were trained?)

- What is your group's experience with the topic and subtopics targeted for this proposal?

- Does the group have experience with topics, populations, or research that are similar those targeted for this proposal?

Project Team Experience

- What are the qualifications of the professional staff that will carry out the proposed program or project?

- For new positions that will be created for this project, provide a statement of minimum hiring qualifications and position description.

Work/Research Plan

Work Plan Overview

- Will new research materials be developed with this program? If so, how will they be developed and produced? If not, will existing materials be used, and how?

- What work will be accomplished, and how much time will be needed to complete this work?

- Will members of a target population be recruited for the project? If so, how and when? Has IRB approval been requested or received?

- Where and how will the planned work take place?

- What are the anticipated benefits (if any) for members of the target population who participate in the project?

- Will any technical assistance be offered to the target population?

- How will the impact of the proposed work be assessed?

- What sort of future capacity-building activities for this project are planned or anticipated?

Work Plan Activities

- What specific activities/steps/tasks are needed to implement the proposed project?

- For each activity, what steps will be conducted and who will do those?

- When will each activity be done and what will be the anticipated result of the activity?
- If this is a training grant:
  - What subjects will be taught?
  - How many trainees per class?
  - How many hours per course and what will be the location of the training?
- If this is a technology development grant, what will be the proof of concept?
- If this is a research grant, what research questions will be answered?
- What facilities and resources are needed for this project?
- Where will this project be conducted?

Work Plan Quarterly Projections (Jan–Mar, Apr–Jun, Jul–Sep, Oct–Dec)

- If this is a training grant:
  - About how many technical assistance sessions will be provided per calendar quarter?
  - About how many classes will be conducted per calendar quarter?
  - About how many employers and/or employees will be trained per quarter?
  - About how many trainee contact hours will occur per quarter?
- What methodology did you use to develop your projections?
- What are the total work plan activity items for a whole year?

Materials

- Will new materials be developed for the proposed project? If so, what type of material (flyers, poster, training manuals)?
- What is the timetable for developing and producing the new material?
- If no new materials will be developed, what previously developed material will be used? Will this material need to be approved by the sponsor?

Evaluations

- How will training sessions be assessed?
- How will learning be assessed?

- How will training impact be assessed?

- How will quarterly reports be developed?

- How will final and annual reports be developed?

- If the group is seeking funding for multiple years, how many total years will funding be needed?

- How will the program be funded once grant funding has ended?

Section 2
Managing the Proposal Work

Planning for Proposal Development

Many tasks must engage the investigators and all others who contribute, and staying organized and productive under the stress of unrelenting deadlines is challenging. There are a variety of models for successful proposal submission. The most important ingredient is a team approach in which all involved are contributing their strengths, knowledge, and talents in a coordinated fashion. Building effective and efficient teams also takes time and requires a lot of communication. The "Proposal Development Tasks Discussion Checklist" (Table 8) can be used to clarify responsibilities either for general, default processes within a department or center or for preparation of a particular proposal.

If you have attended a regional conference of the National Science Foundation, you will recognize "ask early, ask often" as the mantra of NSF personnel repeatedly urging principal investigators to touch base with agency personnel as proposals are prepared. This is good advice and applies to many, many sponsors. The documents that follow will help you prepare for these conversations.

- When you e-mail a program officer to request a phone appointment, it is a good idea to send a concept paper with this e-mail, and the advice that follows in "Developing a Concept Paper" will help you develop this document.

- When you place your call, probably the first thing after you introduce yourself will be to give your elevator pitch to succinctly remind the program officer of your project. The prompts in "Four Sentences to Focus Your Elevator Pitch" can help you develop your elevator pitch if you are having troubling boiling your idea down to just a few sentences.

- Finally, the points in "Contacting a Program Officer" should help you to focus the purpose of your call and plan to get the most out of it.

TABLE 8

Proposal Development Tasks Discussion Checklist

Timeline	Tasks	PI	GWC	Dept/Ctr	Division
Several months before the deadline	• Identify departments involved. • Register with sponsor and/or e-system. • Develop and write concept paper. • Contact sponsor's program officer. • Request grant writing assistance. • Identify appropriate department and division (dept/ctr and division) grants personnel. • Inform the PI about dept/div and institutional procedural requirements. • Ensure PI is aware of assistance available from dept/div personnel. • Inform dept/div personnel of intent to submit a proposal and provide guidelines or funding opportunity number. • Communicate regarding dept/div procedures related to proposal submission. • If limited submission, ensure internal procedures are followed and approval to submit is secured. • Investigate funding program (priorities, tone, funding history, strategic match, etc.) • Read guidelines for Eligibility Required sections and content Review criteria F&A limits Budget limits Terms requiring legal review Letters of support/commitment • Create proposal timeline. • Clarify applicable F&A rate(s) with sponsored programs office.				

TABLE 8

Timeline	Tasks	PI	GWC	Dept/Ctr	Division
Several times before submission	• Read the guidelines for 　Priority funding areas 　Submission requirements 　Budget requirements and limits 　Formatting requirements and page limits 　Required narrative sections and content 　Documents/sections required besides narrative 　Letters of support/commitment 　Appendices/optional submission materials 　Legal language requiring signature 　Potential problem areas • Communicate with program officer. • Identify and engage collaborators. • Construct and review draft documents: 　Abstract 　Narrative 　Budget narrative 　Project timeline 　Figures and tables • Communicate as needed with sponsored programs office regarding procedures. • Communicate regarding specific departmental requirements for budget or other. • Communicate regarding specific school/college requirements for budget or other. • Draft budget with PI and/or grant writing consultant. • Track requests for collection of text and other documents. • Review and edit drafts to align with guidelines: review criteria and background knowledge of the funding program.				

(Continued)

TABLE 8

(Continued)

Timeline	Tasks	PI	GWC	Dept/Ctr	Division
2–4 months before deadline	• Make a list of areas of possible concern. • Draft, request, and collect letters of support/ commitment. • Draft figures and tables. • Identify key personnel. • Identify colleagues for friendly review. • Generate complete draft proposal for friendly review. • Coordinate getting materials to and from friendly reviewer(s). • Review and edit draft to align with guidelines: review criteria and background knowledge of the funding program.				
1–2 months before deadline	• Finalize other required documents (e.g., biosketches, facilities, current and pending support). • Itemize friendly review suggestions into a checklist. • Do more drafts. • Respond to suggestions from friendly review. • Establish shared credit distribution. • Review and edit draft to align with guidelines: review criteria and background knowledge of the funding program.				
2–4 weeks before deadline	• Provide dept/div grants people with information for grants database, including mailing instructions, guidelines, abstract, budget, shared credit information, and budget justification. • Enter proposal into the grants database, obtaining other departments' information as needed.				
1–3 weeks before deadline	• Coordinate preparation of e-submission package. • Proof complete proposal package. • Collect internal approval signatures. • Collect financial disclosure forms for key personnel if sponsor is NIH or NSF.				
10 days before deadline	• Complete any departmental review processes. • Submit complete package to division for approval.				

TABLE 8

Timeline	Tasks	PI	GWC	Dept/Ctr	Division
3–7 days before deadline	• Finalize/proof complete proposal package: Check content and placement of figures. Check pagination. Check special characters in the text. Check printing of color content in black and white. Check institutional information. Make sure the internal and proposal budgets and justifications are the same. Check numbering of references. Write out any special instructions for sponsored programs office. Request tracking number for hard copy proposals. • If the proposal is to be submitted in hard copy, assemble the proposal. • If proposal is to be submitted electronically: Make sure all the required fields are completed. Check to see that all required files are named correctly and are in the right format (PDF, Word, or whatever is required). • Make copies for the agency (if hard copy), sponsored programs office, department personnel, PI, co-investigators, and grant writing consultant. • Communicate review approval to PI and grant writing consultant.				
Five days before it must be shipped or e-submitted	• Submit the proposal to sponsored programs office: Internal approval signatures Proposal (copies for sponsor and sponsored programs office) Internal budget Guidelines Subcontract information, if applicable				
After submission	• Track delivery of hard copy proposal. • Track successful submission of electronic proposal via agency website. • Follow-up e-mails and communication with program officer. • Complete compliance activities (IRB, etc.).				

PI–Principal Investigator/Project Director; GWC–Grant Writing Consultant; Dept/Ctr–Department or Center Communicating with Program Officers

Developing a Concept Paper

Organize your thoughts for productive discussion with a program official. This should be 1–3 pages in length. The following is taken directly from a National Institutes of Health document providing guidance for concept papers (NIH, National Institute on Drug Abuse, 2007):

- **Grant Purpose.** Briefly, relate the type of mechanism (R01/R03/R43 etc.), amount and duration of the grant, and which institutes/centers/agencies you think might be interested in funding your project.

- **Problem and Significance.** Explain why the literature/your research leads you to think this topic needs study. Relate the payoff to science AND to public health. Mention what makes your project unique and innovative, especially in light of any similar projects identified in RePORT and the refereed literature.

- **Question.** Derived from the scientific literature, describe the theories and model(s) that will guide your hypotheses, and specify what hypotheses you will test.

- **Design and Analysis.** Describe the population (age range, gender, race, selective characteristics), interventions, controls, measures, etc., that will enable testing your hypotheses. Estimate the required sample and power (N, levels of analysis). Justify the statistical approach that will ensure a fair test of your hypotheses.

- **Team and Logistics.** Indicate how your career stage, expertise, and experience qualify you to lead a project of the size, scope, and technology proposed. Name key collaborators (co-investigators, consultants, and organizations) who will help the project succeed. Mention the organizations whose cooperation you will need to access subjects/data/equipment/field sites, and indicate any people or organizations who have agreed in writing to participate/support the project.

- **Urgency.** If you are trying to initiate work within a time-sensitive window, indicate the scientific and public health justification for an early award and the consequences of a delayed award.

Four Sentences to Focus Your Elevator Pitch

Define a problem

For example: Our grant writing consultants have been shearing alpacas for four hours every Tuesday afternoon since the beginning of the fall semester.

Explain why this is a problem

For example: Shearing alpacas is inherently unproductive, taking valuable time away from faculty-student contact, publication, service, and research activities, and making the alpacas cold in the winter months.

What is a possible solution to the problem?

For example: I will create and evaluate a 12-step counseling program to help grant writing consultants recover from their addiction to shearing alpacas.

How could the research be conducted?

For example: I will survey a representative sample of students, faculty members, and administrators in our department, conduct qualitative interviews, and use observational techniques.

Contacting a Program Officer

Why Talk to a Program Officer?

- To confirm that your application fits the program

- To assess the level of enthusiasm about your research and discuss potential topics

- To ask about funding opportunities

- To help you decide which grant type or program is appropriate for you

- To seek advice on preparing an application

- To ask about compliance issues

- To ask about investigator-initiated research:

    - Topics of interest

    - New scientific directions

    - Existing and new priorities that do not yet have published funding opportunities

- To find out if there are any relevant programs in another part of the agency

- To find out about requesting assignment to a specific review panel or agency program

- After your proposal has been reviewed:

    - To answer any questions about the review or summary

    - To get insights into the discussion of your application at the peer review meeting

    - If you did not receive a fundable score, to figure out how much to revise before resubmitting

    - If the funding decision on your application is deferred until later in the fiscal year, to stay in touch and check on its status

    - To clarify the agency codes on your review

    - If reviewers seem to disagree, to find out which was the stronger feeling in the room

(NIH, National Institute of Allergy and Infectious Diseases, 2011a)

Best Practices for Contacting a Program Officer

- Be courteous and professional at all times.

- Make an appointment at your mutual convenience.

- Know the role of program officers at that particular agency. Do not ask them to go where they cannot go.

- Be concrete and specific.

- Develop a concept paper and send it to the program officer before the meeting.

- Be on time and be prepared.

- Have someone else listen in on the conversation and take notes.

- After you meet in person or by phone or correspond by e-mail, send an e-mail thank-you to the program officer with an indication of the next steps you plan to take.

Sample Questions for the Program Officer

- Do you feel this concept paper is appropriate for the funding opportunity?

- Do you have alternate recommendations for data sources?

- How much preliminary data do I need?

- Do you have recommendations for refining my aims/objectives?

- Do you have a recommendation about an appropriate review panel or agency program for my application?

- What areas are you interested in funding?

- Should I contact you again before submitting my application?

- Do you have any other recommendations?

Managing Proposal Development

The three sample proposal development timelines that follow ("Narrative Timeline for Proposal Development," Table 9: Timeline for Proposal Development: National Science Foundation, and Table 10: Proposal Timeline: Engineering Information Foundation) show different format options, timeframes, and types of proposals. Formatting options are to some extent a matter of taste but also reflect the complexity of a given proposal or project team. The more people, the more details you will need in order to keep everyone on the same page as to who is responsible for which parts of the proposal by what deadlines. The tasks we list overlap somewhat from one proposal to the next, but the differences may help you identify and anticipate tasks that apply to your own proposals.

Finally, we include a sample of the kind of table that we typically use to track the materials for a given proposal (Table 11: Materials Tracking Table). Note that we have codes built into the table for tracking our requests, drafts, proofing—all the stages that each document will go through as it is finalized for inclusion in the proposal.

Narrative Timeline for Proposal Development

May 15	Finalize written vision and mission statements for the center as a whole and the South African part of the center. SharePoint site, including all key investigators, is set up.
June 1	Finalize organizational chart, attaching names to each item. Finalize partners to be included in the center.
June 15	Determine what research subprojects and cores will comprise the grant. Determine theme of center. Finalize process for selecting pilot projects. Finalize training plans. Detail administrative structure. Notify key investigators and core leaders.
	Center director, along with co-investigators, meets with partners. Inform them if cost match commitments will be needed. Meet with appropriate administrative personnel to inform them of this activity and to obtain space commitment and resource commitments for the center.
June 21	All investigators submit the following to the grant writing consultant:

- Biographical sketch

- Resources form

- A paragraph or so summarizing each investigator's strength and experience, to be used in the overview narrative

- Financial disclosure form

PI and co-investigators provide evidence of substantive departmental and institutional support and "umbrella" resources forms for the two lead institutions.

July 1	Compliance language completed:

- Inclusion of women, children, and minorities

- IRB and/or animal use approvals

- Biohazards

- Intellectual property

Investigators return corrected biographical sketches to the grant writing consultant.

July 15   Complete (though not necessarily polished) drafts of subproject and core narratives and budgets due to the grant writing consultant.

PI assigns each research project a number (I, II, III) and each core unit a capital letter (A, B, C). These designations should not change as the grant is built. The number and letter assignment will reflect the order in which the research projects and core units are presented in the application research plan.

The grant writing consultant returns biosketches and resources forms to investigators to proof.

July 21   Complete draft of center proposal posted for development of synergies across projects and cores. This draft also includes the first draft of the narrative for the umbrella sections:

The Main Body of the Application. The introduction should concisely present the proposed research strategy, including background information leading to the request for program project support, a description of the aims of the program project, benefits to be achieved by funding as a program project grant, special program resources, and overview descriptions of activities and functions of each core unit and subunit, emphasizing areas of coordination.

Organization and Administrative Structure. (No specific instructions in PHS 398.) Describe in detail and by diagram, if appropriate, the chain of responsibility for decision making and administration, beginning at the level of principal investigator. Indicate investigators responsible for individual projects and how the projects are planned, coordinated, and evaluated. Describe roles of advisory groups of local or outside consultants. Describe relationships between the center and other research, academic, and administrative units of the institutions, such as centers, institutes, departments, and central administration.

August 1   All investigators provide feedback on/revisions of proposal draft to the PI and the grant writing consultant for multidisciplinary approach, responsiveness to agency areas of emphasis, innovation and significance, synergy, etc.

Final budgets, budget narratives, cost match commitments, and subcontract agreements due to the PI and the grant writing consultant.

August 7   Complete draft of total proposal—narrative, budgets, budget justifications, bios, resources, letters of support and commitment, abstract for overall center—posted for review by all investigators.

Budgets and narratives submitted to divisional grants office for review.

Required number of copies of appendix materials due to the grant writing consultant. Every page should be labeled in upper right-hand corner with the PI's last name, first name, and middle initial.

August 15   Final comments on draft proposal due to the PI and the grant writing consultant.

Center key-personnel list prepared.

Finalize table of Use of Core Units by Component Research Projects.

Face Page prepared.

Cost match request application is turned in to Office of Research.

August 21   Final revisions incorporated into proposal.

Proposal is paginated and table of contents is finalized.

Complete Checklist page.

Enter proposal into internal grants system and solicit required signatures.

August 25   Application materials submitted to sponsored programs office.

TABLE 9

Timeline for Proposal Development: National Science Foundation

National Science Foundation Transforming Undergraduate Education in Science, Technology, Engineering and Mathematics (TUES) (formerly CCLI); Type Two Proposal

> TUES Program page: http://www.nsf.gov/funding/pgm_summ.jsp?pims_id=5741
> Guidelines: http://www.nsf.gov/publications/pub_summ.jsp?WT.z_pims_id=5741&ods_key=nsf10544
> NSF Grant Proposal Guide: http://www.nsf.gov/publications/pub_summ.jsp?ods_key=gpg
> NSF FastLane: https://www.fastlane.nsf.gov/fastlane.jsp
> MU Review Deadline: January 7, 2011; Sponsor Proposal Submission Deadline: January 14, 2011

Item	Responsible person(s)	Date	Status
Initial budget meeting		Aug. 4	Done
Create timeline (including proposal requirements list)		Aug. 16	Done
Sponsored programs office notified of intent to submit		Aug. 16	
Revise timeline		Sept. 3	Done
Identify partner institutions		Sept. 17	
Initial budget draft completed		Sept. 22	
Draft scope of work, letters of commitment for partner institutions, and institutional endorsement; send drafts to partner institutions for initial review and feedback		Sept. 27	
Second budget draft completed		Nov. 1	
Final copies of scope of work, letters of commitment for partner institutions, and institutional endorsement; send to partner institutions for official completion		Nov. 1	
Official letters of commitment due from partner institutions; institutional endorsement due		Nov. 17	
Obtain letter from department chairs indicating cost match commitments		Nov. 17	
First draft of project narrative, budget narrative, summary, references, facilities, and supplementary documentation due; circulate summary/narrative for feedback		Nov. 29	
Submit campus cost match proposal		Dec. 2	
Request CVs from senior personnel, including PIs at partner institutions, to create biosketches, etc.		Dec. 2	
Feedback on summary/narrative due		Dec. 8	
Biosketches completed		Dec. 20	
Final budget completed		Dec. 20	

TABLE 9

Item	Responsible person(s)	Date	Status
Request information for entering proposal in internal grant system		Dec. 20	
Conflict of Interest forms due		Dec. 22	
Collect internal approval signatures		Dec. 27	
Finalize all proposal parts; submit to divisional grants offices; upload proposal to NSF Fastlane system		Jan. 7	
Transmit completed application to sponsored programs office for review		Jan. 7–11	
Submitted electronically through NSF Fastlane		Jan. 11–14	

TABLE 10

Proposal Timeline: Engineering Information Foundation

Women in Engineering Program
   URL: http://www.eifgrants.org/info/index.html
   Deadline Date to Sponsored Programs: February 20, 2012
   Deadline Date to EIF: February 28, 2012
   Mailing address and contact information:
      180 West 80th Street, Suite 207
      New York, NY 10024–6301
      (212) 579–7596
      (212) 579–7517 fax
      info@eifgrants.org

Due date	Item or activity	Responsible party/parties
F, Jan 6	Arrange for friendly review by a colleague for January 26–31	PI
F, Jan 6	Request statements of qualifications and experience from all key personnel	Grant Writing Consultant
F, Jan 6	Request IRS determination letter regarding tax status from sponsored programs office	Grant Writing Consultant
F, Jan 6	Download financial statements from campus website	Grant Writing Consultant
F, Jan 6	Draft letters of commitment (if applicable) and send out	Grant Writing Consultant
M, Jan 9	DRAFT due of Project Description (Problem Statement, Goals and Objectives, Approach, and Summary)	PI
F, Jan 13	Key personnel statements due to the GWC	All key personnel
M, Jan 16	DRAFT Work Plan due	PI
W, Jan 18	DRAFT Directors and Key Personnel sections due	PI, Grant Writing Consultant
F, Jan 20	DRAFT Budget and Budget Justification due	PI, Grant Writing Consultant
T, Jan 24	Letters of commitment due to grant writing consultant	Supporters
T, Jan 24	DRAFT Cover Letter due	Grant Writing Consultant
R, Jan 26	Send draft to peer reviewer	PI
T, Jan 31	Review comments due	Peer Reviewer
T, Feb 7	Budget and Budget Justification finalized—NO MORE CHANGES	PI, Grant Writing Consultant
W, Feb 8	Enter proposal in local grant system	Grant Writing Consultant
R, Feb 9	Collect approval signatures and financial disclosure forms	Grant Writing Consultant
W, Feb 15	IRS determination letter and financial statements due	Sponsored Programs

TABLE 10

Due date	Item or activity	Responsible party/parties
W, Feb 15	All documents and sections due for final formatting:	
	• Cover letter	PI
	• Project Description	PI
	• Work Plan	PI
	• Directors and Key Personnel	PI, Grant Writing Consultant
	• Financial Statements and Sources of Support	Grant Writing Consultant, Sponsored Programs
	• Tax Status letter	Grant Writing Consultant, Sponsored Programs
W, Feb 15	All signatures and financial disclosure statements due	Grant Writing Consultant
F, Feb 17	Combine and paginate application package	Grant Writing Consultant
M, Feb 20	Complete package due to sponsored programs office for review	Grant Writing Consultant
M, Feb 27	Deadline for submission via mail to EIF	Sponsored Programs
T, Feb 28	EIF submission receipt deadline	

TABLE 11

Materials Tracking Table

Project title	
Agency	

R = Requested, I = Information received, F = Formatted, P = Sent back for proofing, C = Complete

Institution	Name	CV/ Bio	Current & completed	Research description	Financial disclosure	Trainees	Other	Capacity	Effort	Shared credit

Section 3

Developing Your Proposal

Proposal Logic

Chapter 8 describes the logical argument that lies at the core of any grant proposal (see "Proposal Logic" section). Reviewers expect to be convinced of the broad importance of the central need or problem to be served by the project, the validity of the proposed approach to addressing this need, the objectives that will be accomplished during the term of the project toward addressing the overall goal and need, the strategies for accomplishing those objectives, and the results of the project. These results must then be tied back to the progress they represent toward the overall goal, for solving the original need or problem.

The agency's forms, the specified content, the formatting requirements, the work of coordinating efforts of other team members—the many concerns of proposal development can make it easy to get distracted from the core argument that holds all the pieces together for the reader. We have found the following worksheet, "Moving from the Larger Context to the Details," to be a quick way to lay out the skeleton of a project's logic to guide the more detailed writing.

Moving from the Larger Context to the Details

The Research Goal:

Feasibility and Timeliness:

Aims/Objectives:

  1.

  2.

  3.

Methods/Tasks:

  1.

  2.

  3.

  4.

  5.

  6.

  7.

  8.

  9.

10.

Results:

Benefit:

Proposal Outlines

As explained in Chapter 5, it can be cumbersome to try to compose a proposal, all the while paging back and forth to various sections of the sponsor guidelines to be sure that all of the sponsor's requirements and priorities are addressed. Generating a proposal outline such as the one that follows for a proposal to the Engineering Information Foundation can pull all that information into a single document that makes it much easier for you to assign sections of the proposal to members of your team.

Sample Proposal Outline: Engineering Information Foundation

All text indicated as general guidelines, program guidelines, and review criteria below were taken directly from the Engineering Information Foundation website: http://www.eifgrants.org/info/apply.html.

Women in Engineering Program
<General guidelines> First page—Cover letter on the organization's letterhead
    <<NEW PAGE>>

Proposal Title
<General guidelines> Suggested proposal length is three (3) pages, but this is not a requirement.

  A. Problem Statement <General guidelines>

    <Review criteria> An overview of the problem (the statement of the problem should go beyond a listing of the numbers and percentages of women in engineering and engineering prerequisites to address what is behind those numbers).

    A.1. Significance

      <General guidelines> Make a case for why this problem is significant.

    A.2. Related Work in the Field

      <Review criteria> Summarize related work in the field, including similar programs that have been implemented and any impact that has been made.

    A.3. Fit with EIF Fields of Interest

      <General guidelines> Grants are awarded based on a good fit with EIF's fields of interest.

B. Goals and Objectives

<General guidelines> Potential to contribute to what is known about furthering the goals of the program area.

<Review criteria> A listing of program goals and objectives.

<Review criteria> Proposals should include how the program would contribute to the knowledge base of what works and what doesn't in increasing the numbers of women in engineering.

<Program guidelines> <u>EIF goals and questions for the Women in Engineering program area</u>:

> We want to encourage middle-school-aged girls to pursue engineering degrees. We think that the negative effects of gender-related behavior in the classroom ought to be eliminated. Women fail to pursue careers in engineering, and of those who do, the retention rate is unacceptably low. How can we change this? Do you have a project that addresses this problem?

<Program guidelines> Program areas of interest:

1. **Programs to encourage middle school girls in engineering conducted by engineering educators and others that encourage them to prepare for and undertake careers in engineering.** The Foundation is particularly interested in new programs or modules, which, if they are found to be effective, will be continued within the applying institution(s). These programs supported by the Foundation are expected to test their effectiveness, to examine program impact on participant educational and career plans and on their SMET participation and achievement.

2. **Programs designed to improve the retention rate of undergraduate women in engineering.** These may cover such diverse areas as classroom, climate, learning behaviors, classroom pedagogies, and academic and social support programs. It is expected that the programs will examine their impact on SMET achievement.

C. Approach

<General guidelines> Why is the approach recommended the best one to solve it?

C.1. Proposed Activities

C.2. Program Evaluation

> <Review criteria> An evaluation plan that makes explicit how the impact of the project on participants will be tested.

C.3. **Sustainability**

<General guidelines> Potential for continuing past the funding period.

<Review criteria> A plan for continuing the program after the funding period.

D. **Summary**

<General guidelines> Overall quality of the project, including its chances to be successfully implemented.

<<NEW PAGE>>

Supporting Information

Budget <General guidelines> No overhead is allowed.

<General guidelines> We tend to support smaller projects.

<Program guidelines> **Middle School Girls**—$5,000–$15,000 per year for up to three years.

<Program guidelines> **Undergraduate Women**—$5,000–$25,000 per year.

<<NEW PAGE>>

Work Plan <General guidelines> Potential for continuing past the funding period.

<Review criteria> A statement of work tasks to be accomplished, including a timeline and a management plan.

<<NEW PAGE>>

Directors and Key Personnel <General guidelines> List of directors of the organization and key personnel.

<Review criteria> A listing of staff qualifications.

<<NEW PAGE>>

Financial Statements and Sources of Support

<<NEW PAGE>>

Tax Status <General guidelines> IRS determination letter.

Evaluation

Project evaluation can be tricky. To thoroughly evaluate a given project would often mean initiating a separate research project. On the other hand, to limit the evaluation effort and budget too much can yield token effort that does not produce useful information. The sample evaluation questions that follow illustrate several points. First, evaluation can be structured around research questions or hypotheses, just as the rest of the project is. The lists of questions address the need to report to most sponsors on the implementation process as well as monitoring the actual products of a given project. The focus group questions address a typical sponsor concern related to projects that involve people: securing stakeholder input. Finally, sponsors are often concerned with formative and summative evaluations, and are sometimes also interested in any grantee plans for impact evaluation.

Although the "Sample Evaluation Questions" list that follows provides a useful model of one approach to planning for the evaluation of your project, there are certainly other options. Some sponsors, for example, require logic models that include evaluation strategies. Research proposals usually incorporate evaluation strategies into the methods sections under such headings as "Expected Results." Regardless of how or where in your proposal you present your evaluation strategies, we hope that the model that follows will help you think about the kinds of questions that would be relevant to your particular project.

Sample Evaluation Questions

Formative Evaluation Questions

- Are activities being completed according to the project timeline?
- Are the data sources adequate to measure the objectives?
- Will the numbers of participants/subjects/repetitions be sufficient to provide reliable and valid data? Are project personnel meeting expectations in this area?
- Is the data being collected, recorded, and analyzed accurately?
- Have project personnel been adequately trained to perform the work?
- Are project personnel following all compliance protocols?
- Are project resources being utilized as proposed?
- Are any problems being identified and adequately corrected?

- Is communication among project personnel enhancing or degrading activities?
- Are subcontractors/project partners performing assigned duties adequately?
- Are preliminary project results meeting expectations?
- Are funds being monitored and spent appropriately?
- Are all sponsor reports/requirements being completed?
- Are project personnel participating in appropriate dissemination activities?
- Are all stakeholders being adequately informed about project progress?

Summative Evaluation Questions

- Have all activities been completed according to expectations? Were all objectives met as proposed?
- Have all data been adequately collected, recorded, and analyzed?
- Did problems/obstacles surface which prevented results from meeting expectations?
- Did surprises surface which enhanced or degraded project activities?
- Have all project outputs and deliverables been completed as proposed?
- Were all funds spent appropriately? Were all compliance protocols followed?
- Have all sponsor reports/requirements been fulfilled?
- Are project personnel continuing to disseminate results?
- Have all stakeholders been adequately informed about the project?
- Are the project's short-term outcomes being sustained?
- Do the project's conclusions reinforce or contrast with similar conclusions from previous research?
- Did the project make advancements toward meeting the goal?
- Were future collaborations enhanced through communication with project partners? Did project partners fulfill expectations?
- Was the budget adequate to complete all project activities?
- Has the project enhanced the future funding competitiveness of project personnel?

- Are project activities able to be replicated by researchers in other locations?

- Are project results generalizable to other fields of study?

Impact Evaluation Questions

- Has the project made contributions to the field of study?

- What impacts may occur because of project activities?

- Are the project's long-term outcomes sustainable? What steps should be taken to sustain/enhance these outcomes? In what ways could these long-term outcomes be measured?

- Have new areas of research or activity been exposed by project results? What potential new stakeholders may be interested in project results or activities?

- What changes are anticipated to the field of study or to society in general?

Budget Justification

The sample budget justification that follows is provided to help give you an idea as to the level of detail that should be provided to allow reviewers to understand your numbers and to provide a sample of a readable format for this part of the proposal.

Budget Justification for Terrytoons University

Note: All costs are increased 3 percent per year to account for inflation.

Personnel

Dr. Phlapyer Wings (2 calendar months' effort per year) is the **Director of the My-T Mouse Center**. He has extensive experience with generating knockout mice and developed the Zymogwin procedure which is used world-wide for transilectomies. He has published prolifically on the development of sharwings and ebbernoodles. Dr. Wings collaborates with ornithologists, zoologists, and educators on projects related to mammalian flight. He will be directly responsible for statistical analyses of data collected in experiments in aims 1, 3, and 4. He will coordinate the work done at Terrytoons University, the subcontracted work done at Unique University, and the Cores. He will also be responsible for writing all progress reports and supervising the postdoctoral fellow. ($120,000/year base salary × 2/12 = $20,000 per year)

Dr. Pearl Pureheart, Postdoctoral Fellow (12 calendar months' effort per year) has been a part of the Wings lab for two years, bringing experience with the Maximowz procedure as well as extensive work with anthropomorphism. Dr. Pureheart will perform the gene replacement regimen and other experiments for Aims 1 and 3 as well as assisting with data management. She will also supervise the undergraduate student researchers. ($40,000/year base salary × 12/12 = $40,000 per year)

Two Undergraduate Student Researchers (1 calendar month effort each per year) will assist with basic lab procedures and preparing mice for surgery. ($10/hr. × 175 hours × 2 students = $3,500 per year)

TABLE 12

Total Personnel Costs

Year 1 Request	Year 1 Cost Match	Year 2 Request	Year 2 Cost Match	Year 3 Request	Year 3 Cost Match

Fringe Benefits

Fringe benefits are calculated at the University's federally negotiated rate of 30 percent for full-time employees. No fringe benefits are calculated for the undergraduate student researchers.

TABLE 13

Total Fringe Benefits Costs

Year 1 Request	Year 1 Cost Match	Year 2 Request	Year 2 Cost Match	Year 3 Request	Year 3 Cost Match

Equipment

A Flimsadiddle microscope will be purchased in Year 1 for use in the insertion phase of the Maximowz procedure. A quote of $11,200 for this microscope is attached. Having this microscope in the Wings lab relieves the team from paying fees to use the Biochemistry Department's microscope which would add more than $8,000 in fees over the course of the project. As this equipment would be used for other projects as well, the University will fund half of the cost, requesting only $5,600.

TABLE 14

Total Equipment Costs

Year 1 Request	Year 1 Cost Match	Year 2 Request	Year 2 Cost Match	Year 3 Request	Year 3 Cost Match

Travel

Collaboration travel funds: Funds are requested for the PI and Postdoctoral Fellow to coordinate research efforts with the team at Unique University in Iowa. This subcontract team will be responsible for Aim 2 in Years 2 and 3 of the project. Two 2-day trips a year are planned for Years 2 and 3 (600 miles per round trip $\times$ $0.525/mile $\times$ 2 trips; 2 hotel rooms $\times$ $100 per night $\times$ 1 night $\times$ 2 trips; $42 per diem $\times$ 2 days $\times$ 2 people $\times$ 2 trips) for a total request of $1,366 per year for Years 2 and 3.

Travel to scientific conferences: Funds are requested to support participation in the US Knockout Science Conference where research results from this project will be presented. Estimated costs for a three-day trip to this conference include $800 for airfare, $42 per diem, $100/night for lodging, $50 for ground transportation, and $300 for conference registration ($1,476 per year).

TABLE 15

Total Travel Costs

Year 1 Request	Year 1 Cost Match	Year 2 Request	Year 2 Cost Match	Year 3 Request	Year 3 Cost Match

---

Materials and Supplies

Two **Mouse Landing Strips** with safety stripes, computer interface, and software will be purchased to monitor the distance traveled for each flight. These landing strips also measure food consumed per day and directly upload results to the computer. A quote for these strips is attached ($1,200 each, or $2,400 total in Year 1 only).

Five enzyme kits are required each year to perform the Maximowz procedure. At $850/kit, this is $4,250/year. Fluorescent antibodies will be utilized for the mouse dance procedures. Only half the mice will be subjected to this procedure. At $30/mouse for 180 mice, antibodies will cost $5,400/year.

Disposables (plasticware, gloves, reagents, etc.) are estimated to cost $3,500/year. Laboratory chemicals will cost about $5,000/year.

TABLE 16

Total Materials and Supplies Costs

Year 1 Request	Year 1 Cost Match	Year 2 Request	Year 2 Cost Match	Year 3 Request	Year 3 Cost Match

Subcontract with Unique University

A subcontract to Unique University will be required in Years 2 and 3 for the analysis of the sentient mouse hyperation in Aim 2. The Unique team has the expertise and equipment required to do this portion of the work. The PI and Postdoc will visit with the Unique team twice a year to coordinate processes and results.

Subcontract Personnel Dr. X. Ray Vision (0.5 calendar month effort per year) will serve as the PI for Unique University's portion of work. He has extensive experience in hyperation analysis as well as serving as an expert on flight simulation with Marvelizing Filmation. He will oversee the Graduate Research Assistant as well as provide expertise for the mouse dance procedures being done at Terrytoons University. ($60,000/year base salary $\times$ 0.5/12 = $2,500 for Years 2 and 3)

A **Graduate Research Assistant** (3 calendar months' effort per year) will perform the lab work required for the hyperation analysis including the use of the Hanns-Downe dance simulator. ($30,000/year base salary $\times$ 3/12 = $7,500 for Years 2 and 3)

Subcontract Fringe Benefits Fringe benefits are calculated at Unique University's federally negotiated rate of 35 percent for full-time employees. Medical insurance is provided to the GRA for $1,227.50 per year. Tuition is also provided for the GRA and is listed under Other Direct Costs.

Subcontract Materials and Supplies Hyperation analysis requires the use of four Haydonical Ablation Kits each year at a cost of $502.25 each ($2,009 total per year). Chemicals, plasticware, and reagents will cost about $3,100 in Years 2 and 3.

In addition, in Year 3, 200 hyperation instellagatory blankets are required for the final step of the analysis at a cost of $13 each, totaling $2,600.

Subcontract Other Direct Costs Tuition fees for the Graduate Research Assistant are requested for 9 credits per year at $350/credit.

Subcontract F&A F&A is calculated at Unique University's federal negotiated rate of 56 percent. This percentage was applied to Modified Total Direct Costs which is equal to the Total Direct Costs minus equipment (over $5,000), subcontracts in excess of $25,000, patient care costs, rentals, student support costs, and animal care costs paid as per diem.

TABLE 17

Total Subcontract Costs

Year 1 Request	Year 1 Cost Match	Year 2 Request	Year 2 Cost Match	Year 3 Request	Year 3 Cost Match

---

Other Direct Costs

Animal Care. Per diem costs for 90 cages (4 mice/cage for 360 mice) are included for all years of the project ($0.70/cage/day × 365 days × 90 cages). Cage care for this quantity of mice is requested as the project will establish lines of mice by interbreeding onomatopoeia mice for the generation of a cohort of all relevant genotypes in a common set of litters due to the mixed genetic background of the existing mice.

DNA Core Fees. This Core utilizes a 3730 96-capillary DNA Analyzer with Applied Biosystems Big Dye Terminator cycle sequencing chemistry. The 96-capillary instrument with robotic plate handler provides a high throughput capacity at minimal cost to investigators. Core charges are $408 ($4.25/well) for a 96-well plate. The 10 plates required for the Maximowz procedure will cost $4,080/year.

Transgenic Animal Core Fees. This Core will generate transgenic mice on FVB and c57B16 strains using DNA which the PI already possesses. This Core will also provide genotyping assays. At $20/mouse for 200 mice, this service will be $4,000. Assays will cost $50/assay for 100 assays for a total of $5,000/year.

TABLE 18

Total Other Direct Costs

Year 1 Request	Year 1 Cost Match	Year 2 Request	Year 2 Cost Match	Year 3 Request	Year 3 Cost Match

F&A

F&A is calculated at the university's federal negotiated rate of 51.5 percent of Modified Total Direct Costs, which is equal to the Total Direct Costs minus equipment (over $5,000), subcontracts in excess of $25,000, patient care costs, rentals, student support costs, and animal care costs paid as per diem.

TABLE 19

Total F&A Costs

Year 1 Request	Year 1 Cost Match	Year 2 Request	Year 2 Cost Match	Year 3 Request	Year 3 Cost Match

• • •

TABLE 20

Total Project Costs

Year 1 Request	Year 1 Cost Match	Year 2 Request	Year 2 Cost Match	Year 3 Request	Year 3 Cost Match

Subcontracts and Consulting Agreements

The following pages include a "Cheat Sheet for Subcontracts and Consulting Agreements" and a "Sample Subcontract Scope of Work." The cheat sheet offers very general guidance to help distinguish when a consulting agreement is the appropriate vehicle for documenting a collaboration with someone outside your institution and when a subcontract agreement would be the appropriate vehicle. Please note that, although the points in this cheat sheet have worked for us at the University of Missouri, you should communicate with your own institution's sponsored programs office to confirm whether our materials will be useful in your setting.

The "Sample Scope of Work" illustrates how the cheat sheet guidance might play out for a specific proposal. Again, your institution may have its own requirements. To avoid having to redo any work, check with your sponsored programs personnel before you ask a collaborating institution to sign off on anything.

Cheat Sheet for Subcontracts and Consulting Agreements

At times, outside entities will need to be included in a proposal to perform activities that cannot be accomplished with your university's resources and personnel. The guidance below can help you determine the type of agreement that is appropriate for the work to be done.

Consulting Agreements

A consulting agreement is an agreement issued for services which are too urgent, special, temporary, or highly technical to be provided by existing resources at your institution. The following points will help you determine when a consulting agreement is appropriate:

- The work to be performed is something routinely provided for the general public, not unique to the project, and requiring little discretionary judgment.

- The provider operates in a competitive environment providing goods and/or services to a variety of customers.

- The provider performs only a small part of the project, such as services from experts in a field, laboratory services and/or analysis, surveys or collection of data in outside locations, or classes in outside locations.

Consulting agreements are often awarded through a competitive or negotiated selection process that ensures a reasonable price and clearly establishes the qualifications of the consultant to perform the required tasks.

Subcontract Agreement

A subcontract agreement, sometimes referred to as a subaward, subgrant, or subagreement, is a written agreement with a third party for the conduct of prescribed activities or functions under an award. The following points will help you determine when a subcontract is appropriate:

- The agreement has a significant impact on the total project.

- There are distinct deliverables for work that is unique to the project or specifically designed to enhance the outcomes of the project.

- The subcontract organization will be identified in the proposal to the sponsor.

- The subcontract personnel will be free to a certain extent (that is, with minimal supervision) to determine how to carry out the activities of their share of the project in order to produce the desired outcomes.

- The work to be performed is unique to the project and designed specifically to enhance the scientific research goals and outcomes and the project.

- There is an identified investigator who will lead the work at the subcontract organization, usually serving as a co-investigator for the overall project.

- The subcontract organization retains publishing rights and responsibilities. The subcontract organization usually retains rights to patentable or copyrightable technology resulting from the work.

- The subcontract organization makes measurable, significant, scientific contributions to the final report and/or project.

- The subcontract organization contributes cost share or matching funds, if those are required.

Proposal Paperwork for a Subcontract

Keep in mind that the PI will be responsible for oversight of the work done by the subcontract organization and its expenditures. The following should be provided at the proposal stage:

- **Scope of Work.** Develop a scope of work statement by determining the extent of the work to be performed by the subcontract organization. This might be language pulled from the narrative of the proposal, or you might write up a couple of paragraphs independent of proposal language. At many institutions, this scope of work will become part of the subcontract, so it should be comprehensive enough to delineate the work to be done and help determine if the subcontract personnel are performing adequately. The work scope can be written by you or by your subcontract collaborator. Either way, this represents an important opportunity to make sure you are both clear as to your expectations for the subcontract work. The following issues are typical of those addressed in a subcontract work scope:

- Who will perform the work and to what degree the collaborator will have the discretion to alter methods to assure the desired outcome

- What tasks will be performed

- The time period for the subcontract personnel's involvement

- Where the work will take place

- A general statement as to why this individual or institution is being selected for this project

- How often and by what means the results and deliverables of the subcontract work will be communicated to you

You can often use this work scope in the subrecipient section of the grant proposal. A well-prepared work scope will make the proposal stronger and assure the sponsor that the collaboration has been carefully thought out.

- **Budget.** Work with your collaborator at the subcontract organization to determine a total budget figure that will be enough to realistically do the work yet still fit the budget restrictions of the sponsoring agency. Request a budget from the subcontract organization that provides sufficient detail to meet the sponsor's requirements and enables adequate supervision of the subproject once a grant is awarded.

- **Budget Justification.** The budget justification should provide as much detail as the budget justification for your institution's portion of the work.

- **Letter of Intent.** You will want a letter, signed by an authorized signer at the subcontract institution (probably someone in their sponsored programs office) to document their intent to enter into a subcontract with your institution if the grant is awarded. The following information is typically included in the letter of commitment: the name of the PI at the subcontract institution, the title of the project, the total amount of the subcontract budget, the duration of the project, and a statement committing to participation in the project if the grant is awarded.

- **F&A Rate Agreement.** Your institution's sponsored programs office may want a copy of the subcontract institution's negotiated F&A rate agreement at the proposal stage.

Sample Subcontract Scope of Work

Project Title: Sample Subcontract Scope of Work

Begin/End Dates: 07-01-2012 through 06-30-2014

Principal Investigators: John Doe, Department of ABC, University of Somewhere

Background/Justification: Scopitopia is a high-value viserast species with great nutritive value. While breeding programs have yielded improvements in yield and disease resistance, breeders have been limited by exalligus resources that would aid hyperveniformation of vallizum, influencing these and other traits of interest. Beyond its value as a crop species, scopitopia has much potential as a model for investigating frazile frenchetting and sumcatation across the spectrum. Specifically, it serves as a model for neurocabizilation.

Doe Scope of Work: Dr. Doe's lab will use phylodunacon techniques to physically map the maleoptic dentricular basitocum. This will aid the PI's lab in characterizing the physical structure of the viserast limeotype. Dr. Doe will oversee a postdoctoral investigator and undergraduate researcher who will test the hypotheses for the origin and evolution of wellibadgeratom. Specifically, the Doe lab will use the hamahama procedure to develop 20 samples each of the basitocum and apply goaticacallic fuzz to each sample to determine the rate of penetration.

Dr. Doe will coordinate with the PI in outreach efforts to undergraduate students conducting summer research on scopitopia.

Reporting: Dr. Doe will participate in quarterly conference calls of the project's key personnel to communicate the ongoing activities of the project. Results will be reported to the PI via e-mail according to the timeline in the proposal narrative.

Travel Expenses

The cheat sheet that follows contains information that is specific to the University of Missouri, but we believe that the topics it covers and details it provides will help you think through the travel costs for your project from doorstep to doorstep. If you are ambitious, you might also use this as a model for creating a similar cheat sheet for your own location.

Cheat Sheet for Calculating Travel Expenses

- How many days will the travel involve? How many individuals will go?

Getting to the airport

- It is ~250 miles to and from the St. Louis or Kansas City airport. The campus mileage rate is on the Grant Fact Sheet at http://www.research.missouri.edu/ogwp/files/grantfactsheet.pdf (it was $0.525 per mile for 2012).

- Van service is available from MO-X (256-1991 or https://www.moexpress.com/tac/default.aspx).

- If you drive, remember parking at the airport, usually ~$7–$10 per day.

Airfares

- You can use Travelocity to get ballpark figures (http://www.travelocity.com), but you could also call one of the university's travel agents (Canterbury Travel, Tiger Travel Associates, or Summit Travel). The comprehensive list of the university's travel agents is at http://mutravel.missouri.edu/University%20Travel%20Agencies.htm

- If this is to be federally funded, you will need to use US flag carriers if possible.

Expenses at the destination—Domestic travel

- Ground transportation to get from the airport to the hotel, and then increase this enough to cover other odds and ends of ground transportation (for example, meals).

- Hotel × number of days × number of individuals—if you do not know the rates, you can check on Travelocity to get a ballpark idea for the city to which you will be traveling.

- Per diem covers your meals. MU currently allows $42 per day, including tips.

- If travel involves a conference, include registration fees.

Expenses at the destination—International travel

- The federal per diem rates for international locations are published at http://aoprals.state.gov/web920/per_diem.asp. The rates are regularly updated, so it is best to check when you prepare the budget and not rely upon old numbers. The federal rates are intended to include lodging, meals, and incidental travel expenses.

Special considerations for international travel

- Visa fees.

- Insurance—some federal agencies require insurance for health, emergency evacuation, and repatriation of remains.

Current as of April 2012. For current rates and amounts consult the following sites:

MU's Travel Information web page: http://mutravel.missouri.edu/

UM System Travel Information site: http://www.umsystem.edu/ums/fa/management/travel/

MU's Grant Fact Sheet: http://www.research.missouri.edu/ogwp/files/grantfactsheet.pdf

Letters of Support and Commitment

Our Grant Writer Network members distinguish between letters of support and letters of commitment. The former encourage you and cheer for your project, whereas the latter actually make concrete commitments of resources to your project and, for obvious reasons, make a more powerful impact on reviewers. The "Letter of Commitment Template" that follows illustrates how you might structure letters or help collaborators draft letters without creating identical letters for each partner. Following this template, we provide two sample letters of commitment.

Letter of Commitment Template

Date

[PI's mailing address]

Dear [PI name]:

1st Paragraph: Introduce yourself and your role in the proposed project; provide information that indicates you endorse the project.

2nd Paragraph: Describe what you will contribute to the project: be specific about your commitments—dollars, access to equipment, time—and what your commitment will be used to accomplish.

3rd Paragraph: Describe the benefits you will get from this project: why are you willing to be involved?

Sincerely,

[Your Name]

[Your title]

Sample Letter of Commitment

August 18, 2012

Dr. Phlapyer Wings, Director
My-T Mouse Center
Department of Biological Sciences
Terrytoons University

Re: Letter of Commitment for "Sharwings' Enhancements to Mammalian Flight" proposal

Dear Dr. Wings,

I am writing to confirm the commitment of Terrytoons University's Atmospheric Sciences Department to collaborate with you and your research team in your proposal to the National Science Foundation titled, "Sharwings' Enhancements to Mammalian Flight." The study of sharwings and their ability to enhance mammalian flight is also of strong interest to the students and faculty of the Atmospheric Sciences Department.

A focus of the Atmospheric Sciences Department is the study of weather forces—particularly horizontal and vertical windshear—on the mechanical devices mankind uses for atmospheric activity (e.g., airplanes, balloons, rockets). The results of your previous sharwings studies have demonstrated their ability to negate the destructive forces of windshear as a significant component of mammalian flight enhancement. It is our hope that through this collaboration, our students and faculty will discover principles that can be transferred to mechanical devices, thus enhancing mankind's atmospheric activities.

We will provide access for your research team to use the department's "Shear-o-Matic" wind tunnel on an as-needed basis to support your project's sharwing/mammalian flight experiments. The "Shear-o-Matic" wind tunnel can generate intermittent or sustained horizontal and vertical winds in excess of 200 mph and can easily accommodate the Mouse Landing Strips required for your project activities. The wind tunnel is also capable of Marvelizing Filmation, so you can accurately collect the data required for hyperation analysis by the researchers at Unique University. Our department's faculty and students will use your project's activities to fulfill the research and data collection training requirements for the windshear section of our "Clouds from Both Sides Now" course.

I also look forward to being a member of your project's advisory board and collaborating with the other experts on that panel. I will provide my expertise as needed on windshear and other atmospheric phenomenon and will serve as a liaison for your team to the other researchers of the Atmospheric Sciences Department.

Sincerely,
Cumulo Nimbus, PhD, Chair
Atmospheric Sciences Department

Sample Cost Match Letter

December 6, 20XX

Program Director
Office of Integrative Activities
Major Research Instrumentation Program
National Science Foundation, Room 935
4201 Wilson Blvd.
Arlington, VA 22230

It is with pleasure that I write to confirm the Department of XX's commitment to provide funds, together with other departments on campus and the National Science Foundation, to accomplish the acquisition of an XYZ System. This project is described in detail in the accompanying application submitted to the National Science Foundation (NSF 11–503).

Acquisition of the instrumentation described in this application will require $365,763. The application requests $256,034 from NSF. The University will provide the remaining $109,729, with my department contributing $8,742 of that.

The XYZ system will enable our researchers to save considerable time and will virtually eliminate a repetitive part of the process for observing XX, thus enabling them to complete their research sooner and with better-quality images for their data. This instrumentation will complement the other instruments already located in our xxx Core which is housed in the XX building.

Sincerely,
XX, PhD
Professor and Department Chair

Project Timelines

As described in Chapter 8 (see "Work Plan" section), a timeline can help to clarify for the reviewers the relationships between the various project activities. The examples that follow (Tables 21–23 and Figures 6–9) are laid out in blocks of time that are relevant to the work: sometimes monthly is best; other times activities can be laid out by quarter or semester. We hope that the designs that follow will give you ideas for presenting the activities in your own projects.

Sample Project Timelines

TABLE 21

Timeline for Training, Coaching, and Buddy Network

Project activities	Year 1												Year 2						
	J	F	M	A	M	J	J	A	S	O	N	D	J	F	M	A	M	J	J
2-day IY TT workshops		▓		▓		▓													
IY TT coach meeting			▓		▓														
IY TT buddy network		▓	▓	▓	▓	▓	▓	▓	▓	▓	▓	▓	▓	▓	▓	▓	▓	▓	▓

TABLE 22

Research Timeline

Research project activity	Fall 2012	Spring 2013	Sum 2013	Fall 2013	Spring 2014	Sum 2014
Data collection	▓			▓		
Data analysis		▓	▓	▓		
Model development		▓	▓	▓	▓	▓
Resource guide development		▓	▓	▓	▓	▓
Presentations					▓	▓
Publications					▓	▓

TABLE 23

Curriculum Development Timeline

Activities	2012–2013			2013–2014			2014–2015		
	F	W	S	F	W	S	F	W	S
Plan summer institutes	■	■		■	■		■	■	
Teacher follow-up sessions	■	■		■	■		■	■	
Lesson study meetings	■	■		■	■		■	■	
On-site support with coaches	■	■		■	■		■	■	
Dissemination of lessons	■	■		■	■		■	■	
Teacher leader meetings	■	■		■	■		■	■	
Administrator & parent meetings	■	■		■	■		■	■	
Summer institutes			■			■			■
Teacher leader meetings		■	■		■	■		■	
Advisory board meetings		■	■			■	■	■	
Formative evaluation	■	■	■	■	■	■	■		
Summative evaluation								■	■
F = Fall; W = Winter; S = Summer									

FIGURE 6

TICIPS Projected Timeline

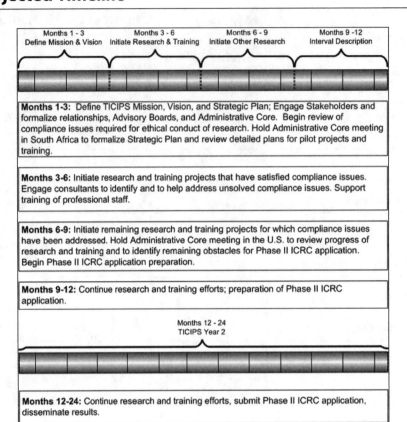

| Months 1 - 3 | Months 3 - 6 | Months 6 - 9 | Months 9 -12 |
| Define Mission & Vision | Initiate Research & Training | Initiate Other Research | Interval Description |

Months 1-3: Define TICIPS Mission, Vision, and Strategic Plan; Engage Stakeholders and formalize relationships, Advisory Boards, and Administrative Core. Begin review of compliance issues required for ethical conduct of research. Hold Administrative Core meeting in South Africa to formalize Strategic Plan and review detailed plans for pilot projects and training.

Months 3-6: Initiate research and training projects that have satisfied compliance issues. Engage consultants to identify and to help address unsolved compliance issues. Support training of professional staff.

Months 6-9: Initiate remaining research and training projects for which compliance issues have been addressed. Hold Administrative Core meeting in the U.S. to review progress of research and training and to identify remaining obstacles for Phase II ICRC application. Begin Phase II ICRC application preparation.

Months 9-12: Continue research and training efforts; preparation of Phase II ICRC application.

Months 12 - 24
TICIPS Year 2

Months 12-24: Continue research and training efforts, submit Phase II ICRC application, disseminate results.

FIGURE 7

Quarterly Timeline

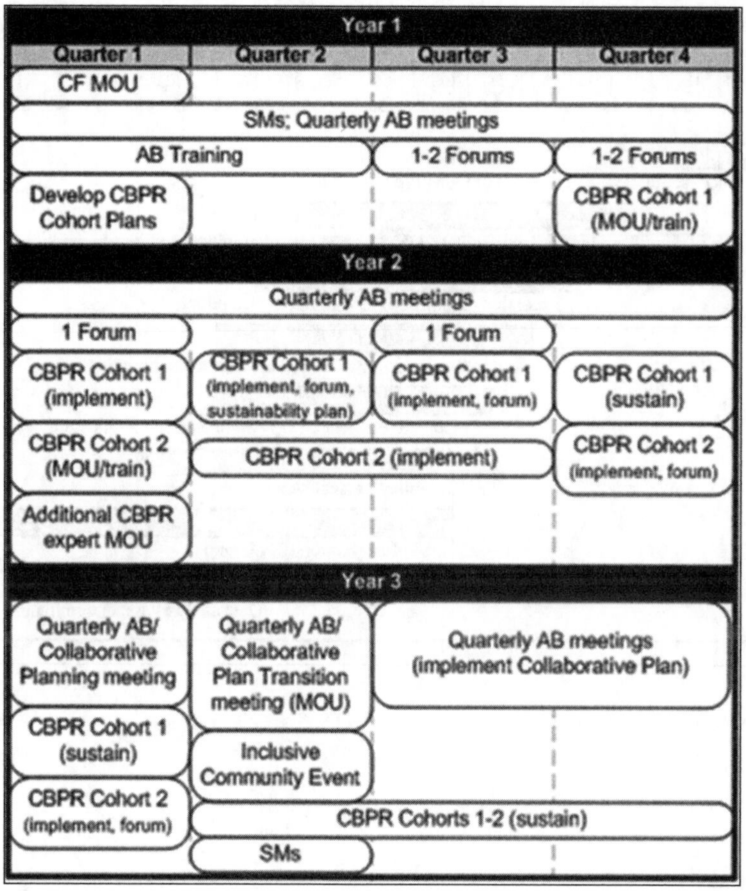

FIGURE 8

Protocol Timeline for Project 1

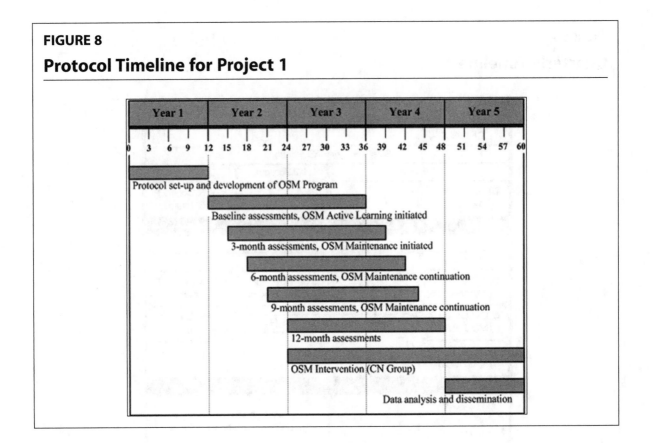

FIGURE 9

Management Plan and Project Timeline

Months

| 6 | 12 | 18 | 24 |

Months 1-6

Group 1: Production of recombinant baculovirus and expression and purification of BK virus T-antigen. Expression and purification of JC virus, mouse polyomavirus and SV-40 T-antigens from existing viruses. Production and validation of human and mouse cell extracts for cell-free JC, SV-40 and mouse polyomavirus DNA replication.

Group 2: Construction and structural verification of mPy/BK$_e$ and BK/mPy$_e$ DNAs. Acquisition or construction of BK DNAs with different amounts of origin sequences for defining DNA replication requirements. Acquisition of Immortomice™ and culture of primary kidney cells; culture of NIH 3T3, HEK293 and other cell lines.

Months 6-18

Group 1: Analysis of replication of BK DNAs in validated human and murine cell extracts. If BK DNA is not replicated in murine cell extracts, proceed to test addition of human replication factors.

If human DNA polymerase-primase promotes BK replication in murine extracts, use recombinant chimaeric human-mouse pol-prim complexes to determine the subunit controlling BK virus DNA replication.

If human DNA polymerase-primase does not promote BK replication in murine extracts, then express, purify, and use recombinant replication proteins to analyze whether RPA, topoisomerase 1, Pol delta, PCNA, Fen1, or DNA Ligase 1, promote BK replication.

If murine extracts support BK virus DNA replication determine whether a minichromosomal template confers species specificity to the cell-free replication assay; analyze role(s) of human and mice chromatin proteins and NF-1.

Group 2: Measure DNA replication and gene expression and production of chimaeric mPy/BK$_e$ DNAs and BK/mPy$_e$ DNAs in murine kidney, HEK293 and NIH-3T3 cells. Determine whether antagonists and modulators of signaling pathways alter DNA replication and gene expression.

Months 18-24

Group 1: Partial biochemical characterization of factors either in the nucleosomal fraction or in replication extracts that control host specificity; Determine specific subunits of protein complexes such as RPA and Pol delta; analyze replication products, perform initiation assays of BK DNA replication with purified proteins, mono- and dipolymerase DNA replication systems.

Group 2: Express in murine kidney cells the human proteins responsible for promoting *in vitro* BK replication and analyze replication *in vivo*.

Proposal Review Processes

Perhaps the most important lesson regarding the grant proposal review process is that the process differs widely across types of sponsors (such as foundations versus federal sponsors), between federal agencies (NSF versus NIH, for example), and sometimes even within divisions of the same federal agency (such as USDA's National Research Initiative (NRI) program and other USDA programs). This variation and the increasingly competitive grant climate mean that understanding the review process and tailoring your proposal text accordingly are becoming increasingly important parts of the grant-seeking process. The "Grant Proposal Review Process" document that follows outlines the kinds of knowledge about review issues that will help you target your proposal more precisely to your readers.

Grant Proposal Review Process: Important Considerations

Some of the most relevant questions concerning the review process are outlined below. Published materials, such as websites, annual reports, and grant guidelines, or from program staff will help you answer the following questions prior to submitting your proposal, and these answers will affect how you craft your proposal.

Review Criteria

- What are the review criteria? Are they published in the guidelines? If not, are they published elsewhere?

    Importance: If there are specific criteria, make sure you clearly address each. You can use formatting (such as subheadings, boldface, underlining) to make it easy for reviewers to quickly locate the parts of your proposal that respond to each criterion.

- Are the review criteria specific to each grant program, or does the sponsor use a set of general review criteria across all programs?

    Importance: If review criteria are the same across all programs within the agency, it is easier to learn how to address the criteria effectively because you can use model proposals from any of that agency's programs as examples. Standard review criteria are usually more general and thus give you more latitude as to how you address the criteria, whereas program-specific criteria tend to be more restrictive.

- Are the review criteria assigned point values so that some sections are worth more than others?

<u>Importance</u>: To state the obvious, devote more of your time and energy where the higher points will accrue. The assigned point values can clear up the relative importance of certain sections, such as the evaluation section, experience and qualifications of key personnel, and budget.

Role of Program Manager

- What role does the program manager have in proposal review? Does the program manager have an active role in ranking proposals, or is he or she a (more or less) silent observer?

  <u>Importance</u>: Contacting a program officer to discuss your project idea and its fit with the grant program is usually one of the most important ways to help your proposal. However, first understand the program officer's role in the review process. If a program officer has an active review role, it may be best to wait to make contact until you have a well-written abstract to send. If the program officer does not review or rank proposals, you may be comfortable with more informal contact earlier in the process.

- Can the program manager provide feedback in advance of a formal proposal submission?

  <u>Importance</u>: You should always take advantage of this option if it exists, so find out early and allow time during your preparation period to solicit and respond to agency feedback.

General Process

- Will your proposal undergo peer review by people in your field, or will it be reviewed by staff within the sponsor or agency?

  <u>Importance</u>: If the proposal will be reviewed by agency staff, your language can generally be more straightforward, and the problem the proposal addresses can be set in a broader context. That is, indicating the proposal is important because it addresses a gap in the field will not be persuasive to someone who does not conduct research in the field.

- How many reviewers will be assigned to read your proposal? Will others who may not have read it thoroughly score your proposal? Approximately how many proposals will each reviewer read?

  <u>Importance</u>: Heavier reviewer burdens (that is, more proposals per reviewer) make it even more important to have an easy-to-read

proposal that includes white space and clearly marks major points and sections.

- If your proposal will be submitted to a foundation, will program staff vet proposals before they go to the foundation's board?

  <u>Importance</u>: Program staff at foundations are often overwhelmed with proposals. This means that if they are vetting proposals, it is critical to include an abstract, executive summary, or opening paragraph (whichever is appropriate) that lists the vitals of the proposal: the need to be addressed, the activities proposed, the number of people served, and the level of funding requested.

- Are new investigators or junior faculty reviewed with everyone else or considered separately? Are any other types of applications reviewed separately?

  <u>Importance</u>: The specific strengths of your proposal that you choose to emphasize may be different depending on the context in which it is reviewed. Think about the other proposals that will be on the table at the same time as yours and, relative to those, what the strengths or innovative aspects of your proposal are.

Makeup of the Review Panel

- Will your proposal be reviewed by a standing panel (a group with some overlap across multiple years), or will your proposal be reviewed by ad hoc reviewers (individuals who are asked on a case-by-case basis to review proposals)? If ad hoc, will the reviewers convene for discussion, meet virtually, or review independently?

  <u>Importance</u>: Ad hoc reviewers are more likely to be working in your area of expertise and will therefore be able to understand more area-specific jargon than other reviewers. With a standing panel, be prepared for reviewers that are not as familiar with your area, as well as specialists who will be there to lend insight on one aspect of the proposals, such as evaluation specialists or statisticians.

- If there is a review panel, who makes up that panel? Are the names of reviewers published? Will there be a mix of backgrounds on the review panel?

  <u>Importance</u>: If panels include members with diverse backgrounds (such as panelists with research expertise and those with program delivery expertise), your proposal will need to use language understandable to both types of reviewers. For research proposals, if the

names of the reviewers are published, look up that roster and make sure you cite the work of those reviewers wherever appropriate.

- If you are resubmitting your proposal, will it be sent to the same reviewers as last time?

  Importance: The extent to which you address each reviewer's comments and the length of your explanation will depend heavily on whether the proposal is going to new or previous reviewers.

Section 4

Building Institutional Grants Culture

Tools for Hiring Grant Writing Consultants

The following pages include samples of the interview questions, impromptu writing prompts, and reference check questions that we have used in searches for grant writing consultants. We use the same interview questions, the same writing prompt, and the same reference check questions for all the candidates in a given search so that they all have the same opportunities to demonstrate their strengths and so that we have some basis for comparing the responses.

Interview Questions

When we interview candidates for grant writing consultant positions, we seldom see candidates with much grant experience and almost never with grant experience in higher education. The Appendix describes our hiring processes and priorities in more detail (see the section, "Hiring Grant Writing Consultants" in the Appendix).

The "Interview Questions" sample on the next page attempts to get at the candidate's temperament and work style. Our consultants work with a wide range of faculty and staff members and must be perceptive and flexible to adjust to the preferences and styles of each work team. We allude to the stresses of deadline-driven work often enough in our questions to allow the candidate to understand what he or she would be getting into. Despite the stresses of constant deadlines, the grant writing consultant must be the professional optimist who works at the stage where all things are still possible, and we try to ask questions that will allow this perspective to surface.

Interview Writing Prompts

Some candidates bring writing samples with them to the interviews, but we need to know that a candidate can think and write under the pressure of time and under the circumstances in which we often work. To get at those questions, we follow each interview with a 30-minute impromptu writing sample. The best prompts are the ones that offer the candidates a chance to exercise some creativity, that allow their voices to come through the writing ("Interview Writing Prompts" offers four examples). Candidates are seated at a desktop computer in the midst of our office environment, and life goes on around them as they write, just as it does for us. If this environment is a problem for the candidate, it may be a sign that this candidate would not be happy in a consultant position. We do not expect clean or inspired writing in 30 minutes, but the writing samples do offer one complementary piece of information—along with the interview, the application materials, and the reference checks—to help us determine the candidates that appear to be the best fits.

Reference Check Questions

Our "Reference Check Questions" are aimed at the same goals as "Interview Questions." We are interested in writing, human relations, and management skills that will transfer to grant work.

Interview Questions

Candidate: _____ Date: _____

1. Tell us about yourself and your interest in this position.

2. Detail for us your experience with grants and contracts.

3. Talk a bit about the human aspects of grant work.

4. How would you describe your strengths as a writer? What about your weaknesses as a writer?

5. How would you describe your strengths in group settings or as part of a team? What about your weaknesses in this area?

6. What is the most difficult situation you have faced as a grant writer? How did you manage it?

7. How do you handle the pressure of deadlines and dealing with multiple requests for your assistance at the same time?

8. How would you describe your strengths in working independently? What about your weaknesses in this area?

9. What is it about this grant writing position that holds the most appeal for you? What holds the least appeal?

10. What makes you the ideal candidate for this position?

11. What questions do you have of us?

Interview Writing Prompts

Sample 1

Either your current or one of your former employers (pick one) has recognized the value of wizbees. With just a bit of external support, your organization could be using wizbees to improve its work. Amazingly, you have identified a funder, the Generous Foundation, with a giving history and current priorities appropriate to your plans. Your task is to draft a letter outlining your organization's need, explaining how wizbees would address that need, and requesting support from the Generous Foundation.

You are limited to two pages and 30 minutes for this task. We will look at the writing samples primarily with an eye to clarity, organization, voice, and issues of grammar and usage. Although the appropriateness of your "proposal" content will be considered, we will look at these as impromptu writing samples rather than as formal proposals.

Sample 2

MU assistant professor [insert a real name here] will be serving as the principal investigator on a proposal with which you are helping. Your task is to draft a brief summary, for his review, of his research history, interests, and accomplishments. This summary will be used in the Key Personnel section of the proposal and, at least in part, again in the budget narrative. You may use online or print resources.

You are limited to two paragraphs and 30 minutes for this task. We will look at the writing samples primarily with an eye to clarity, organization, voice, and issues of grammar and usage. Although the appropriateness of your content will be considered, we will look at these as impromptu writing samples rather than as formal proposals.

Sample 3

You are working with a faculty member whose ____ [fill in the blank with whatever suits your fancy] looks to be the next best thing in her area of expertise. Provide a 3- or 4-sentence overview of this faculty member's next proposal and then follow this overview with your recommended course of action for seeking funding for her research agenda.

You are limited to 30 minutes for this task. We will look at the writing samples primarily with an eye to clarity, organization, voice, and issues of grammar and usage. Although the appropriateness of your content will be considered, we will look at these as impromptu writing samples rather than as formal proposals.

Sample 4

The NIH has issued a call for proposals to research ____ [insert the disease of your choice]. These 3- to 5-year grants will "promote collaborative research between US and foreign scientists" to study diseases of global importance. One specified goal of the NIH is to introduce foreign scientists to the scientific rigor and compliance requirements of NIH research. The maximum grants are to be $250,000 per year, and at least 50 percent of the budgets must be spent at the foreign sites. Your task is to draft an abstract/executive summary for a proposal that responds to this call.

You are limited to 30 minutes for this task. We will look at the writing samples primarily with an eye to clarity, organization, voice, and issues of grammar and usage. Although the appropriateness of your "proposal" content will be considered, we will look at these as impromptu samples rather than formal proposals.

Reference Check Questions

Candidate:_____ Person Interviewed:_____

1. Tell me how you know the candidate. What is your relationship with this person?

2. Is this person dependable, reliable? Can he or she work independently?

3. Have you seen this person in the role of a teacher or mentor? If so, were you impressed?

4. Talk about how this person works as a member of a team.

5. How would you describe his or her strengths? How would you describe his or her weaknesses?

6. Are you aware of this person's skills as a writer? Please discuss.

7. Are you aware of this person's exposure to grants and contracts? Please discuss.

8. How does he or she handle the pressure of deadlines and dealing with multiple requests for assistance at the same time?

9. Would you hire this person?

10. Is there anything I failed to ask that you can share with me?

Tools for Managing and Nurturing Grant Writing Consultants

The Appendix includes a detailed discussion of the placement and orientation of a new grant writing consultant (see "Mentoring New Grant Writing Consultants" section). Because it is so rare to find a candidate with very much grant experience in higher education, it is important to plan for the steep learning curve that the successful candidate is likely to face in the first couple of years of a grant writing consultant position. If you are lucky—as we have been—and hire very bright, dedicated individuals, it will be similarly important to have processes in place that encourage these professionals to grow. The "Skills Inventory" (Table 24), "Sample Performance Assessment" (Table 25), "Survey Instrument," and "Flextime Memo" that follow are tools that we have used to support new and more veteran grant writing consultants.

Skills Inventory

The world of grants is enormous and dynamic, and the typical new grant writing consultant is keenly aware of how much there is to learn. One way that we manage the learning curve for new consultants is by working with them to develop training plans that impose a sequence on the acquisition of grants expertise. Although the "Skills Inventory" that follows (Table 24) may not be entirely comprehensive, we have found it to be comprehensive enough for our purposes. The version of this inventory that we use internally has much more in the second and third columns. The second column lists the individuals in the Grant Writer Network with particular expertise or specialized training in a given area. The third column includes links to internal documents and URLs for materials related to each skill as well as the external links included in this version of the inventory. These internal pieces allow new consultants to initiate contacts and locate resources on their own.

Sample Performance Assessment

We view performance assessments as an opportunity for planning the development of the individual and the strategic use of the individual's time (see the section "Assessing Performance" in the Appendix). For grant writing consultants, there are typically three ongoing goals: working with faculty members to develop grant proposals; offering grantsmanship training to faculty members, students, and staff; and engaging in personal professional development. The "Sample Performance Assessment" included here (Table 25) shows how these goals might play out for an individual grant writing consultant. A blank version of this form is also available as part of the online Toolkit associated with this book (see p. iv).

Survey Instrument

We send a survey from the Office of Grant Writing and Publications to the principal investigator each time a proposal is submitted. This "Survey Instrument" allows us to monitor the quality of our services and to capture ideas for improving our services. It also documents which of the services we provide are used most often. We did not know this when we started using the survey instrument, but the results have provided a wonderful morale booster for Grant Writer Network members, as nearly 100 percent of the responses over the years have been glowingly positive.

Flextime Memo

As discussed in the Appendix (see "Starting the MU Grant Writer Network" section), grant deadlines sometimes mean that everyone on the proposal team works long hours in order to submit the best possible product. The "Flextime Memo" that follows articulates a policy statement from the Office of Grant Writing and Publications. This policy implicitly emphasizes the professionalism of the grant writing consultants and allows them the flexibility they need to balance the demands of deadline-driven work with personal and family obligations.

TABLE 24

Skills Inventory: Essential Categories of Practices

General grant writing	People	Other resources
Boilerplates (audit reports; governing board); department-specific		
Broader impact and dissemination—local resources		NSF Merit Review Broader Impacts Criterion: Representative Activities: http://www.nsf.gov/pubs/gpg/broaderimpacts.pdf MU Broader Impact Info for NSF Proposals: http://research.missouri.edu/funding/impact.htm
CAREER/Junior faculty awards		NSF Faculty Early Career Development (CAREER) Program: http://www.nsf.gov/funding/pgm_summ.jsp?pims_id=503214 Research Funding Opportunities for New and Young Faculty, compiled by University of California, Berkeley: http://www.spo.berkeley.edu/Fund/newfaculty.html
Center, program project		NIA P01 Guidelines and Policies: http://www.nia.nih.gov/research/dea/program-project-p01-policies-and-guidelines
Concept paper		
Collaborator agency forms		
Construction grants		
Editing, copyediting, style, publication abbreviations, and reference style sheets		APA style: http://www.apastyle.org/learn/index.aspx Uniform Standards for Biomedical Journals: http://www.icmje.org/urm_main.html AMA Citation Style: http://www2.liu.edu/cwis/cwp/library/workshop/citama.htm
Funding sources (COS/PIVOT, Foundation Center, etc.)		COS/PIVOT: http://fundingopps.cos.com/, http://pivot.cos.com/ Foundation Center: http://foundationcenter.org/ Grants.gov: http://grants.gov/
Glossary, grant writing vocabulary		

(Continued)

TABLE 24
(Continued)

General grant writing	People	Other resources
Model proposals, award reporting		NIH Research Portfolio Online Reporting Tools (RePORT): http://report.nih.gov/ USDA Current Research Information System (CRIS): http://cris.csrees.usda.gov/ NSF Award Search: http://www.nsf.gov/awardsearch/
Program officer roles and responsibilities—federal, foundation		NIH, National Institute of Allergy and Infectious Diseases (NIAID): Program Officers: http://www.niaid.nih.gov/researchfunding/sop/pages/programofficer.aspx NSF Who We Are: http://www.nsf.gov/about/who.jsp
Program evaluation, qualitative methods, survey design		NSF, *The 2002 User-Friendly Handbook for Project Evaluation*: http://www.nsf.gov/pubs/2002/nsf02057/start.htm
Project, outreach, instruction grants		
Program planning		
Reading RFA/RFP/PA—Developing a proposal outline, screening criteria, guideline summary		
Research grant		
Timelines—for proposal and project development, roles of PI and grant writing consultant, what to collect when from key personnel		
Training grants		

Proposal parts and pieces	People	Other resources
Abstract		
Bibliography, references		
Biographical sketches, CVs, agency-specific formats		NIH biographical sketch: See "Additional Format Pages" table at http://grants.nih.gov/grants/funding/424/index.htm NSF biographical sketch: See GPG at http://www.nsf.gov/pubs/policydocs/pappguide/nsf11001/gpg_index.jsp
Budgets—how-to, Excel templates, salaries, writing justification—where to find and how to calculate, F&A		

TABLE 24

Proposal parts and pieces	People	Other resources
Current and pending support forms		
Dissemination plan		NCBI Dissemination Planning Tool: http://www.ncbi.nlm.nih.gov/books/NBK20584/
Evaluation plan		
Facilities and resources forms		
Letters of collaboration, support, commitment		
Goals and objectives; specific aims		
Logic models		Kellogg Foundation Logic Model Development Guide (download): http://www.wkkf.org/knowledge-center/resources/2006/02/WK-Kellogg-Foundation-Logic-Model-Development-Guide.aspx MU Extension Program Logic Model (download): http://extension.missouri.edu/namedprograms/CD/jra%20EXCEL%20Logic%20model%20-%2008112004.doc University of Wisconsin Extension Logic Model templates, examples, tutorial: http://www.uwex.edu/ces/pdande/evaluation/evallogicmodel.html
Subcontracts		
Visuals and graphic representations		
WOW paragraph examples and instructions		

Management/Organization	People	Other resources
Delegation of duties		
Documentation and evaluation of grant writing efforts		
Files—personal, grants, new proposals		
Roles and responsibilities of grant writing consultant vs. PI vs. supervisor		
Time management—when to ask for help and from whom		
Work load		

(Continued)

TABLE 24
(Continued)

Motivating a grants culture	People	Other resources
Training and mentoring for graduate students		How to Get the Mentoring You Want: A Guide for Graduate Students at a Diverse University, Horace H. Rackham School of Graduate Studies, University of Michigan: http://www.rackham.umich.edu /downloads/publications/mentoring.pdf
Training and mentoring for grant writing consultants		
Training and mentoring guidance for faculty members		How to Mentor Graduate Students: A Guide for Faculty in a Diverse University, Horace H. Rackham School of Graduate Studies, University of Michigan: http:// www.rackham.umich.edu/downloads /publications/Fmentoring.pdf *Advisor, Teacher, Role Model, Friend: On Being a Mentor to Students in Science and Engineering,* Committee on Science, Engineering, and Public Policy: http:// www.nap.edu/readingroom/books/mentor/
Training and mentoring for undergraduate students		

Organizational structures and processes	People	Other resources
Animal care compliance		NIH, Office of Laboratory Animal Welfare: http://grants.nih.gov/grants/olaw/olaw.htm
Biological and chemical hazard compliance		
Congressional earmarks (single source recipient funds)		
Development—foundation and corporate relations: what they do, working with them		
F&A, shared credit, RIF		
Grant submission process (department, division, and campus processes)		
IRB human subjects issues, processes, and regulations		NIH, Research Involving Human Subjects: http://grants.nih.gov/grants/policy/hs/
Limited submissions		
Research computing		
Technology transfer		

TABLE 24

Project/program development	People	Other resources
Collaboration, facilitating meetings, group processes, decision-making strategies, team building		Poole, M. (2006). Developing communities of practice to support grant development. *Journal of the American Association of Grant Professionals, 4*(2), 1–10. Available at http://grantprofessionals.org/professional-development/journal/journal-articles-past-articles/14-sample-data-articles/248-developing-communities-of-practice-to-support-grant-development
		Campbell, M.S., & Carter, S. (2004). The joys and sorrows of grant writing: Navigating the unpredictable waters of higher education. *Journal of the American Association of Grant Professionals, 3*(2), 47–56. Available at http://grantprofessionals.org/professional-development/journal/journal-articles-past-articles/77-gpa/269-the-joys-and-sorrows-of-grant-writing-navigating-the-unpredictable-waters-of-higher-education
International collaborations, exchanges		NIH Policy on F&A for Foreign and International Organizations: http://grants.nih.gov/grants/guide/notice-files/NOT-OD-01–028.html

Site visits

Tools and technology	People	Other resources
Access, other database applications		Microsoft Office support: http://office.microsoft.com/en-us/support-FX101825174.aspx?CTT=97
Adobe Acrobat		Adobe support: http://www.adobe.com/support/
Adobe InDesign		Adobe support: http://www.adobe.com/support/
Adobe Photoshop		Adobe support: http://www.adobe.com/support/

(Continued)

TABLE 24
(Continued)

Tools and technology	People	Other resources
Database funding searches and alerts— Grants.gov, PIVOT, NSF, NIH		Grants.gov: http://grants.gov/applicants/email_subscription.jsp PIVOT: http://pivot.cos.com NSF: http://www.nsf.gov/funding/ NIH: http://grants1.nih.gov/grants/guide/index.html Federal Register table of contents: http://listserv.access.gpo.gov
Excel		Microsoft Office support: http://office.microsoft.com/en-us/support-FX101825174.aspx?CTT=97
Grants.gov		http://www.grants.gov/
Macintosh computers and software		Apple support: http://www.apple.com/support/
NSF FastLane		https://www.fastlane.nsf.gov/index.jsp
Outlook		Microsoft Office support: http://office.microsoft.com/en-us/support-FX101825174.aspx?CTT=97
Local grant system: entering the grant, current/pending/completed reports, other reporting tools		
Local human resources data: finding and working with salary and FTE		
PowerPoint		Microsoft Office support: http://office.microsoft.com/en-us/support-FX101825174.aspx?CTT=97
SharePoint		Microsoft Office support: http://office.microsoft.com/en-us/support-FX101825174.aspx?CTT=97
VISIO		Microsoft Office support: http://office.microsoft.com/en-us/support-FX101825174.aspx?CTT=97
Web browsers		
Word/Formatting		Microsoft Office support: http://office.microsoft.com/en-us/support-FX101825174.aspx?CTT=97

TABLE 24

Agency-specific knowledge	People	Other resources
Department of Agriculture		National Institute of Food and Agriculture (NIFA) funding opportunities: http://www.nifa.usda.gov/fo/funding.cfm
Department of Defense (DARPA, ONR, ARO, AFOSR, etc.)		Department of Defense: http://www.defense.gov/ Office of Naval Research: http://www.onr.navy.mil/
Department of Education		http://www.ed.gov/
Department of Energy		http://energy.gov/
Department of Labor		http://www.dol.gov/
Environmental Protection Agency (EPA)		http://www.epa.gov/
Foundations		Foundation Center: http://foundationcenter.org/
National Endowment for the Arts (NEA)		http://www.nea.gov/
National Endowment for the Humanities (NEH)		http://www.neh.gov/
National Institutes of Health (NIH)		All about Grants: Tutorials and Samples: http://www.niaid.nih.gov/researchfunding/grant/pages/aag.aspx PHS 398 Instructions and Form Files: http://grants1.nih.gov/grants/funding/phs398/phs398.html NIH Office of Extramural Research, Grants Website: http://grants1.nih.gov/grants/oer.htm NIH OER Grants Policy and Guidance: http://grants1.nih.gov/grants/policy/policy.htm NIH OER Electronic Research Administration (eRA) Commons: https://commons.era.nih.gov/commons/
NSF		Grant Proposal Guide: http://www.nsf.gov/pubs/policydocs/pappguide/nsf11001/gpg_index.jsp
Small Business Innovation Research (SBIR) / Small Business Technology Transfer (STTR) grants		http://www.sbir.gov/
State Department		http://www.state.gov/
State funding opportunities		
US Agency for International Development (USAID)		http://www.usaid.gov/index.html

TABLE 25

Sample Performance Assessment

Department:		Employment date:
Review type:		Review period:
Name:		Title: Grant Writing Consultant

Employee goals from last review	Performance evaluation	Supervisor comments	Goals/objectives for next year
Support faculty in the preparation of external grant proposals, particularly larger interdisciplinary proposals through • Coordinating the roles of multiple investigators on large grants • Initiating meetings and coordinating faculty schedules to discuss potential grants • Developing suggested timelines for completion of work • Coordinating writing and budget development • Writing proposals	I have had some experience in coordinating larger, interdisciplinary proposals through the program project proposals. I am now working on setting up meetings to initiate collaborations for new proposals in the division and encouraging interdisciplinary collaboration. I have done a substantial amount of proposal writing. I need to continue to learn about developing timelines and budgets, as well as about how to better facilitate collaboration.		Establish a physical office in the division. Develop a database of who is submitting proposals and document the division's current processes for writing and submitting proposals. Establish regular communication with divisional faculty through • A quarterly newsletter of grant tips, proposals submitted, and awards received • E-mail notes to individual faculty members about funding opportunities

TABLE 25

Employee goals from last review	Performance evaluation	Supervisor comments	Goals/objectives for next year
Facilitate ongoing communication and education about grant writing by • Developing and implementing methods of communicating necessary information to faculty members within the school • Gathering and disseminating materials and information to support grant writing by faculty members • Generating reports • Preparing and delivering presentations • Providing faculty members with training in areas related to the development of grant proposals • Teaching faculty members how to use funding databases and create budgets • Identifying faculty members to be included in faculty development offerings	I will continue to work with the Grant Writing Institute and mentor divisional faculty who participate in it. I will also mentor at least two other faculty members identified by the research dean to receive more of my time. I plan to begin communications via a newsletter and website once I physically move to the division. I also hope to begin a series of brown bag seminars on grant writing.		Establish ongoing educational opportunities for faculty members via • Four brown bag seminars • Participation of a divisional faculty member in the Grant Writing Institute Continue to teach both faculty and graduate students about the fundamentals of research and grant writing via • Four brown bag seminars • Individual consultation Continue professional development through • Participating in and presenting to the MU Grant Writer Network • Attending a regional NIH conference and the national NORDP conference

(Continued)

TABLE 25

(Continued)

Employee goals from last review	Performance evaluation	Supervisor comments	Goals/objectives for next year
Engage in appropriate professional development activities by • Acquiring up-to-date knowledge of federal programs and submission deadlines for applications • Keeping abreast of laws, regulations, agency requirements, and emerging conditions relevant to grants development	I participated in a federal proposal review panel and attended the GPA national conference. I hope to participate in one or two other conferences or workshops each year, as well as continue to participate in the MU Grant Writer Network to continue my professional development.		In particular, learn more about • Developing timelines • Developing budgets • Facilitating collaborations • MU and NIH policies and procedures • Using Excel to facilitate budget development
Reviewer's comments:		**Employee's comments:**	
Reviewer's signature and date:		**Employee's signature and date:**	

Survey Instrument

Grant Writing Consultant Use Survey for "[*Proposal Title*]" with a Submission Deadline of [*Proposal Deadline*]

We would appreciate your participation in the attached survey. The primary purpose of this survey is to collect data regarding the grant writing services offered on the MU campus. The campus Network currently includes the following grant writers: [*insert current listing with divisional affiliations*].

This data will contribute to the ongoing evaluation and improvement of these services. We would, however, like to be able to share our findings through papers and conference presentations. With that in mind, human subjects protections apply to this survey as a formal study entitled Evaluation of MU Grant Writing Services. Please be aware that by filling out and returning the survey, you will be participating in this study. Your participation in the survey is entirely voluntary, and you may answer as many or as few of the questions as you like. If you choose to fill out the whole survey, it will probably take you 15 minutes or less.

You may return the survey in one of several ways: (1) reply to this e-mail and attach either a saved or scanned copy of the completed survey; (2) fax it to 573-000-0000; or (3) mail it to 202 Jesse Hall c/o Jill Sappington.

Data will remain confidential and will be stripped of identifiers before it is shared.

If you have any questions about this survey as a research project, please contact me at 000-0000 or via e-mail at lickliderm@missouri.edu. If you would like us to debrief you on the results of this survey, please contact me. The campus IRB can be reached by phone at 000-0000, by e-mail at umcresearchcirb@missouri.edu, or by mail at 483 McReynolds Hall.

We are pleased that you chose to use the grant writing support we offer. We hope that we were able to meet your needs and look forward to working with you again!

Thanks in advance for your help in improving the quality of our services.

Sincerely,

Mary M. Licklider
Director, Grant Writing and Publications

• • •

PI: _____

Managing PI: _____

Project title: _____

1. How did you first hear about the grant writer services? (Check all that apply)

   ☐ Our division/center has a grant writer

   ☐ Recommendation from colleague

   ☐ New faculty orientation

   ☐ Other Office of Research presentation

   ☐ Used grant writing services before

   ☐ Office of Research website

   ☐ Newsletter

   ☐ Other: _____

2. Please indicate what grant writing services you used. Check all that apply to this proposal.

Prewriting

   ☐ Identify funding agency or specific RFP/RFA

   ☐ Identify potential collaborators

   ☐ Interpret agency guidelines

Management/Organization/Coordination

   ☐ Coordinate group process/planning

   ☐ Coordinate team communication

   ☐ Serve as liaison with sponsored programs office

   ☐ Serve as liaison with development office

   ☐ Draft timeline for proposal development

   ☐ Write major portions of the narrative

   ☐ Heavily edit/reformulate the narrative

   ☐ Copy edit/proofread text

Fiscal (Budget)

   ☐ Draft budget

   ☐ Draft budget justification

   ☐ Prepare cost match requests

Supporting materials

☐ Draft/edit biographical sketches

☐ Draft WOW paragraphs

☐ Draft abstract/executive summary

☐ Draft/edit resources & facilities information

☐ Draft letters of support & commitment

☐ Design graphics, figures, tables, etc.

☐ Draft project timeline

☐ Verify/edit bibliographic references

Forms

☐ Prepare agency-required forms

☐ Complete grants management system data entry

☐ Collect internal signatures

☐ E-submission

Other

☐ Draft letter of intent

☐ Draft concept paper

☐ Paginate finished proposal

☐ Make/deliver copies of final product

☐ Software support with Word, Excel, Acrobat, or Sharepoint

3. How much was the total request (direct and indirect, all years) for this project?

☐ < $10,000

☐ $10,000–$50,000

☐ $50,000–$100,000

☐ $100,000–$500,000

☐ $500,000–$1,000,000

☐ >$1,000,000

4. Overall, how would you characterize the grant writing consultant's involvement in developing this proposal?

☐ Heavy   ☐ Medium   ☐ Light

5. Do you think that your proposal has an increased chance of funding because of grant writing consultant help?

   ☐ Yes   ☐ No

   Why or why not? (Use additional space if needed)

6. How would you categorize the flow of communications with your grant writing consultant?

   ☐ Excellent   ☐ Satisfactory   ☐ Improvement needed (please explain)

7. What, if any, obstacles were encountered in developing this proposal, and how were they resolved? (Use additional space if needed.)

8. What, if any, lessons were learned in the course of developing this proposal?

9. How could the grant writing consultant have better assisted you in developing this proposal? (Use additional space if needed.)

10. What was the most helpful thing the grant writing consultant did to support the development of this proposal? (Use additional space if needed.)

11. Do you intend to use MU's grant writing services in the future?

    ☐ Yes   ☐ No

12. If yes, will you ask for and use other services you did not request this time?

    ☐ Yes   ☐ No

    Please explain.

13. Would you recommend grant writer services to other faculty members?

    ☐ Yes   ☐ No

Flextime Memo

TO: Office of Grant Writing and Publications Personnel
FROM: Mary Licklider
DATE: August 5, 2004
RE: Time

Effective immediately, the Office of Grant Writing and Publications (OGWP) will implement the following practices:

Flextime—OGWP personnel are expected to work at least 40 hours per week and to be available to the campus community as needed during MU's regular business hours. That said, many of us can work some of our time outside normal business hours without compromising the level of service we provide. As a general rule, hours should be worked between 6:00 a.m. and 7:00 p.m. Monday through Friday. Exceptions should be checked with me.

Work-from-Home Option—When personal circumstances make it a more efficient choice, OGWP employees may opt to work from home. This is an option offered for the convenience of the employee, so it doesn't imply that MU will provide or maintain your home computing equipment or Internet access. Although there are days when we simply need to be at home to get the most accomplished, much of our work does require us to be available to faculty on a drop-in basis, so we'll need to exercise this option judiciously.

Let me know if you have questions. I hope these practices will give you the flexibility to continue to be as amazingly productive as you have been *and* to allow you to achieve a comfortable balance between your work and personal lives.

Afterword

Summing It Up

Mary Licklider

I OPENED THIS handbook, in the Preface, with the claim that if you work anywhere in higher education and have responsibilities related to submitting and running grant-funded projects, this handbook is for you. I hope you have found that claim to be true. Grant funding in higher education supports a wide, wide range of work. Instructional projects build and improve our curricula. Outreach projects help the K–12 enterprise improve the quality of its teachers and administrators and prepare its students for the rigors of postsecondary work and education. Grants for research and creative work generate new knowledge that helps us better understand ourselves and keeps our world moving forward, while funding for technology transfer and creative productions and installations move that knowledge and understanding into communities to improve lives around the world. Grant work is an inherently optimistic endeavor: it assumes that we can make a difference, can better understand the world, can conquer the world's thorny questions and problems.

The Vision Thing

A corollary of this optimism is that there tends to be a certain messiness about the work for which we seek grant funding. Those who are uncomfortable with ambiguity will find discomfort at every turn in the grant world. We seek funding for that which has not been done, a territory that comes without clear road maps. I hope that this handbook has helped you impose a degree of order on the processes you use to march into the unknown. The contexts that Susan Hazelwood and I explained in Chapter 1 can embed your grant work in larger visions for your institution, the sponsor, and your scholarly career. Clear targets won't necessarily straighten your path, but they can go a long way toward making sense of the detours.

A clear sense of purpose can also make the inevitable declinations at least a little less painful. If the planning work of the proposal process moves your project forward, as it should, then a declination from the sponsor is disappointing but will not mean the proposal was a waste of time. Your focus on longer term goals has obvious utility as you examine potential sponsors and their funding programs, weighing the match between your agenda and theirs. Key points from Chapter 2 reinforce this approach:

- Invest time up front in funder research and the development of targeted e-mail funding alerts.

- Use funder research and tools such as the "Deal or No Deal" worksheet in the Toolkit (Section One, Table 7) to assess the match between your agenda and a given funding opportunity.

- Don't waste the time of sponsor personnel asking for information that is available on the web, but don't hesitate to contact sponsors with the questions that remain after you have read their published materials.

- Every contact with sponsor personnel represents an opportunity to build or damage your relationship with that sponsor. Treat e-mails, phone calls, visits, proposals, and reports accordingly.

Investing Your Time

Besides the "vision thing," a central take-home message of this handbook is to be conscious and purposeful with the very limited resource that your time represents. In addition to providing a critical lens for examining funding opportunities, clear priorities can guide your efforts to tap campus resources, as Bob Glidewell and Diane Oerly explain in Chapter 3, and to engage in collaborative endeavors, as Sherri Sachdev explains in Chapter 4.

Awareness of the strategic planning priorities of the campus and your department will allow you to make informed approaches to campus leaders as you request support for your projects. Campus policies on grant-funded facilities and administrative costs and salaries will be key factors as you consider what you will need from the sponsor in order to do the work. Learning who is available to help with proposal preparation, administrative details, and fiscal management may allow you to do more than you thought, and in any case it will help you pace your own work more realistically:

- Take time to investigate the resources your institution offers that could help you develop and strengthen your grant proposals.

- Teach yourself to hand off work that doesn't require your specialized knowledge or skills.

Awareness of your priorities and those of your institution can also guide your responses to collaborative requests and your own initiation of such requests. As Sherri Sachdev emphasizes, collaboration adds a layer of complexity to a project; there's little to be gained from collaboration for collaboration's sake. Collaboration that allows us to address the work more thoroughly or to take on more complex problems, on the other hand, carries a great deal of value. The trick is to enter into collaborative endeavors with the understanding that communications must be explicit and ongoing:

- Engage collaborators when this will strengthen the work.

- Expect all members of a collaborative team to articulate their expectations and assumptions up front. Expect collaborations to require up-front negotiation and ongoing communication.

- Use a proposal outline to pull together sponsor requirements and review criteria and to assign portions of the writing to helpers and collaborators.

- Use a proposal development timeline to keep collaborators on track and to avoid last-minute rushes that will compromise the quality of the proposal.

Form Follows Function

Your grant-getting agenda will be shaped by the goals you set at each stage of your career. The work of a particular project will dictate its structure, such as whether a collaborative team is needed. The "form follows function" dictum is helpful as you shape your grant-getting agenda and your collaborative relationships with others on and off campus, and it is also useful in designing, writing, and editing your proposal documents:

- Write for an educated lay reader.

- Allow enough time to finely hone the abstract toward the goals of building interest in and excitement about the proposed project.

- Structure the project description as a logical funnel that leads the reader from a broader problem to the aspect of that problem to be addressed, through previous approaches to the issue, to your proposed solution, and finally into the details of your work plan and expected results.

- Take the Goldilocks just-right approach to your budget: not too much, not too little, just enough to do the project well.

- Use formatting to support the ideas in the proposal and to move the reader smoothly through those ideas.

Building the Campus Culture

Grant writing may be optimistic work, but it's not for the fainthearted. If your experience follows the norm, your proposals will be declined about twice as often as they receive awards. Don't give up. Read the reviews, put them away, then get them out again once the sting of rejection isn't quite so sharp. Discuss the reviews with the sponsor's program officer if that is an option, and add to that conversation the advice that Susan Hazelwood and Diane Oerly provide in Chapter 11 to figure out how to strengthen the proposal for resubmission.

When signals for an award are favorable at last, use the "limbo" time that Elizabeth Miller describes in Chapter 12 to prepare yourself to become the manager of the funded project and to prepare your team to begin work immediately once the award notice arrives.

Consider, too, how you can contribute to the grants culture on your campus. Volunteer to serve on review panels, as Sara Vassmer suggests in Chapter 11 ("Becoming a Reviewer: Selected Funding Agencies"), but don't let it end there. When you get back to campus, send a note to your collaborators and departmental colleagues summarizing what you learned about the review process and agency priorities. Lobby for funding to bring grantsmanship experts to campus for workshops, to hire grant writers, and to include formal grantsmanship training in graduate education, as I suggest in the Appendix.

It is probably obvious by now that my own optimism extends to a firm belief that an individual really can make a difference. Whether through the results of your grant-funded work or through ideas for improving the campus grants culture, we hope you have found that our ideas and approaches will help you make a difference in your world. If you have suggestions for future editions of this handbook or questions of me as its editor, I can be reached via e-mail at lickliderm@missouri.edu.

Best of luck with your next proposal!

Building a Grants Culture: A Word to Campus Leaders

Mary Licklider

THERE HAS BEEN plenty written in recent years about how the culture of higher education—and to at least some extent American culture at large—has shifted (Figure 10). The traditional image of the college or university faculty member is of the lone investigator or scholar, slogging away in the lab or the library. That rarely describes today's work.

Traditional versus Emerging Paradigms

Laboratories are staffed now by teams; studies in the physical, social, and life sciences almost always involve collaborative assemblies of expertise. Books in the humanities may still be published under a single author's byline, but take a look at the acknowledgments pages and it becomes obvious that here, too, collaboration is the norm. My perception is that the easy questions have pretty much been answered. It's the hard stuff that's left—the issues that fall between the disciplines or even outside the traditional disciplines altogether. To address these issues, we have to learn to talk and work across traditional organizational boundaries: across departments, across institutions, across languages, and across cultures.

Some say that e-mail and social networking applications like Facebook precipitated the flattening of organizational hierarchies. Because anyone can communicate with anyone else within the organization without going through a gatekeeper, the distinctions between the levels of the traditional hierarchy are fading. I wonder if, in scientific and scholarly collaborations, the organizational hierarchies have simply become irrelevant. If I am the only participant from my department on a particular team, it is not my departmental status that is really pertinent, but rather the expertise I bring

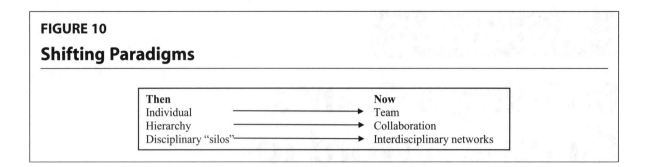

FIGURE 10

Shifting Paradigms

Then		Now
Individual	⟶	Team
Hierarchy	⟶	Collaboration
Disciplinary "silos"	⟶	Interdisciplinary networks

to the team. The work drives who should logically lead this effort or the next rather than some externally assigned status. This means that scientific and scholarly collaborations today tend to be associations of equals.

To succeed in a collaborative environment, the individual scholar must develop and maintain interdisciplinary networks of colleagues whose expertise can be tapped and to whose work the individual might contribute. The nerdy scientist or scholar with poor social skills, the individual who communicates in jargon and only with those in the same field, who has little to do with others outside the field—this traditional stereotype will have trouble succeeding for very long in today's environment.

Implications for Individual Faculty Members

Collaborations are harder to manage than individual work. Collaborators must be identified and cultivated. Work must be coordinated to keep the project moving forward efficiently. Work across disciplines experiences glitches in communication because of the variance in the respective languages and approaches of individual disciplines.

Collaborative projects are inherently larger, involving more people, more time, more institutions. These projects require unique and sometimes highly nuanced leadership skills from faculty members who came to their positions by virtue of their training and scholarship rather than their personnel management skills. It seems a wonder that all this isn't enough for the individual faculty member with responsibilities for teaching, service, and research/scholarship to run screaming into the night.

Implications for Institutions of Higher Education

Institutions of higher education can make this all easier, and we can begin by making it easier for faculty members to understand grants culture. If we define *culture* as the beliefs and customs of specific groups of people, then it is easy to see that the world of grants has its own culture. Each organization or institution has its own grant processes: who writes the text, who creates the budget, who has to sign off on the project, who actually submits the proposal to the sponsor, who is authorized to negotiate with the sponsor. There are external regulations that govern grants: sponsor rules, human and animal subjects protections, export controls, conflict of interest regulations, accounting practices, audits. Budgeting is fraught not only with a multitude of esoteric rules, but also with unwritten expectations: percentages of effort or person months that should be requested from the sponsor, the total request amount that a given sponsor will consider reasonable, whether the colleague down the hall should be paid for consultations. Deliverables vary across sponsors, ranging from a marketable product to social service programming to journal articles. Success rates vary widely from sponsor to sponsor and even from program to program for some sponsors.

Despite the complexity of grants culture and the ubiquity of the expectation that faculty members participate in this culture, faculty members in the humanities are often left more or less on their own to develop an understanding of this culture (Figure 11). Whereas graduate students and postdocs in the sciences are often involved in proposal preparation, this is rarely the case in the humanities. Faculty members in these disciplines can pick up the processes and regulations, but they tend to struggle with the unwritten elements of grants culture. Making some of this more explicit could go a long way toward encouraging humanities faculty members to seek grant funding. Just understanding that a no from a sponsor is simply a step on the way to funding and that proposal work itself is a positive, funded or not, is news to many in these disciplines. Workshops and support from a grant writing consultant can be especially valuable in these fields.

FIGURE 11

Grants Culture across the Disciplines

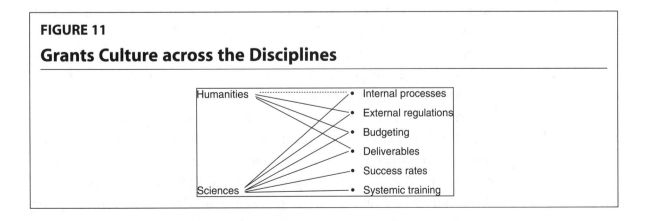

In addition to more consciously and conscientiously bringing our graduate students and postdocs into grants culture, higher education also has control of its own internal processes and expectations. Those can be made to support or hinder grant writing, and they can likewise be made to support or hinder collaborative activities. At MU, a system of shared credit designates each investigator's intellectual contribution to a given grant proposal. These shared credit percentages also translate into internal Research Incentive Fund (RIF) dollars as a grant award is implemented. At the end of each fiscal year, an amount equal to 25 percent of the facilities and administration costs that have been recovered for a grant-funded project is awarded to the departments participating in that project. Those funds are divided according to the shared credit percentages designated for each investigator involved in the project. If an investigator has a dual appointment, portions go to each department. Research Incentive Fund monies are intended for use as the name implies. Sometimes the RIF is rolled back into a project as a cost match; sometimes it is used to keep a lab running between periods of grant funding; the decisions about how to use RIF are made at the department level.

For departments with heavy teaching responsibilities, policies for buying out teaching time can have a profound effect on a faculty member's decision whether to pursue grant funding. This is particularly true in the humanities, where many funders do not pay the full costs of facilities and administrative expenses. If there were a policy, however, to use a portion of salary savings on such proposals toward teaching replacement costs, it would be easier for these faculty members to think about submitting grant proposals because work in the humanities tends to be more time-intensive than materials- and equipment-intensive.

Likewise, promotion and tenure policies need to be examined for implicit stances on collaboration and grant writing. It seems ridiculous to insist that junior faculty members work entirely on their own until they are tenured—and their professional habits are established—and then suddenly expect them to be ready to engage in collaborative work upon securing tenure. Likewise, faculty members who are punished in the promotion and tenure process for submitting grant proposals that are not funded will simply choose not to submit any.

Training grants and other complex proposals will have very little attraction for the individual faculty member if there is no staff support for coordinating collaborators and collecting required data, regardless of the prestige that accrues to the institution for such awards. We need to think about our reward and recognition systems and how they either support or subvert institutional goals and priorities.

The Need for Grant Writing Consultants

Some years ago, I was sitting next to a woman at one of the regional NIH grants conferences, and we were exchanging pleasantries—where we were from, what we did there, that kind of thing. She asked what I did at the University of Missouri, and I told her that I was a grant writer and that I helped faculty members with their research proposals. She looked at me for a long pause and then said, "That's cheating," and went on to say that those proposals are supposed to represent the work of the faculty member. My response was to explain that I did not think that was really the case anymore. As you no doubt gathered from Sherri Sachdev's overview in Chapter 4, the days of the lone investigator are pretty much over. What a proposal represents now is that the principal investigator or project director is capable of assembling and leading a team with the expertise needed to do the proposed work well.

At MU, this often means that a grant writing consultant is part of that team. There is plenty of literature out there to document the amount of time faculty members in US higher education are spending on activities other than research and other creative activities. It was hard enough to juggle teaching, service, and research when the latter was primarily a solo activity. It takes even more time and energy, along with an additional set of human relations and administrative skills, to recruit, coordinate, and manage group projects. One of the primary roles of the grant writing consultant is that of project manager, the *project* being the grant proposal. We identify funding opportunities, help assemble the appropriate expertise, assign writing tasks, pull budget numbers together, knit disparate pieces of writing into a coherent whole—we peel off everything we can to allow the faculty members to focus on the science and scholarship. When we put this in the context of the dramatic decrease in recent years in the size of the nation's ranked faculty, it seems obvious that we need to do everything we can to make the very best use of each faculty member's time.

Rob Duncan's boxed piece on the vice chancellor's perspective mentions the transaction costs of engaging in projects that reach outside the home department, division, or institution. This is not a trivial concern and cannot be addressed by adding an administrative assistant or giving the faculty member a graduate research assistant. A good grant writing consultant understands grants culture, university culture, the research process, and project management. This is not just a warm body with another pair of hands. This is a mature professional with a skill set that complements the faculty member's expertise.

Perspective of the Vice Chancellor for Research

Robert V. Duncan

I can't claim to be the one who had the foresight to give Mary Licklider permission to start the MU Grant Writer Network. That claim rests with one of my predecessors, Jack Burns. I can, however, say that when I joined MU as the new vice chancellor for research, the importance and value of the Grant Writer Network were immediately obvious. This Network is a key piece of the institution's central nervous system. The grant writing consultants are dispersed into the campus's colleges and centers, but they come together each week and in day-to-day communications, sharing what they know about the research endeavors and priorities of their home units. Together, they know as much about the whole of the institution's research enterprise as anyone, and they take that knowledge back to their home units and to the scientists and scholars with whom they work, all nodes on that nervous system. This permits MU to structure larger interdisciplinary efforts by introducing faculty researchers to one another and by discussing with them new larger-scale research efforts that they may decide to pursue. This also makes administrators aware of the full complexity and extent of our university research enterprise.

MU boasts an unusually interdisciplinary culture that has been developed and sustained by our most competent and visionary faculty members. The grant writing consultants nurture this culture by lowering the transaction costs for faculty members as they reach across departments, colleges, and institutional boundaries to collaborate.

Finding Grant Writing Consultants

Whether the label is *grant writer, research development professional, proposal development specialist*, or something else, the bottom line is that this is an emerging profession. According to the 2011 survey of the National Organization of Research Development Professionals, 70 percent of research development offices have been in place for less than six years, and 67 percent of research development personnel have 10 years of experience or less in the field. The median number of positions in a research development office is three. I have said on any number of occasions that no little kid tells his or her parents that he or she wants to be a grant writing consultant when he or she grows up. So rather than looking for experienced grant writing consultants, we look for a transferrable skill set.

• First of all, grant writing consultants must be strong writers. Much of what a new grant writing consultant needs to know and be able to do can be taught, but not this.

• Grant writing consultants also need administrative and leadership experience. For a team proposal, the selection of the principal investigator or project director is often a strategic decision. The lead individual's biographical sketch communicates to the reviewer about the most important expertise, the primary field of the project, and the institutional commitment to the project. From this strategic perspective, the best fit for the lead role is not always clear until the work on the proposal is thoroughly under way. In these situations, the grant writing consultant often serves as a sort of surrogate leader until the choice of the real principal investigator or project director becomes clear: It is much easier to take over the leadership of a project if this does not entail taking the project away from another faculty member. Everyone knows from the start that the proposal will not be going to the sponsor with the grant writing consultant as project director. In this project management role, the grant writing consultant needs to be comfortable and experienced in managing people and anticipating the work that needs to be done.

• Grant writing consultants should have teaching experience. As teachers, we must typically think through a task analysis in order to assess where our students are and what steps will be needed to get them from wherever they are to where they need to be. We find that this kind of task analysis parallels nicely the grant writing consultant's need to assess the status of the faculty's grant culture at a more global level as well as the more granular kind of analysis entailed in planning work on a particular grant proposal.

• Grant writing consultants should have done research themselves. We need to interact with faculty clients as peers who understand the vagaries of the research endeavor. We often find ourselves advising young faculty members, helping to define a research agenda beyond the immediate tenure goal and to create a funding strategy to serve that agenda. These faculty members seem to find it easier to admit gaps in knowledge or skills to grant writing consultants, who have no roles at all in the promotion and tenure process, than it might be to address the same issues with departmental colleagues or faculty mentors.

• This is not to say that the grant writing consultants need expertise in the same areas as those of the faculty members that the consultant will support. The grant writing consultant's expertise lies in the process, not the content, of the work. There is no need to duplicate the expertise of the faculty scholars. In fact, we benefit from having an outsider's perspective. We do not come to the work or the proposal with the same assumptions as the faculty scholars, which is to say that we likely have much the same perspective as reviewers will have. This outsider perspective is also useful when we need to "translate" between faculty clients and the compliance and grants personnel on campus.

- Finally, grant writing consultants need mature people skills. The grant writing consultant treads a fine line between passionate commitment to the success of the proposals and the funded work and remembering that the proposals are not our own. We must work hard, give our best advice, attempt to seal any logical holes in the proposal's argument, and take the time to present the ideas in the most readable form. But when the principal investigator wants to do something else, the grant writing consultant needs to swallow hard and let go. It is the principal investigator's career and work, not ours. Besides this paradoxical commitment/detachment, the grant writing consultant's role also entails extracting information from a wide range of individuals on tight timelines, representing the project director and the institution to external collaborators, communicating budget cuts to members of the team, and any number of other opportunities to complicate the project director's life with poor decisions. Mature people skills are essential to avoiding these risks.

Grant writing is very human work. The grant writing consultant must be sensitive to the needs and work styles of the faculty teams. I tell new consultants that it is part of the job to be the chameleon on the team. We need to ask questions and observe consciously and then adjust the proposal processes to fit the faculty members involved. The goal is to keep the investment of faculty time and effort focused on the things only they can do by virtue of their special expertise.

Hiring Grant Writing Consultants

The hiring process is critical to finding individuals who can succeed in the work. The two-tiered process we use at MU may take a little longer, but this investment on the front end has been a big part of keeping our annual turnover rate among our grant writing consultants well below 10 percent.

We start with a conversation with the hiring unit about what the goals will be for the position. Then we tweak the position description to reflect these goals and post the position. The Office of Grant Writing and Publications pays for an ad in the local paper to advertise the position. I put together a screening committee of a grant writing consultant or two and me as the director of the Grant Writer Network. We review all applications and then meet to decide which candidates we want to interview. Interviews entail a standard set of questions such as those included in Section Four of the Toolkit ("Interview Questions").

Following each interview, we take a 30-minute impromptu writing sample from each candidate. We provide a prompt for this sample such as the ones included in Section Four of the Toolkit ("Interview Writing Prompts"), and we situate the candidates at a computer in the midst of the traffic and conversations of the office—in other words, we give them a taste of the work context. Following the interviews, the screening committee meets again to discuss the relative strengths and weaknesses of each candidate. We generally select two to five finalists whose references we will check. We call references and ask a standard set of questions as well as any questions specific to a particular candidate that came up as a result of the interview. Again, a sample of a standard set of questions is included in Section Four of the Toolkit ("Reference Check Questions"). Finally, we meet to settle on finalist candidates, usually two to five, all of whom we are confident could succeed as grant writing consultants.

Then I draft a cover memo to the hiring unit in which I summarize our process and our perceptions of the relative strengths and weaknesses of each of the finalists. I rarely, if ever, rank the finalists. From our perspective, the hiring decision almost always comes down to the hiring division's priorities and culture. Rather than a ranking, my memo, either implicitly or explicitly, communicates that if one skill or quality is more important to the division, the candidate strongest in this area would be the best choice. If a different skill or quality is more important, then the candidate strongest in that area would be the best choice. I always leave open the option that, if none of the finalists seems a good fit, we will go back to the candidate pool and try to identify a better match. I attach this cover memo to the writing prompt and all the application materials from these finalists: their application forms, résumés, cover letters, writing samples, and thank-you notes. This package then goes to the hiring unit, and we step out of the process.

In some cases, the hiring unit's process involves a single interview with an individual or committee; other times it entails a series of interviews. The other grant writing consultants and I are not part of this stage of the search, nor do we inquire about it. I believe we know best what a grant writing consultant looks like, and the hiring unit best knows its own culture. By combining forces, we have significantly raised our odds of finding the best fits for the grant writing positions at MU. In fact, we have in the last couple of years had several openings for what I would consider fairly attractive leadership positions within MU's Grant Writer Network. In conversations with individual grant writing consultants about these openings, I was more than once told, "I just don't know that I want to apply for that. I'm really happy where I am."

Getting New Grant Writing Consultants Started

In at least some institutions of higher education, there seems to be an unwritten rule for staff personnel that, in order to get a substantial raise in pay, the individual must change job titles. If you can forgive me a brief detour onto a personal soapbox, the resulting movement of staff from position to position costs the institution a great deal in recruiting and training costs. With this in mind, we created three grant writing titles: Grant Writing Consultant 1, Grant Writing Consultant 2, and Senior Grant Writing Consultant. It takes about 18 to 24 months for a new grant writing consultant to learn the research agendas, funding sources, and work styles of the faculty members in the unit—in other words, it takes 18 to 24 months to really get useful. Without some sort of career ladder, we worried about falling into a situation in which we were just training grant writing consultants to go into private consulting rather than keeping our personnel.

The grant writing consultant is a strategic position. Where proposals are developed, plans are made for investments of faculty time and other institutional resources. When proposals are funded, institutional resources are invested further to implement the projects. Proposal development entails serious costs and, even in the rare circumstance when a sponsor funds 100 percent of the project costs, there are still opportunity costs for the institution. To invest those institutional resources most effectively and efficiently, *the grant writing consultant must report to the individual responsible for establishing and implementing the unit's research agenda.*

As the director of the Office of Grant Writing and Publications at MU, I have approval authority for use of the grant writing consultant titles, and the proposed reporting relationship for a new grant writing position has caused me to withhold approval for a grant writing title more often than anything else. On the surface, it seems to make sense to have the grant writing consultant reporting to the fiscal manager for the unit (grants are money, right?) or to the unit's grants and contracts manager. Those options might work if you want your fiscal or grants managers to make decisions about the unit's programmatic priorities. If this is not the case, however, the grant writing consultant needs a direct reporting line to the research chair, center director, research dean, or whoever sets those priorities.

Another reason this reporting relationship is critical is to provide the grant writing consultant with bureaucratic cover. Faculty members can be very insistent about the importance of their own projects. The discrepancy between the status of faculty and that of staff at most institutions of higher education makes it very difficult for a new grant writing consultant to tell a faculty member that the consultant's time is already booked and that limited if any help is available right now. The grant writing consultant needs a supervisor who can back these decisions. A grant writing consultant spread too thin is an unhappy person with a graduate degree who is being paid to fill out forms—not a good investment for the institution. To be effective, the grant writing consultant needs clear priorities that enable informed decisions about where to invest time and bureaucratic backing when the inevitable conflicts arise about whose project gets that investment this time.

As a side note, I can add that at MU, we very seldom respond with a flat no to anyone who asks for help. We can usually offer some limited help, offer to make the project a priority for a later deadline cycle, or recommend a freelance grant writing consultant. I maintain a list of freelancers whose work we trust, and we have an extra workstation in my office where freelancers work. We have found that our faculty clients have been *much* happier with freelance support when we bring the freelancers into our office, where we can answer questions and provide at least some guidance for the work.

After 14 years of hiring and mentoring grant writing consultants, my perception is that the first year or so in a grant writing position entails a learning curve that is roughly equivalent to the acquisition of a master's degree. In a year. So this is a stressful time for the new employee, yet paradoxically during the first several months, there often does not seem to be very much to do, particularly if the position is new. Faculty members are not accustomed to having this help; the grant writing consultant does not know the faculty and how best to help them; the grant writing consultant worries that he or she will soon be unemployed. Then the adoption-of-innovation curve hits that near-vertical period, and the grant writing consultant is afraid to say no to anyone, having so recently not had enough to do. The consultant falls into working regularly into the night and through weekends, a pattern that almost ensures errors of fatigue and impatience.

There are lots of opportunities in the first year to set precedents that will establish positive and lasting working relationships and to communicate institutional investment in priorities. The flip side of these opportunities is that, if they are poorly handled, the grant writing position can essentially be sabotaged to the point where it fails, and I have seen this happen.

Mentoring New Grant Writing Consultants

The key to the first couple of years of a grant writing position lies in effective mentoring and engaged supervision. The "Skills Inventory" (Table 24) in Section Four of the Toolkit can be used to develop a training plan. The mentor works with the grant writing consultant to identify the skills and knowledge needed immediately and to create a plan for acquiring them. It is not unusual during the first year to run through a cycle of two or three such plans, with the grant writing consultant becoming progressively more independent in identifying and managing his or her own professional development. One effect of the training plans is to relieve the new grant writing consultant of at least some of the self-imposed pressure to know everything at once. The training plan gives implicit permission to let go of some of that and take things in turn.

Besides facilitating this more didactic professional development, the mentor can also play important roles in clarifying and perhaps also modeling the grant writing consultant's place in the organization. By joining the grant writing consultant's periodic meetings with the supervisor, the mentor can sometimes ask questions that a new employee, no matter how experienced, would be unlikely to ask: What are your priorities for this position? Because there will only be time to support one of these two proposals, which is more important to the unit? By shadowing the grant writing consultant and being shadowed by the consultant in meetings with proposal development teams, the mentor can demonstrate and provide feedback on development of meeting agendas, creation of follow-up e-mails, strategies for keeping meetings on track, strategies for extracting information from team members, and the like.

Regularly scheduled meetings with the mentor will allow topics to naturally bubble up for discussion and advice before situations reach the crisis stage. Grant writing, by its deadline-driven nature, can easily become a high-burnout field. One of the mentor's roles must be to make it easy for the new grant writing consultant to ask for help and to make it acceptable to recognize his or her limits. Shallow or error-ridden grant writing support is worse than none at all—the grant writing consultant must know where to seek help and how to manage the resource that his or her time represents so that it accrues the maximum benefit for the institution and the faculty clients.

Assessing Performance

The "benefit" that we provide, however, may or may not come in the form of grant dollars. Because grant writing consultants seek money in the form of grant awards, it may be tempting to evaluate consultants based upon the grant dollars they secure. Grant writing consultants are not development personnel. The goal for development personnel is to raise money for the institution. The goal of a grant writing position is to support the research, instruction, and public service endeavors of the faculty.

For the grant writing consultant's time to be invested well, the detailed planning and collaborative team-building that happen as a grant proposal is developed must be ends in themselves. In the best of circumstances at well-funded sponsors, overall success rates for competitive grant proposals will hit maybe 32 percent. For some programs, particularly for very large awards and for awards in the arts and humanities, success rates can be as low as 5 or 6 percent. Put another way, this means that in the very best of circumstances, about two-thirds of grant proposals will be turned down. If we are doing this only for the money, we might do better to take out a CD at the local bank or take up day trading. If we are strategically investing institutional resources in proposals for work that the institution wants to do and probably will eventually do anyway, then the proposals themselves will move the institution forward.

If the grant writing consultant were evaluated based upon the grant dollars received, this would encourage the consultant to help only on proposals that are most likely to be funded, regardless of the importance of the work to the institution. Never mind helping the promising young faculty member learn the ropes. Never mind helping to build a relationship with a new funder, knowing that the first couple of proposals may not be funded. Never mind the smaller humanities fellowships.

All this is not to say that the grant writing consultant's help will not allow faculty members to pursue more and larger funding opportunities than they might otherwise consider. As best I could determine, the University of Missouri before 1998, when we initiated our Grant Writer Network, had in its history received one center grant, one program project grant, and one construction grant. Since then, we have received 10 construction/renovation awards and 14 program project and center grants and renewals. The MU faculty did not suddenly get smarter or more ambitious. The grant writing consultants simply enabled faculty members to attempt these more complex proposals that they could not realistically have taken on without help.

This brings me to another reason that grant writing consultants should not be evaluated based on the dollars awarded: the consultant should never, ever, be placed in a position of taking credit for faculty ideas. The grant writing consultant can facilitate the proposal getting out the door, particularly larger and complex proposals that faculty members would not otherwise have time to develop. The grant writing consultant can also add maybe three or four percentage points to the score by spit-shining the presentation. A strong presentation cannot make a weak idea fundable, but a poor presentation can take a good idea out of the running. A strong presentation can push a good idea over the line into the "funded" category. At bottom, though, the creativity and ideas remain the faculty member's.

So how to evaluate the grant writing consultant? Look at the goals and priorities of the position. In our Network, there are typically three ongoing goals for most of the positions:

- Support faculty members in securing external funding for their research and scholarship.

- Provide grantsmanship training activities for the university community.

- Engage in professional development activities to stay abreast of the field.

As part of Section Four of our Toolkit, we share the performance evaluation form I use for the grant writing consultants who report to me. The online Toolkit (see p. iv) includes both a blank template form and a filled-in sample; the sample is also included in this handbook (Table 25: Sample Performance Assessment).

In addition to the individual performance assessment, we send a survey instrument from my office to the principal investigator after each proposal is submitted. Surveys are returned to my office, and results remain anonymous but not confidential. We tally the results each year as a way of monitoring the work of the Grant Writer Network as a whole and of refining the services we offer. The "Survey Instrument" is also included in Section Four of the Toolkit.

Starting the MU Grant Writer Network— Beginner's Luck

I came to the University of Missouri in 1998, the first hire of a new vice provost for research whose charge was to reinvigorate a research enter-prise that had stagnated under a long series of interim appointees. I had previously been an English teacher and department chair and then the grants coordinator for the local school district. This bit of personal history is important because K–12 education, at least in my experience, has a relatively flat culture in which all the adults operate on fairly level status. Despite having worked in higher education in student and adjunct positions and of course having been a student through several degrees, the hierarchical nature of the culture in higher education had escaped me. So when I came to MU and began working with faculty members and administrators, I called them by their first names. I liberally edited writing that was given to me to revise. I flexed my hours to meet deadlines. In short, I interacted with the other adults as peers and had no idea that, as a member of the staff, I was supposed to be deferential to those in faculty positions and rigid in my office hours.

I have since learned that higher education really does not have much of a paradigm for professional staff. At least to some extent, it is fair to say that *professional staff* is to many in higher education an oxymoron: one is expected to be one or the other, professional or staff. In the early years, more than one faculty member started to ask me why, with a terminal degree, I would want to work as a grant writing consultant and then caught themselves before the question was all the way out, realizing the value judgments implied by such a question. So I have to say that the relationships I established with the vice provost and my faculty clients were in the beginning largely a result of ignorance and dumb luck.

It is important for the grant writing consultant to be able to interact with faculty clients as a peer. We have knowledge and skills that parallel and complement the faculty member's. To make the proposals as logically bulletproof as possible, we must be able to integrate our grantsmanship and writing skills with the disciplinary expertise of the faculty member. This kind of teamwork can happen best between peers rather than when part of the equation is considered inferior.

We were further lucky in starting our Grant Writer Network in that my undergraduate degree is in English and my graduate degrees are in education with a focus on organizational dynamics and change. I came to MU with K–12 experience that had included roles that regularly took me into the local business community. Within six months, we hired Susan Hazelwood as a second grant writing consultant who eventually became the associate director of our Network. Susan's background is in biology, and she had already worked at MU for nearly 20 years when we hired her. So with our first two positions, we had both "town" and "gown" experience and familiarity with both humanities and life science disciplines. We did a lot of "translating" for each other early on, and learning the languages of each other's worlds helped us to be much more effective with our faculty clients.

We were lucky, too, in that the interdisciplinary culture at MU was extremely fertile ground for growing the Grant Writer Network. Cynics would say that the culture was as interdisciplinary as it was because the curriculum was a mile wide and an inch deep: faculty members had no choice but to reach out across departmental lines to find the expertise they needed. Perhaps. My sense is that there was much more to it than that. MU is both Research 1 (now "Research University/Very High") and a land grant institution. MU's extension program is considered a national model. The sense that we will do what we need to do in order to solve real problems for real people runs deep here. There is a certain aw-shucks Midwest humility that makes collaboration easier. The almost immediate success and the rapid growth of the Grant Writer Network suggest to me that MU's investigators had taken the single-investigator grant about as far as they could. They needed to work together to address the questions and needs they saw, and they recognized grant writing consultants as exactly the tool they needed.

And finally, we were lucky that the timing so soon after the arrival of the new vice provost and his subsequent restructuring of the Office of Research allowed him to say yes when I asked for a half salary each year to seed new grant writing positions. Our offer to the campus was that if a division, department, or center would commit long term to a full-time grant writing position, we would pay half of the salary and benefits for the first year and 5 percent thereafter. This communicated the priority of the central administration, and it also lowered the risk to units. That said, I think that an ideal arrangement would be to extend the half-and-half support to two years before dropping back to 5 percent.

A realistic expectation for a new proposal is to work on the proposal and submit it in the first year and then wait six to nine months for a funding decision, at which time the proposal is turned down. The proposal is then revised and resubmitted sometime late in the second year, followed by another six- to nine-month wait. With a solid proposal and a little luck, the project is finally funded in the third year. When I talk to administrators about investing in grant writing positions, I tell them not to expect any dollars to come in from proposals in which the grant writing consultant is involved until at least the third year. So it would be more logically consistent if the central salary support could run through the second year rather than dropping off after the first year.

Besides lowering the risk of investing in a new position, the salary support buys what I have rather indelicately referred to as "meddling rights." In a culture that lacks much of a tradition to fall back on for handling professional staff, the fiscal involvement of my office has allowed me to mentor the supervisors as they establish priorities for their grant writing consultants, integrate the grant writing positions with those of existing grants and contracts personnel, and figure out how to assess the grant writing consultants' performance. Keeping a bit of a hand in as the new grant writing positions evolved positioned me to share information about structures in different campus divisions. As our Network grew, I was able to share these local models as options or tap the personnel involved for advice to others on campus.

I also keep an eye on salaries across the Network. I try to send an e-mail memo each year to the supervisors and grant writing consultants that summarizes the work of the year: the number of proposals the group worked on, the number of grant writing positions, the numbers of workshops conducted and workshop registrations attracted, and the like. I also note the salary range and mean salary for each level—Grant Writing Consultant 1, Grant Writing Consultant 2, and Senior Grant Writing Consultant—and comment on the normal time in rank for the Grant Writing Consultant 1 position (12–24 months). The online Toolkit includes University of Missouri's position classifications for all three of these positions (see p. iv).

The Grant Writing Consultant 1 position is seen as something of a training position, and we do what we can to encourage promotion to the next level at an appropriate pace. Otherwise, each time a new position opened, it would likely set off a string of domino openings as grant writing consultants moved from position to position in order to be promoted. I believe this kind of turnover would have a negative effect on the ability of the Network to serve faculty needs. It takes a year or two to figure out who is doing what research, where funding can be found for that research at that stage of the faculty member's career, and how best to support the work style of the individual faculty member. Turnover for the sake of promotion would disrupt those working relationships and reset the learning curve to zero.

We also use our meddling rights to track the workloads of the individual grant writing consultants. Grant writing is deadline-driven work. One way we mitigate the potential for burnout is by devoting one of our weekly staff meetings each month to sharing our upcoming deadlines with each other. When it looks as though someone will have a heavy confluence of deadlines, we look to see who will have a lighter load and could pitch in. Another way we mitigate the potential for burnout is by sharing with each new grant writing consultant and supervisor a memo that I issued a number of years ago laying out policies for flextime and working from home. This memo is included in Section Four of the Toolkit ("Flextime Memo"). Although grant writing consultants are not for the most part hourly employees (more on this shortly), neither are we university slaves. If we are to devote weekends and nights to meeting deadlines from time to time, we ought to be able to attend our kids' Halloween parties at school or to work from home in order to be there for the repair guy. I suppose this may come back around to the luck I referenced earlier, but in 14 years of building the MU Network, I have never seen the policy abused. The time issue simply has to cut both ways if we are serious about respecting the individuals and the work they do.

At MU, the Grant Writing Consultant 1 position is hourly. I worried about this when human resources initiated it, but in hindsight, I think it is a good thing. Either we tend to hire type A personalities, or individuals drawn to grant writing tend to be type A. I can't say which is the chicken and which is the egg. It works out the same either way, and beginning grant writing consultants tend to want to know and be able to do everything right away. They tend to be hard on themselves about what they do not know and about how much longer it takes them to do things than it takes the experienced members of the Network. Supervisors of new grant writing consultants likewise know very little about what a reasonable workload should look like. Starting out on an hourly basis seems to help both the consultant and the supervisor to learn what is reasonable or doable. Without the requirement to track hours, there would be an increased tendency to take on too much, compromising the quality of the work and starting the employee down a path of unsustainable expectations.

In this context, it should be logical that one of the lessons of the mentoring period for each grant writing consultant is to learn to let go. Somewhere in graduate school, I think, we seem to learn that it is somehow a sign of weakness to ask for help. We just need to drag the work off into a cave, put our heads down, and work till it's done. The problem with this is that in grant writing, the work is almost never "done." To be a strong grant writing consultant, we have to learn to gauge the work so that it does not just get done, but gets done well and in time to correct the inevitable oversights. And we have to come to an understanding that leadership is work, too, not just clutter that gets in the way of work. On a large proposal with multiple faculty members, often at multiple institutions, the lead grant writing consultant on many days does little else but manage e-mail traffic and play the role of the conductor—setting the pace, timing the roles of the other players, controlling the volume and intensity, assigning parts. To do this work, the grant writing consultant sometimes has to learn to let go of the budget, the editing, and the other on-the-ground tasks in order to concentrate on the overhead view of the proposal as a whole. Even more often, the consultant has to have the "helicopter" capacity to move between the two views easily and regularly. Mentoring and an explicit expectation of shared workloads can make this comfortable and the work sustainable.

In the early days of the MU Network, the grant writing consultants' supervisors would periodically ask me if a given commitment was coming from my 5 percent of the grant writing consultant's time. I cannot remember the last time anyone raised that issue. Since the beginning of the MU Network, there have been at least two grant writing consultants, and now five, in the central campus Office of Grant Writing and Publications. This means that there are at any given time two to five full-time equivalents available to work on campus-level proposals and to help divisional grant writing consultants. The math works in favor of the units, so there is little reason to worry about other units or the campus getting more than 5 percent of your unit's investment in a grant writing consultant.

When there simply is not enough capacity within the Network to handle a particular proposal, we can recommend a freelancer. We help to shepherd the person through the HR process to be added to the payroll system. By housing the freelancer physically in our office, we can answer questions, overhear conversations, and guide the work. This has consistently worked well.

Network Synergies

Besides sharing workloads, we have engaged in several additional strategies to generate synergies among the campus grant writing positions. An obvious motivation is that grant writing can be lonely work. A grant writing consultant is typically the only one in his or her unit. We meet weekly for 90-minute staff meetings. We use these meetings to share ideas as well as to monitor workloads. At each year's annual retreat, we decide how we will use the staff meeting time during the coming academic year. One constant is a regular time for each person to share what he or she is working on and has coming up in the near future.

Another constant is that I report information from the Office of Research senior staff meetings and the meetings of the campus Council of Research Administrators (mostly the divisional research deans). Collectively, the Network probably knows more about the research under way on campus at a greater level of depth than anyone else. Adding campus-level concerns and priorities to the mix positions us as a valuable part of the campus's "central nervous system" (see "The Vice Chancellor for Research's Perspective" earlier in this Appendix). We can help connect investigators with potential collaborators. We can catch opportunities for broader interdisciplinary projects that other perspectives may not be positioned to see. We can see redundancies that may not be obvious from higher or lower altitudes.

A third constant has been that Network staff meetings are used for our own professional development. We bring in experts from around campus. We tour specialized campus facilities. We share our individual expertise. Most of this would not be possible for a single grant writing consultant to do on his or her own. By sharing responsibility, we all learn more than we would otherwise.

Paradoxically, we can also allow ourselves to know less about some things because of the existence of the Network. The world of grant writing is huge and extremely dynamic. One person cannot keep up with it all. Because we are a network, we can be confident that new opportunities or sponsor changes will not slip by us. When Shelley Hilton took the job as the grant writing consultant in the College of Engineering, then-research dean Noah Manring asked her to place a priority on work with new faculty members. Shelley became the campus expert on the National Science Foundation's CAREER program, and the numbers of MU applications and awards have climbed. When I get a question about the CAREER program, I refer the individual to Shelley. Elizabeth Miller, the grant writing consultant for the College of Human Environmental Sciences, has an eye for graphic design and a mind for graphic information. She is the Network's go-to person when we struggle with an informational graphic.

We each have our niche strengths, and we track these for new grant writing consultants in a separate column of the "Skills Inventory" that lists the go-to grant writing consultant and any internal documents related to a given skill (see Table 24 in Section Four of the Toolkit). We know more as a group than any one consultant can know, and that knowledge gives us confidence that we can find almost any answer that a faculty client needs. In fact, several of us have had the experience in meetings that when we say we do not have the answer to a question but will look into it, someone chimes in with "Check with your Network. Someone there probably knows."

We maintain an e-mail distribution list of Network members and a SharePoint site of Network resources. The distribution list sees daily use with quick questions, funding opportunity notes, and requests for help.

The SharePoint site stores the collective knowledge of the group, including a library of several hundred biographical sketches, all formatted to match so that our proposal teams actually look on paper (or on screen) like teams; an archive of submitted proposal files; slides and notes for workshop presentations; and all manner of other odds and ends. Thankfully, the search function on SharePoint works well.

We meet for a full-day retreat each summer at an off-campus location, usually someone's home. I maintain a folder into which ideas for retreat conversations are filed over the course of the year. Typical topics include how we will use our staff meeting time for the coming year, plans and processes for mentoring new grant writing consultants, survey results from the previous year, evaluations from the campus-level workshop series, and campus-level or Network needs that we have observed. The retreat yields objectives and action items for the coming year. In fact, this book actually grew out of a retreat action item. We realized that we had accrued a good deal of useful material on our SharePoint site, but that much of it needed a context in order to be useful to anyone external to the Network. We also realized that our SharePoint site had become one of those closets for which opening the door entails some personal risk and that some housecleaning was overdue. The retreat conversation led to a commitment to explore publication of a Toolkit, and the attendant context became this book.

Grantsmanship Training

The MU Grant Writer Network has three audiences and perhaps a fourth for grantsmanship training. Our first commitment is to the MU faculty and staff. For them, we offer three 90-minute workshops each fall and spring semester. Topics vary widely based on suggestions from participants, faculty members with whom individual grant writing consultants work, and current issues in the field. These sessions typically attract a total of about 500 registrations each year.

We also offer an intensive faculty Grant Writing Institute. The Institute entails six full days of instruction and accepts 10 applicants per session. The traditional structure is to begin with a full-day session on the Monday after finals week in May, then follow that with either eight half days or four full days in June, and end with a full-day follow-up session in December. The grant writing consultants provide some of the lectures and facilitate small-group discussions. We bring in guest speakers for such topics as research compliance issues, statistical support services, internal funding programs, and research incentive funds. We have a faculty panel on engaging in collaborative research and another that conducts a mock proposal review. Each participant is also paired with a grant writing consultant for one-on-one support in developing the grant proposal that the participant selects as the focus of the Institute work. This last may seem redundant, but there are still several campus divisions that have not invested in grant writing positions, and others have placed priority on larger, interdisciplinary proposals rather than support for smaller proposals or beginning investigators. So one-on-one grant writing support is not always available to participants in their home units.

Until recently, applicants were provided a stipend for their participation with the expectation that they would devote full-time effort to the Institute and the associated grant proposal during the month of June. They were also provided a research budget of $1,000 to support the development of preliminary data. These funds went away when the economy tanked. We receive up to 40 applications each year. In response to this demand, the deans across campus came together in 2011 to create a new grant writing position devoted to providing the Institute three times each year rather than just once. We are very excited about the endorsement that this funding implies, and even more excited about the possibilities of this position. We can envision specialty institutes for the NSF CAREER program, NIH "K" mechanisms, arts and humanities scholars, clinician scientists, and other niche audiences. Stay tuned—as we go to press, we have not yet tried out the translation from summer to the academic year, but we are confident we can make the transition to further improve the services we offer our faculty.

In the last several years, we have also sponsored a national webinar in which federal agency personnel speak to federal research priorities for the upcoming fiscal year and any recent or upcoming grants policy changes (http://research.missouri.edu/federalupdate/). We do this at very low cost by teaming with the National Association of College and University Business Officers (NACUBO). The association provides space in its Washington, DC, offices, which makes it inexpensive for the federal personnel to participate. NACUBO also provides the digital pipeline to stream the webinar to MOREnet, the Internet provider for MU. My office provides logistical support, and we fund the travel and technical expenses for our Academic Support personnel to go to NACUBO to record and stream the presentations and then to process the recordings for posting to the web and for MOREnet to pass the stream along to subscribers nationally. We have been able to break even on this effort by charging a nominal subscription fee. The webinar is a fair amount of work, but it allows our faculty and all of the campus grant personnel free access to presentations that would otherwise cost $1,200–$1,500 per person for travel to the annual conferences of the National Council of University Research Administrators or the Society of Research Administrators.

Our second commitment for grantsmanship training is to ourselves. I encourage grant writing consultants and their supervisors to include ongoing professional development as one of each individual's continuing goals and to develop objectives toward this goal in performance assessments each year. When new positions are created and I am reviewing costs with the hiring unit, I ask for a travel budget of about $1,500 per year so that the grant writing consultant can get to at least one national conference or a couple of regional conferences each year. As a network, we look at upcoming conferences annually and make decisions as to who will go to which events. Ideally, we like to have the Network represented at the national conferences of the National Organization of Research Development Professionals and the Grant Professionals Association; the national Small Business Innovation Research (SBIR) conference; and regional seminars of the US Department of Agriculture, National Institutes of Health, and National Science Foundation. Travel funds have been thin in recent years, and we leverage the one or two individuals we can send to any conference by asking attendees to debrief the group at a staff meeting following their return from the conference.

Our third audience is graduate students, and the fourth is postdoctoral fellows, if you consider them separately from the graduate students. We began some years ago to offer a grant writing course through the MU Truman School of Public Affairs. The course was always full, but student and instructor feedback stressed the impossibility of treating the subject adequately in a 3-credit-hour experience. As a result of our annual retreat discussions, we developed a graduate certificate in grantsmanship (http://truman.missouri.edu/DegreePrograms/GraduateCertificates/Grantsmanship). The certificate program consists of four 3-hour courses: Grant Writing 1, Grant Writing 2, Sponsor Relationships, and Award Management. The first two are "lab" courses that focus on skills development. Student groups are paired with real organizations (either community organizations or faculty labs) to develop grant proposals with their "clients." The last two courses are more traditional content courses. All are offered via the web, and Grant Writing 1 is also offered face to face in the summer.

There are two primary audiences for these courses. Students include those who are or will be working in nonprofits, state and local government, or K–12 schools and whose grant proposals will be focused on programs for these organizations. The second audience for the certificate courses is graduate students and postdoctoral fellows seeking research careers. The courses are deliberately not intended for those seeking to work in research administration or general grant administration. Our scan of available programs found a number of other programs available for that audience. As far as we know, ours is the only graduate program aimed at those who will actually write and implement grant-funded programs.

We handle these courses as we do the Grant Writing Institute. One grant writing consultant serves as the instructor for a course, but we bring in guest lecturers to ensure that the students are exposed to a broad range of perspectives, expertise, and opinions. In the first two courses, a grant writing consultant is assigned to each student group and provides professional feedback on draft documents at two points in each course. Yes, the instructor could do this, but the instructor could not turn the documents around in 24 to 48 hours as we can with one document per consultant. And the grant writing consultants do not influence the students' grades; they serve truly as mentors for the student groups and as such have been a very popular element of the courses.

The grant writing position classifications do not include teaching responsibilities, and my office does not receive general operating funds to offer courses. With the sustainability of the program in mind, we set up the business model for the courses so that most of the tuition dollars that go to the Truman School for these courses flows through to the Grant Writer Network. We use these funds to provide extra-duty stipends to the instructors, mentor consultants, and guest lecturers. We also set aside some of these funds to hire freelance help if the instructor needs some extra support as a result of the time devoted to teaching. Anything that remains goes into our budget for professional development activities.

Conclusion

With the benefit of hindsight, we can see that more than a few things fell in our favor in the early years of MU's Grant Writer Network. Now that we can see more clearly what we did right, I would encourage you to use our experience to make your own luck.

References

Boice, R. (1983). Increasing the writing productivity of "blocked" academicians. *Behaviour Research and Therapy, 20*(3), 197–207.

Boice, R. (1989). Procrastination, busyness, and bingeing. *Behaviour Research and Therapy, 27*(6), 605–611.

Brown, L. G., & Brown, J. B. (2001). *Demystifying grant seeking: What you really need to do to get grants*. San Francisco, CA: Jossey-Bass.

Bunton, S. A., & Mallon, W. T. (2007). The continued evolution of faculty appointment and tenure policies at U.S. medical schools. *Academic Medicine, 82,* 281–289.

Campbell, M. S., & Carter, S. (2004). The joys and sorrows of grant writing: Navigating the unpredictable waters of higher education. *JAAGP, 3*(2), 47–56.

Elbow, P. (1973). *Writing without teachers*. New York, NY: Oxford University Press.

Elbow, P. (1981). *Writing with power: Techniques for mastering the writing process*. New York, NY: Oxford University Press.

Floersch, B. (n.d.). *Federal grantmaking: The long view of history*. Grantsmanship Center. Retrieved from https://www.tgci.com/magazine/govfunding.shtml

Gawalt, G. W. (Transcriber and editor). (n.d.). Transcript: Jefferson's instructions for Meriwether Lewis (ante June 20 1803). *Rivers, Edens, empires: Lewis & Clark and the revealing of America*. Library of Congress. Retrieved from http://www.loc.gov/exhibits/lewisandclark/transcript57.html

Gelsinger, P., & Shamoo, A. (2008, April). Eight years after Jesse's death, are human research subjects any safer? *Hastings Center Report 25*. The Hastings Center. Retrieved from http://humansubjects.energy.gov/news/articles/04002008.EightYears_ac.pdf

Giving USA Foundation. (2011). *Giving USA 2011: The annual report on philanthropy for the year 2010*. Retrieved from www.givingusareports.org

Government Information and Reference Services Unit; Connecticut Agricultural Experiment Station. (2008). *Brief descriptions of Connecticut state agencies*. Connecticut State Library. Retrieved from http://www.cslib.org/agencies/agriculturalexperimentstation.htm

Guimerà, R., Uzzi, B., Spiro, J., & Amaral, L. A. N. (2005). Team assembly mechanisms determine collaboration network structure and team performance. *Science, 308,* 697–702.

Hall, M., & Howlett, S. (2011). *Getting funded: The complete guide to writing grant proposals.* Portland, OR: Portland State University. Seattle, WA: Word & Raby.

Horton, S. R. (1982). *Thinking through writing.* Baltimore, MD: Johns Hopkins Press.

Independent Sector. (n.d.) *Value of volunteer time.* Retrieved from http://www.independentsector.org/volunteer_time

Inter-University Consortium for Political and Social Research (ICPSR). (2009). *Guide to social science data preparation and archiving: Best practice throughout the data life cycle* (4th ed.). Ann Arbor, MI. Retrieved from http://www.icpsr.umich.edu/files/ICPSR/access/dataprep.pdf

Jones, B. F., Wuchty, S., & Uzzi, B. (2008). Multi-university research teams: Shifting impact, geography, and stratification in science. *Science, 322,* 1259–1262.

Kennedy, M. L. (1985). The composing processes of college student writing from sources. *Written Communication, 2,* 434–456.

Korenman, S. G. (2006). Research in humans. *Teaching the responsible conduct of research in humans (RCRH).* Retrieved from http://ori.dhhs.gov/education/products/ucla/chapter2/page04b.htm

Krashen, S. (2002). Optimal levels of writing management: A re-analysis of Boice (1983). *Education, 122*(3), 605–608.

May, J. P. (2005). *Export controls.* Retrieved from University of Missouri, Office of Research website: http://research.missouri.edu/complia/export_about.htm

Morrill Act. (1862). Public Law 37–108; Enrolled Acts and Resolutions of Congress, 1789–1996; Record Group 11. *100 milestone documents.* General Records of the United States Government. National Archives and Records Administration. Retrieved from http://www.ourdocuments.gov/doc.php?doc=33

National Institutes of Health (NIH), National Center for Research Resources. (2009). *Recovery Act limited competition: Core facility renovation, repair, and improvement (G20)* (Request for Applications Number RFA-RR-09–007). Retrieved from http://grants.nih.gov/grants/guide/rfa-files/RFA-RR-09–007.html

National Institutes of Health (NIH), National Human Genome Research Institute. (2006). *Centers for excellence in ethical, legal and social implications (ELSI) research (CEERs) (P50)* (Request for Applications number RFA-HG-06–025). Retrieved from http://grants.nih.gov/grants/guide/rfa-files/RFA-HG-06–025.html

National Institutes of Health (NIH), National Institute of Allergy and Infectious Diseases. (2011a, March 21). *When to contact an NIAID program officer.* Retrieved

from http://www.niaid.nih.gov/researchfunding/grant/checklists/Pages
/checkpo.aspx

National Institutes of Health (NIH), National Institute of Allergy and Infectious Diseases. (2011b, July 8). *Data sharing for grants: Final research data.* Retrieved from http://www.niaid.nih.gov/researchfunding/sop/pages/datasharing
.aspx

National Institutes of Health (NIH), National Institute on Drug Abuse (NIDA), Division of Epidemiology, Services and Prevention Research. (2007). *Project concept paper for NIH-supported research.* Retrieved from http://www
.drugabuse.gov/about/organization/despr/GrantsInfo.html

National Institutes of Health (NIH), Office of Budget. (2011) *Spending history by institute/center, mechanism, etc. (1983 to present). Mechanism detail, Total NIH, FY 1983–2010.* Retrieved from http://officeofbudget.od.nih.gov/pdfs/FY12
/Mechanism%20Detail,%20Total%20NIH,%20FY%201983%20-%202010.pdf

National Institutes of Health (NIH), Office of Extramural Research. (2010). *Developing your budget.* Retrieved from http://grants.nih.gov/grants
/developing_budget.htm

National Institutes of Health (NIH), Office of Research Information Systems (ORIS), Division of Information Services (DIS). (2010, Dec 17). Success rates, research project grants, Table #205A. *Research project grants (RPG) & other mechanisms: Competing applications, awards, success rates and total funding.* Retrieved from http://report.nih.gov/success_rates/index.aspx

National Science Foundation. (2010, May). *Report to the National Science Board on the National Science Foundation's merit review process: Fiscal year 2009.* Retrieved from http://www.nsf.gov/nsb/publications/2010/nsb1027.pdf

National Science Foundation. (2011, January). *Grant proposal guide* (NSF 11-1). Washington, D.C.: Retrieved from http://www.nsf.gov/pubs/policydocs
/pappguide/nsf11001/gpgprint.pdf

Office of Management and Budget (OMB). (1999). *Circular A-110 revised 11/19/93 as further amended 9/30/99: Uniform administrative requirements for grants and agreements with institutions of higher education, hospitals, and other non-profit organizations.* Retrieved from http://www.whitehouse.gov/omb/circulars
_a110/

Office of Management and Budget (OMB). (2004). *Circular A-21 revised 5/10/04: Cost principles for educational institutions.* Retrieved from http://www
.whitehouse.gov/omb/circulars_a021_2004/

Office of Management and Budget (OMB). (2007). *Circular A-133 revised to show changes published in the* Federal Register *June 27, 2003 and June 26, 2007: Audits of states, local governments, and non-profit organizations.* Retrieved from http://

www.whitehouse.gov/sites/default/files/omb/assets/a133/a133_revised _2007.pdf

Phelps, R. L. (2008, Oct). *What makes an MRI proposal fail, what makes an MRI proposal competitive?* National Science Foundation, Office of Integrative Activities. Retrieved from http://www.nsf.gov/od/oia/presentations/

Poole, M. (2006). Developing communities of practice to support grant development. *JAAGP, 4*(2), 1–10.

Protection of Human Subjects, 45 C.F.R. 46.102(d) (2009). Retrieved from http://www.hhs.gov/ohrp/humansubjects/guidance/45cfr46.html

Second Morrill Act. (1890). Act of August 30, 1890, ch. 841, 26 Stat. 417, 7 U.S.C. 322 et seq. Retrieved from http://www.csrees.usda.gov/about/offices/legis /secondmorrill.html

Silvia, P. J. (2007). *How to write a lot: A practical guide to productive academic writing.* Washington, DC: American Psychological Association.

Strober, M. H. (2011). Communicating across the academic divide. *Chronicle of Higher Education, 57*, 18.

Tocqueville, A. de (1969). *Democracy in America*, ed. J. P. Mayer, trans. G. Lawrence. Garden City, NJ: Doubleday. (Original work published 1835–1840)

Tropman, J. E. (1995). *The Catholic ethic in American society: An exploration of values.* San Francisco, CA: Jossey-Bass.

U.S. Department of Agriculture, Animal Welfare Information Center (2012). Animal Welfare Act. Retrieved from http://awic.nal.usda.gov/government -and-professional-resources/federal-laws/animal-welfare-act

U.S. Department of Health and Human Services (U.S. DHHS), Office for Human Research Protections. (1979). *The Belmont report.* Retrieved from http://www .hhs.gov/ohrp/policy/belmont.html

U.S. Department of Health and Human Services (U.S. DHHS), Public Health Service (2011). *SF424 (R&R) application guide for NIH and other PHS agencies.* Washington, D.C.: Retrieved from http://grants.nih.gov/grants/funding /424/SF424_RR_Guide_General_Adobe_VerB.pdf

University of Missouri Environmental Health and Safety. (2004). *MU biosafety manual.* Columbia, MO: Retrieved from http://ehs.missouri.edu/bio /manuals/biosafety.pdf

van Rijnsoever, F. J., & Hessels, L. K. (2011). Factors associated with disciplinary and interdisciplinary research collaboration. *Research Policy, 40*(3), 463–472.

Weber, M. (1956). *The Protestant ethic and the spirit of capitalism* (T. Parsons, Trans.). New York, NY: Scribner's.

Westat, J. F. (2002). *The 2002 user friendly handbook for project evaluation*. Division of Research, Evaluation and Communication, National Science Foundation. Retrieved from http://www.nsf.gov/pubs/2002/nsf02057/start.htm

Wuchty, S., Jones, B. F., & Uzzi, B. (2007). The increasing dominance of teams in production of knowledge. *Science, 316,* 1036–1038.

Yu, P. (2009, April 3). *Regarding FY10 funding for the National Endowment for the Humanities: Testimony submitted to the Appropriations Subcommittee on Interior, Environment and Related Agencies, U.S. House of Representatives*. Retrieved from http://www.acls.org/uploadedFiles/Publications/PresTalks/NHA _NEHFY10_HouseREV.pdf

Index